T0314894

WE KEPT 'EM FLYING

THE SUPPORT PERSONNEL OF THE WARTIME RAF

Books by the Author

Non-fiction
Bomb on the Red Markers
Fighter! Fighter! Corkscrew Port!
The Fear In the Sky
Through Enemy Skies
We Kept 'Em Flying

Peakland Air Crash Series:
The South (2005)
The Central Area (2006)
The North (2006)

Derbyshire's High Peak Air Crash Sites, Northern Region
High Peak Air Crash Sites, Central Region
Derbyshire's High Peak Air Crash Sites, Southern Region
White Peak Air Crash Sites

Faction
A Magnificent Diversion Series
(Acclaimed by the First World War Aviation Historical Society)
The Infinite Reaches 1915–16
Contact Patrol 1916
Sold A Pup 1917
The Great Disservice 1918

Blind Faith: Joan Waste, Derby's Martyr
Joyce Lewis of Mancetter, Lichfield's Feisty Martyr

Fiction
In Kinder's Mists (a Kinderscout ghost story)
Though the Treason Pleases (Irish Troubles)

WE KEPT 'EM FLYING

THE SUPPORT PERSONNEL OF THE WARTIME RAF

Pat Cunningham, DFM

'Pat, you're an A2 – above-average rated –, you love flying, and you consistently fly more than any other instructor here – so how come you're not better at it?'

Squadron Leader Brian Jones, me boss, Refresher Flying School, RAF Manby

First published 2014 by DB Publishing, an imprint of JMD Media Ltd, Nottingham, United Kingdom.

ISBN 9781780913759

Printed and bound by Copytech (UK) Limited, Peterborough.

Contents

Acknowledgements

To the copyright holders authorising the use of their photographs: Richard Haigh, manager, intellectual properties, Rolls-Royce; Nicola Hunt, intellectual property rights copyright unit, MOD; archives staff, Imperial War Museum; Judy Nokes, licensing adviser, HMSO (Crown Copyright/MOD); archives staff, Royal Air Force Museum. Craving the indulgence of those for whom all contact attempts have failed.

To Malcolm Barrass, whose superlative website Air of Authority is an utterly dependable source.

To Paul Dalling, for editing the manuscript, and to Simon Hartshorne, for creating the book.

To Clive Teale, aviator and grammarian, for proof-reading and technical advice. Similarly to Ken Johnson and Ken Clare for down-to-earth criticism.

To Derby City Council's Housing Standards and Enforcement Services Department for bestirring the periodically lethargic Derwent Living.

To the oncologists of Derby Royal and Nottingham City Hospitals who, early in 2014, advised me against waiting for mainstream publishers to put this book on their list, and not to start another long one, whether as author, or reader ...

To the ever-ebullient – and consistently irreverent – staff of: ASDA/Macdonald's, Spondon; Four Seasons Café, Park Farm, Derby; Croots Farm Shop, Duffield; The Wheatcroft's Wharf Café, Cromford; Caudwell's Mill Café, Rowsley; and in particular, Hobb's Tea Rooms, Monsal Head.

To the National Trust staff at Kedleston Hall for both irreverence and forbearance.

To the immeasurable expedition afforded by Google.

Despite such inestimable assistance, any errors remaining, and all opinions expressed are my own

Pat Cunningham, DFM

Private publications by the Author

'Now We Are Ninety' (tribute to mother ...)

'The Elephant Box, Volumes 1 # 2' (a grandfather's tall tales)

'By Fell and Dale, Volumes 1 # 5' (walker's logs)

'Frozen Tears' (a Polish family's wartime odyssey)

'Flotsam' (short pieces)

'Jetsam' (short pieces)

Autobiographical Series:

'Brat to Well Beloved' (RAF Aircraft Apprentice to Air Electronics Officer)

[And, vice Gilbert and Sullivan ...]

'Apprentice to a Pilot' (RAF pilot training)

'The Kind Commander' (RAF captaincy)

'The Simple Captain' (civil captaincy)

In preparation:

'Frozen Tears' (wartime romance)

'The Ignorant Walker's Companion' (a walker's reflections)

'The Tenant'/'The CEO' (experiences of a housing association)

'Fifty Years Of Peace: 1945-1995' [Celebratory Stones in Derbyshire] (Memoirs of RAF 'peacekeeping' personnel from Malaya to the First Gulf War)

Pat Cunningham,
DFM, BA, Lic Ac, cfs, RAF, 2014

Introduction

Two things inherent in Aviation are the force of gravity and the fact that fliers receive the plaudits while those who enable them to fly remain unsung. In illustration, many people know that Blériot conquered the English Channel, but how many know who gave him his early-morning call, or saw to his pre-flight breakfast? The media carries this further, continuing to extol the military pilot despite the fact that the operational function of the sortie concerned has been exercised by a specialist crew member.

As a saving grace, there is an equal inherency in Aviation that no flier has ever been in any doubt as to the debt owed to the supporting, non-flying personnel. And yet how to express that debt? A reasonable parallel is our attitude to good health: nobody can doubt how much we owe to it, yet who can go through life daily lauding it?

Certainly, the wartime RAF made successive attempts to illustrate the mutual dependency of fliers and ground personnel. A first-line bomber, a Wellington, a Stirling, or a Lancaster, was wheeled onto the tarmac and the fliers – four for the Wellington, seven or so for the others –, were lined up before it. Then, arrayed behind them, were the ranks of the supporting personnel.

Arranged closest to the fliers would be the mechanics – the fitters (engines), fitters (airframes), electrical, wireless, and armament tradesmen; then personnel manning a tractor and bomb-trolley, a fuel bowser, fire and crash vehicles, an ambulance, a staff car, and a crew gharri; hedged about by stores, cooks, and clerical personnel. In the case of the Stirling photograph, fifty-six people.

Yet populous though such assemblies were they never represented anywhere near the total number of those who enabled the fliers to take to the air and do their jobs. Not represented on such assembly photographs would be all those contributing to the task beyond the station's bounds: personnel of the RAF maintenance units – essentially bulk storage depots and major-servicing facilities; of training establishments, both flying and non-flying; of communications networks; of air-defence and control centres, of radar stations; not least of the Service's regional hospitals. Unrepresented too were the various headquarters, rising hierarchically above station level through groups and commands, and staffed from junior officers to the very highest echelon of air officer; also the myriad specialists these needed to oversee present operations and plan future ones; and the teleprinter operators, telephonists, dispatch riders, and postal clerks who passed their orders and instructions down to stations. Absent too were the photographic interpreters and Intelligence gatherers generally, the so-essential meteorological folk, and the administrative staffs supporting all of them. Similarly missing was any representation of government, of the various air members of councils, ministries and directorates. No sign either of the home front, or of the vital nerve-stiffening comfort and morale supplied by families and friends.

Indeed, in enumerating so many omissions it begins to appear that the task of getting a single flier airborne might even be taken to involve the whole nation! Certainly the United States saw it that way, exhorting, not merely the taxpayer and factory worker, but *all* Americans, in adopting the slogan, 'USA, *Keep 'Em Flying*.'

Limiting this appraisal to the RAF itself, however, records show that the wartime Service peaked at 1,023,000 non-flying personnel, and 185,843 aircrew. Also to be taken into account, though, were personnel from Commonwealth and Dominion countries – and early on, even America! –, and such Allied air forces operating under British Command as those of Poland, Czechoslovakia, Free France, and Belgium.

Whatever the exact figure, the one million plus non-flying personnel were employed in over seventy trades. The medical branch aside, these were arranged in five groups, many being open to recruits aged from 18 to as old as 50, each offering progression through the ranks from aircraftman class two to warrant officer.

Apart from the obvious technical occupations like engines and air-frames, trades in 1943 included carpenter, blacksmith, shoemaker, armoured-car crew, torpedoman, and tailor; some trades having such now-quaint requirements as that riggers – airframe technicians – had to qualify in splicing!

Most trades were also available to members of the Women's Auxiliary Air Force, the WAAF, the general recruiting age range being from 21 to 43. Many WAAFs were employed as wireless operators, teleprinter operators, or as plotters. But there were trades too, specific to the servicewoman, notably that of fabric worker (both aircraft and balloons), and of general duties, whose tasks included 'scrubbing and helping to keep the cookhouse clean', 'cleaning and degreasing engineering plants', 'packing small items of equipment for dispatch', and 'messenger work'. There was also cook, clerical duties, driver (motor transport), and clerk (special duties). It should be noted, however, that mundane titles could confuse – perhaps were meant to, indeed – so that a clerk (special duties) might well be employed in a radar control centre, while drivers (motor transport) frequently became party to all levels of secret.

In passing, an aircraftwoman second class (AC2) drew two shillings and fourpence a day [12p] while her male counterpart drew three shillings and sixpence [17.6p]; then, regarding war pay, although both were facing the same conditions of shot and shell, airmen got sixpence a day, WAAFs just fourpence.

Setting aside such of-the-period detail, however, it can be seen that there were trained personnel, both male and female, to meet every requirement needed to get aircraft and crews safely into the air.

The distinction between flying and non-flying personnel, though taken as read above, had been nowhere as clear cut until just two years before the war. Prior to that only pilots had been considered full-time fliers, and even then many non-commissioned pilots had a ground trade which they would revert to after a spell on flying. Observers and gunners, the other two categories of flier, were drawn, as needed, from volunteer airmen who, after a flying duty, would pocket their one or two shillings of flying pay and return to their workshops. That this was a misemployment of highly-qualified tradesmen was one of many shortcomings dealt with during the pre-war expansion of the RAF.

It was equally recognised that dotting from flying duty back to hangar was hardly conducive to building up expertise in the air. As a result, airmen fliers were accepted as specialists and promoted to sergeant. Only this led to resentment, many ground tradesmen having had to wait some twenty years before that rank was granted them.

Despite the new gulfs so opened between fliers and non-fliers, it was still possible for tradesmen to remuster; indeed, several of the airmen in this book originally volunteered as aircrew. Most tradesmen though, had no interest in becoming fliers. Nor is this surprising. As technicians their concern was to delve as deeply as necessary in order to root out whichever gremlin was causing the trouble. Those who flew, in contrast, were only concerned with operating the various systems: nowhere near as demanding.

As for the hazards, periodical flak and night-fighters on the one hand were balanced on the other by unrelenting months of working in draughty hangars or on open dispersals. Then again, as the narratives in this book show, it was far from uncommon for ground personnel too to find themselves enduring direct enemy fire.

This book then, embraces the experiences of those who wanted to fly but fell short medically and so reverted to ground trades, also of those who got their wings but were prevented from flying on operations as the Service's requirements changed. Most of its personal narratives, though, reflect the diversity of opportunity which took personnel of the ground trades to exercise their skills not only in the beleaguered United Kingdom and later in war-torn Europe, but also in the desert and jungle campaigns of the Middle- and Far-Eastern theatres; in one case a female cook reverses the trend, coming to the RAF in Britain via 'Siberia', Uzbekistan, and East Africa!

There are glimpses too of the world outside the Service, with a schoolgirl recalling the mutual warmth between her family and the exiled foreign flier billeted upon them; with another young woman visiting wartime RAF stations as a civilian aircraft-repair worker.

What all the narratives bring out particularly clearly is that it was the ground personnel who underpinned wartime RAF formations, often serving with the same unit throughout both the conflict and their service; in contrast to the aircrew personnel who, in the course of bestowing gallant lustre to a squadron, might stay for under four months. On 12 March 1949 Marshal of the Royal Air Force Sir Arthur Harris, the wartime commander of Bomber Command, paid his own tribute when cabling the 7,000 former personnel attending the first Bomber Command Reunion, particularly greeting 'the ground staffs who kept 'em flying regardless of the miseries of wet and winter'. This book then, is a tribute to the World War Two groundcrews of the RAF and along with them, those who sought to fly operationally but were prevented by circumstance from doing so.

Pat Cunningham, DFM, RAF 1951–1973

1. My Scrambled Brain

Corporal Fred Harris, wireless mechanic

Fred Harris, 1939

The consultant appointed by the War Pensions Agency at Norcross, Blackpool, shook his head.

'Is it true, then, Doc?' I asked, 'no brain?' After all, enough doubt had been cast on the matter since I had left the Raff, and by all manner of people, not least Edna, my wife.

'Oh,' he said easily, 'you have a brain, Mr Harris. And it's all there. Only nothing's where it ought to be!'

It was my daughter, Gilly, who had arranged the consultation, for despite all the welfare issues I had helped sort out during my years as secretary of the local branch of Raffa [RAFA: The Royal Air Forces Association] it had never occurred to me to apply to them on my own behalf. Now, though, she had pointed out – over months of keeping on at me –, the time had come. Only a year before I had lost my beloved Edna, both wife and lifelong friend. And even I had to admit that looking after the flat was becoming something of a handful. But before deciding whether or not to move into supervised accommodation I would benefit from having my mind set at rest.

The Norcross consultant's response put me sufficiently at my ease, and ultimately I took the decision to move into a care home. And my jumbled brain? Well, that was Adolf Hitler's doing. But best I start just a while before that evil little horror came to my notice.

I suppose nowadays I would be classed as a nerd. Back in 1934, though, when I was taken on as a school-leaver at fourteen by HMV (His Master's Voice: the dog quizzically listening to the loudspeaker, remember?), the term was wireless fanatic. I had started by tickling various crystals with a cat's whisker and using my iron bedframe as an aerial. Oh yes! and wearing earphones: that, at least, hasn't changed overmuch, looking about me at youngsters today! By the time I left school, however, I'd graduated to transmitters and receivers, was adept at the morse code, and had a reputation as an amateur-radio ham.

Cat's whisker

I never had to study all that much, for reading other people's circuits and working out my own, tweaking one part of a set to match another, and even constructing and winding my own transformers, came easy to me.

At the time, I was living in Brixton where my father was a tram driver, so it was very convenient to be assigned to the premier HMV store in Oxford Street, at that time acclaimed for the electrical animation across its frontage showing a man putting a record on an HMV turntable.

HMV knew all about my interest in wireless and the swiftly-developing television, but trade practice meant that I had to serve some time as a messenger. For the most part this meant carrying out deliveries between Oxford Street and head office in Hayes, even so special jobs were not uncommon. One that has to stick in my mind, though, came my way when I was just coming up to fifteen.

I was given a written message to deliver to a Mr Butler who held some position in Buckingham Palace, my manager having impressed upon me that I was to hand it to nobody else but Mr B. My first hurdle was the policeman at the gate, who wanted me to leave it with him. I stuck my heels in, however, pimples and all, and eventually he sent for someone who took me into the main building.

Once inside, I insisted my way past two or three other people before, after some delay, a very elegant young woman appeared, a lord's daughter, it turned out. She also, would be only too pleased to make sure my message was delivered to Mr Butler. How I hated not doing what she wanted, and in the face of that smile, for I've always warmed to the ladies! After only a momentary pause, however, she canted her head, led me to an office where she had a brief word with a seemingly very busy gentleman at a desk, gave me another heart-turning smile, and left.

'Well done!' the man said, leaning towards me with outstretched hand, 'I'm Butler, and you've shown remarkable persistence in getting this far.'

Maybe he repeated that to my manager, for shortly afterwards I set aside my messenger's hat and started training as an HMV engineer.

By 1938 war was well on the cards. Late in August, therefore, when I saw an appeal for radio amateurs to join the Civilian Wireless Reserve of the Royal Air Force, I signed on at once. Members received lectures and carried out exercises using our own equipments, the idea being that at some future stage we would be automatically transferred to the RAF Volunteer Reserve. On 30 August 1939, however, as the war clouds grew darker, I jumped the gun and attested to serve a five-year Voluntary Reserve engagement as a trainee wireless operator.

So it was that, on 4 September 1939, the day after war was declared, and having said a 'for-the-duration' farewell to HMV, I reported to No. 9 Training Centre in London, who immediately dispatched me to No. 32 Squadron at Biggin Hill, near Orpington, in Kent. The squadron, receiving the news, can't have been too thrilled, I suspect, for I'd had virtually no recruit training and no formal technical training whatsoever, joining them as an aircrafthand (wireless operator) – in the vernacular, an ACH (WO) –, or general dogsbody (wireless).

My shortcomings notwithstanding, I found the squadron over the moon, having just received Hawker Hurricane fighters. But I too struck lucky, for formally untrained though I was, I found myself working alongside four experienced wireless mechanics, two of whom were former naval radiomen, and being streets more knowledgeable than I was, taught me a lot.

The work was straightforward enough, largely consisting of determining whether a wireless set was working or not. If pressing the transmit button proved it wasn't, then the box was exchanged at the wireless bay and the replacement screwed into the vacant hole: nowhere near as complicated as the backtuning through circuits and fiddling with a cat's whisker I'd been used to. So it was that, just four days before Christmas 1939, my status was regularised, and I became an established aircraftman second class, the lowest rank there was. Now I had rank! So, although still an experienced operator with virtually nothing to operate, I had everything to aim for.

Where the job was concerned, the Hurricanes were pre-flighted, took off, and we went back to our char and wads. When they returned we put down our mugs, saw them in, post-flighted them, then sought out whatever work there was to do: in my case, back to scratching for knowledge in the wireless bay. The overall importance of Biggin in the scheme of things undoubtedly went over my head.

In truth, stations like Biggin Hill, Kenley, Tangmere, and Hornchurch were key to the air defence organization that was to prove so vital to Britain's survival just a year later. Only then would I begin to find out that the 'wireless direction-finding aerials' recently erected on the coast – even us dyed-in-the-wool wireless chaps thought that was all there was to them! – were far more efficient in warning of approaching enemy aircraft than the Observer Corps watchers in their sandbagged bunkers facing the Channel. About all I knew at the time was that alerting messages from any source would be fed to a headquarters and then sent out to the fighter squadrons; squadrons like ours, and the other Biggin Hurricane outfit, No. 79 Squadron. Not forgetting, of course, the other lot, No. 610 Squadron. They had Spitfires.

It was all I needed to know, of course. Fortunately, as I understand it now, the Germans too, took time to find out that the ostensible-wireless towers bore the far-seeing 'eyes' the world was soon to know as radar, and that Biggin Hill was one of the prime 'command and control' centres in the defensive-offensive chain.

My generation had long had an expectation of what modern conflict meant from our fathers' war. Just as in 1914 a British Expeditionary Force (BEF) would move to the Continent. Once deployed it would bring the German armies to a halt, then sit there, leaking blood for as long as it took, until some form of armistice was signed. And the initial weeks of our war, certainly, followed just this pattern. The BEF showed grins and thumbs-ups, and French peasants were all smiles. And then – nothing happened.

It was what we later learnt to call the Phoney War, though we didn't know it then. Any more than we knew that the turmoil that was to overtake us all too soon would eventually be designated the Battle of Britain.

And so we sat there at Biggin, seeing both Hurricanes and Spitfires come and go, noting as they landed that the linen patches sealing their gun muzzles were unbroken, showing that they had not yet brought to the enemy to combat.

On 1 April 1940 – the RAF having been born on 1 April it loved doing things on its birthday! – major construction work began at Biggin. The Spits winged off to Tangmere while both Hurricane squadrons began a series of moves to Gravesend (Hornchurch) and Manston, two other Kentish airfields. I knew at the time that the Works people were putting in a concrete runway and building deep air-raid shelters but I now know their primary task was to upgrade the command and control centre. Anyway, by mid May of 1940, presumably with the work well under way, all three squadrons were moved back to Biggin.

Shortly after our return, as things finally began to happen on the Continent, we became far busier. Our squadrons started flying sorties over Northern France, with detachments operating from Hawkinge, near Folkestone, to give the fighters more airborne time before they needed to refuel. We also did detachments to Manston, the task there being to prevent German bombers from interfering with Channel convoys.

Then, very suddenly, it was all go as the German armies surged forwards, a hectic period with one of our flights being rushed across to bolster a weakened squadron (I believe it was No. 3), signals coming back to us showing them moving from Abbeville, in France, then into Belgium – to Moorsele, then hurriedly rearwards to Merville, in France, and finally, snapping back at the Germans from Manston, before returning to the fold at Biggin.

For the bulk of the squadron too, the days got even busier. I remember nine of our aircraft being sent to patrol the Hook of Holland, while as May 1940 gave way to June they flew cross-Channel sorties to Le Tréport and such places as Le Cateau, and Arras, names so familiar from the previous war. We had successes, but we also took losses, with five of our pilots being killed. Several others survived being shot down, but became prisoners of war. Indeed, one of our aircraft followed suit, for having crashed nearly intact it was subsequently put on display in Leipzig!

A No. 32 Squadron Hurricane displayed as a war trophy in Leipzig

Swiftly, however, the BEF was pushed back to Dunkirk, and suddenly, the evacuation became the centre of our world.

It was now that personalities began to emerge. Our big boss was Squadron Leader John Worrall, who would later become an air vice-marshal but who remained at Biggin as a fighter controller when the squadron moved north [on 28 August 1940]. During his spell in command he really spurred the lads on and although never becoming a high scorer himself, gained the Distinguished Flying Cross (DFC) and saw No. 32 well started in amassing the 102 German aircraft they would account for during their participation in the Battle: under his direct leadership they destroyed forty-three and were granted twenty-two probables.

But it was the very young chaps who suddenly filled out as characters during those early days. Lads like Pilot Officer Daw who would crash-land, slightly injuring himself, but still claim six enemy aircraft. And Flying Officer Mike Nicholson Crossley – not hyphenated, for all that he was a product of Eton and had a real plum in his mouth! – who after the French battles finished up with seven swastikas painted beneath his canopy, including several Bf109s which, as he told me, 'I really had to work for', clearly rating them more highly than sluggish bombers.

On one sortie he strafed troop-carrying transports at Ypenburg Airfield in Holland, drawing strenuous ground-fire. His daring was rewarded, as he got away unscathed, and though later he was twice shot down by enemy aircraft he came bouncing back each time. In June, I think it was, he got the DFC for his gallantry and would later gain a Distinguished Service Order, eventually claiming twenty victories. Promoted, he actually took over as squadron commander but left in April 1941 on a test-pilot posting to the States.

By the time things had settled after Dunkirk, we'd begun to gather the main outline of the defence scheme of which Biggin was a key part, the radar telling headquarters as German aircraft headed for the convoys, then Biggin relaying that information, and Group's resulting orders, to the squadrons. All of little use if the wireless sets in the cockpits weren't working!

Hurricane Transmitter-Receiver, TR9

Spitfire with TR1133 VHF radio

In fact, we were hard pushed. Our Hurricanes had the Transmitter-Receiver TR9 high-frequency sets which had a sadly poor range, and were irritatingly troublesome. We did our best, while looking aside enviously at the Type 1133 VHF transmitter/receiver carried by No. 610 Squadron's Spits. This not only gave clearer signals and better range – using just a spike aerial and doing away with the fussy wire running back to the tail – but was also technically more dependable. Of course, until we got them ourselves we didn't let on to the Spit chaps, for prima donnas that they were, they'd have told us we were jealous. Nonsense, of course, but I have to admit that although our Hurricanes won the Battle of Britain – there were twice as many of them, we could turn them around far quicker, and they scored more kills –, the Spitfire groupies won the propaganda war.

The flurry of business went on into July, indeed, so busy were we that they rested us for a while, but quickly brought us back to Biggin, and to readiness. It was early in August 1940, though, when things took a major turn and the Luftwaffe switched to bombing Fighter Command's airfields. On the squadron we counted the start of the Battle of Britain from the afternoon of 12 August 1940 when our Hurricanes were sent to shoo enemy bombers away from what we now knew were the radar stations.

That morning I had been taken by road to Hawkinge and had only just seen the aircraft scrambled after some high fliers, when some bombers who had crossed the Channel below the radar screen popped up and began to plaster the airfield, luckily, without causing any casualties to our party. The landing area was put out of commission, however, so we were driven back to Biggin.

At the time we counted the day as unusual, but very soon such activity became the norm. Even so, the initial pattern seemed haphazard, with our aircraft being sent first east, then west – often to protect Kenley – as raids came and went. The case was, it turned out, that the Germans had still not grasped that Biggin Hill was key to the defence system and were striking at any airfield that looked large enough to be important.

Whether or not they had finally twigged, we caught the first of several packets on 18 August 1940 when their bombers suddenly appeared overhead. That first real raid seemed to go on for ever, yet later we learnt it lasted just ten minutes. In that time, though, they'd dropped a fair old number of bombs: some said 500! Fortunately, they'd concentrated on the airfield once more, so that for all the nerve-shattering noise they'd scarcely gone when the whole station was out there filling in enough holes to bring Biggin back into operation that same evening.

The real work, of course, was being done in the air, with our now-exhausted pilots being scrambled as many as four times a day. The strain on them was duly noted, for on 28 August 1940 Fighter Command ordered our Hurricanes to Acklington, in Northumberland, for a well-deserved rest.

Better for me, perhaps, had I gone with them. As it was, I remained with a stay-behind party, getting the last few kites fit to travel.

The weather throughout 30 August 1940 had been glorious, and we were all set for a fine evening. It had also been a hectic day, laid on, we joked, just to wave us stay-behinds off, for next morning we expected to rejoin the rest in Acklington.

In mid morning a major raid of over a hundred aircraft had developed, virtually every available fighter in the south being scrambled. Certainly, these kept the first wave back from Biggin airfield, although the poor old village caught it, as did the hospital in the neighbouring hamlet of Farnborough.

In the afternoon there had been a second raid, though we'd been saved that too, the word filtering from the control centre being that the enemy was targeting the coastal wireless masts. Damage to these must have temporarily disrupted the command-and-control system, for when the Luftwaffe came again that evening we actually saw high-flying bombers going over before the siren went.

I'd just finished helping one of No. 610's lads sort out a snag on a Spitfire, for though there was plenty of inter-squadron rivalry there were no unions and we all mucked in, often regardless of both squadron and trade. The job done, we began to make our way to the cookhouse.

We'd discounted the overflying bombers as a threat, having decided they were going for Kenley once again. In fact, although I'm rather hazy on the point, I believe the all-clear had actually gone. Then we heard explosions coming our way, and I realised that some of the bombers had turned back, dived down, and were already running in on Biggin from low level.

They could hardly miss, and as I found out later, did a lot of damage to installations. What they also hit, though, on one pass, was an air-raid shelter packed with personnel. For my part, caught in the open, I saw earth spurting up as they strafed, and retain an impression of black objects tumbling free. But that was all I remember. As, indeed, is fitting for someone who figured in the initial casualty signal as one of forty fatalities.

In Brixton my father was just wheeling his bicycle into the house after his day's work when he saw the telegram boy coming up behind him. The wartime telegram was always dreaded, and this one told him and mum that I had been killed at Biggin Hill and that my body was being held in the mortuary of Farnborough Hospital, Orpington.

Dad being a man of action, he at once gathered up mum and set off for Kent. Highly distressed, the pair of them duly arrived at the hospital, to be met by the sweet-bitter news that, although not dead, I was badly wounded, and in a coma, and not expected to last out the week.

Only later would the gaps be filled in, both for them, and to a certain extent, for me. It seems that after the raid I was found lying face down with the back of my head so shattered that I was taken for dead.

Initially all the bodies were laid out in a Biggin hangar before being transferred to the nearby hospital. And certainly, countless times over the succeeding years I was to re-live a first awakening, seeing so clearly the rows of still shapes in the shadows; picturing anew the horror of that cavernous interior. And yet surely, having been in a coma, any such awakening could only have been in my imagination!

On transfer, the bodies, all forty of them – mine included – were accepted by the hospital. Except that when a new shift came on duty and were set to cleaning up the corpses, a nurse realised that my pulse was still beating. After which, things must have happened in a rush. Clearly the surgeons did their stuff. As did the communications network, reducing the Biggin casualty signal by one fatality. For my part, I remained in the coma for eight solid days.

To round things off at Biggin, however, and indeed, at No. 32 Squadron, the rest of my party stayed on long enough to experience yet another heavy raid just a day or so after I had been struck down. Again the airfield was plastered, but this time the operations room was hit, the nerve centre, as I now know, not only of Biggin but of much of the defence organisation.

A noteworthy outcome of that particular raid was that three of the station's WAAFs were decorated with the military medal for their courage. Two of these were awarded to teleprinter operators who remained at their posts with rubble all around them and most telephone lines down. The third WAAF, armoury telephonist Sergeant Joan Mortimer, not only completed her assigned task but then took it upon herself to brave the many unexploded bombs (one of which went off, spilling her over!) and used red flags to mark out a safe landing strip off the cratered runway for our returning fighters. Worthy women all! As for the key operations centre, that opened for business again just a short time later in, of all things, a village shop!

WAAF plotters at Biggin Hill

WAAF military medal recipients Sergeant Joan Mortimer,
Flight Officer Elspeth Henderson, and Sergeant Helen Turner
(ranks when photographed)

As for No. 32 Squadron, although they arrived at Acklington as the most successful of the fighter squadrons engaged, they had flown their last Battle of Britain sortie. Four months later, in December 1940, when they were moved south again, they were employed in flying defensive patrols outside the main Battle areas. On occasion, however, they carried out offensive operations, notably when they escorted a force of Fairey Swordfish in the unsuccessful attempt to stop the German capital ships *Scharnhorst*, *Gneisenau*, and *Prince Eugen* in their Channel dash from Brest. Then, in February 1942, they re-trained as a night-intruder unit, and from the July were employed on such sorties over France.

In November 1942 they took part in Operation Torch, the invasion of Morocco and Algeria, subsequently helped drive the Germans out of Africa, supported the Greek government against a Communist takeover, and as the war in Europe finished, moved first to Palestine, and then to Egypt. I was retained on strength, on paper, until August 1942, but apart from a semi-social visit I was able to make while they were poised for some departure or other from Middle Wallop in early 1941, the parting of our ways had come.

In all, it was to be October 1941 before I was fully cleared by the doctors, a good fourteen months after being wounded. In the early days I still had a long way to go, so rejoining the squadron was out of the question. And throughout my recuperation, periods of sick leave were interspersed with medical checks. Clearly though, the medics thought it best to keep my now-scrambled brain from idle mischief, so as early as 23 May 1941 I was posted to RAF Carew Cheriton, near Tenby, in Pembrokeshire.

Hardly the most propitious of places to have sent me, perhaps, for less than six weeks earlier twelve of their airmen had been killed when station sick quarters had been bombed. But who knows! perhaps it was some form of far-sighted therapy, an embryo, wartime version of counselling, maybe ...

Carew Cheriton, I found, was home to a Coastal Command radar-trials unit, but although I made myself useful to them, I became increasingly involved with the build up of what would some months later open as No. 10 Radio School, where many more wireless-oriented tasks were called for. The school trained aircrew wireless operators, so once it was up and running, ensuring that its Anson and Oxford radio equipments stayed serviceable kept me busy.

In September 1941, although still essentially untrained, I had been promoted to aircraftman class one, and a month later to leading aircraftman (LAC), enabling me to impress the ladies by my sleeve badge of a two-bladed propeller. As for the upgrade to LAC, when examined I'd scored 82%: so what, I wondered, would my score have been if I'd had a full brain!

In July 1942, however, I was warned for overseas, given two weeks' embarkation leave, and sent to No. 2 Personnel Despatch Unit at Wilmslow, on Cannock Chase. Having been kitted out with khaki drill, been documented, and given an armful of jabs, I was then left to kick my heels until, on 24 August, I was finally allocated a sailing draft, and told that I was bound for the Middle East.

The voyage out was a protracted affair, and for the most part, better forgotten. From the Clyde we were taken way out into the Atlantic in order to avoid U-boats and long-range German bombers. Indeed, we had to go further out than was normal even for wartime convoys in order to avoid the vast fleets from both America and Britain that were supporting Operation Torch (just to confirm, the British-American invasion of French North Africa). In fact, had the lads from No. 32 Squadron, who were part of Torch, got their fingers out and had the Mediterranean open we could have steamed straight through to Alexandria. But then, without me along … As it was, we had to go around the Cape. Though long and uncomfortable, however, the circumnavigation did bring us the not-to-be-missed bonus of replenishing at Durban. And what a bonus!

Durban's Lady in White, contralto Perla Siedle Gibson

From being sung in by Durban's Lady in White [see Glossary] – she would also sing us out! – and our sheer delight in seeing a capital city lit to the heavens after so many months of Britain's blackout, to the wonderful scenery, and to the even more wonderful hospitality afforded us by the lovely, and so elegant, ladies of Durban, it was a two week break to kill for.

We spent Christmas there, but not the New Year, for idylls pass swiftly, and all too soon it was back to airless 'H' deck, way below the water line, as we ploughed up the Red Sea to disembark at Port Suez, at the southern end of the Suez Canal. It was 2 January 1943, a full two months after leaving the Clyde. And three days later, after a road journey that rivalled the Atlantic transit for discomfort, I reported to RAF Helwan, just east of Cairo.

Fred Harris, 1943

I'd have preferred being with the squadron, who by now, were supporting the eastward slog through Tunisia, but life at RAF Helwan would have been hard to beat. As an established – that is, peacetime – Canal Zone station it had among its facilities a swimming pool, showers, an open-air cinema, married quarters, and a school, even a local village within easy walking distance to give colour. And for longer off-duty periods, Cairo was only ten miles distant.

The major tenant, I found, was the RAF's Middle-East Signals School, where for two months I carried on much as before, changing wireless boxes in Anson and Oxford trainers as required. But now the RAF finally decided to allow me to remuster from aircrafthand (wireless/operator) to a hands-on maintenance trade in which I could legitimately delve into the innards of any set that gave trouble. So, from March until late August 1943 it was heads down on a conversion course from which I emerged as a fully qualified wireless mechanic.

Now that I had the bit-o'-paper to supplement both my amateur-radio experience and that I had gained since joining up, they were able to promote me to corporal. Which meant that, as I would say at the time, instead of changing boxes myself, I now told other airmen to do so. In all seriousness, though, it meant that for the balance of what was to be my two years here I became responsible for both the technical expertise and the domestic harmony of a section of some seven wireless lads, and thereby for the well-being of the radios of any aircraft, established or visitor, that came our way.

The job hardly changed when, on 8 February 1945, I was posted down to Ballah, some way north of Ismailia, and adjacent to the Ballah Cut-Off – the cut-off, and the Great Bitter Lake, further south, being the only places where ships could pass on the canal.

Looking from RAF Ballah, north of Ismailia, a ship on the Suez Canal

RAF Ballah was the Middle-East's Central Gunnery School, but the switch from the Signals School merely meant that I was once again keeping fighting machines, rather than trainers, up to scratch, Hurricanes, Spitfires, and now Kittyhawks, and such bombers as Blenheims, Bostons, and Marauders.

In the main, life was smooth enough, but that there were tensions over and above the World War now raging to its finale in both Europe and the Far East was brutally brought home to me when I arranged an outing for my section to the Great Bitter Lake. The lakeside location was one accepted as secure for bathing, so we dumped our clothes beside those of other groups, and ran down to the water. After a while of skylarking in the shallows we took to the deeps and began a race. Proving to be the strongest swimmer there, I eventually forged ahead of the rest. Then, seeing that they had turned back, I followed. So it was that I was facing their way as they walked back up the beach. And as the landmine exploded among them …

It might well have been a stray, of course, with so many millions laid. Though at this juncture it was equally likely to be a booby trap, or what would now be called an IED – improvised explosive device. What was certain was that back then the nationalists were no longer playing about.

Again, let me leave the trauma. It was all too much like Biggin. And as at Biggin, it had to be lived with, painful though that was …

Undoubtedly the tragedy coloured my view of what, until then, had been a very happy posting, but just weeks later, on 8 May 1945, the war in Europe was over. In due course, therefore, I found myself aboard a trooper, but this time steaming through the Mediterranean, rather than around the Cape. Nor was there any need to loop out into the Atlantic.

In 1939 I had signed on, not 'for the duration' but for five years, my anticipated release date being 29 August 1944, except that at that time, because they'd let their war drag on, I'd still been swanning it in the Canal Zone. Being in Release Group A, however, I might have expected a swift release once I became tour-ex. Certainly, I was hopeful when, as early as 2 January 1946, with my disembarkation leave over, I was called for processing to RAF Hednesford, Staffordshire – No. 104 Personnel Despatch Centre (PDC). It was not to be until early April, however, that I was actually demobbed. Even then, I had a Reserve commitment until 30 June 1959, though when I was released from that I doubt they even bothered to tell me.

In all then, I spent six and a half years 'with the Colours', as the army say, with three and a half of them overseas. And I had been so lucky. Saved from a landmine by an facility for swimming; strafed in the open, and left for dead, yet with not so much as a headache in the years since. What I did have, though, and increasingly used as time went by, was a ready excuse for muddle-headedness: what else with only half a brain?

Lucky, of course, to be permitted the years I was able to spend in so many, and such varied, pursuits, and in the love of the family I gathered about me. And lucky too that the Norcross consultant was able to clear my mind and supply official confirmation that I had made my way since 1940, if not with exactly half a brain, at least with one that was well and truly scrambled.

Fred Harris, 2012

2. A Life Worth Living

Sergeant Don Illsley, fitter 2 (airframes)

Had it not been for my headmaster I would have left school at fifteen and become a motor mechanic. He was dubious, however, about my plan, and proposed that it might be better to get my school certificate, then join the RAF as an aircraft apprentice. My love of cars being equalled only by my love of aeroplanes, I acquiesced at once. So, having achieved a high pass in the school cert, I successfully sat the RAF entrance exam and on 5 September 1939, just two days into the war, reported to RAF Halton, in Buckinghamshire.

I would have been a pre-war joiner had it not been for a fortnight's hiccup with my vaccination appointment, and this proved significant, for as all the vacancies in my trade of choice, that of Fitter Grade 2 (engines), were filled, I had to settle for Fitter Grade 2 (airframes).

Under the RAF aircraft apprentice scheme, fifteen to seventeen-and-a-half-year-old 'Brats' did a three-year technical training course, attesting to serve for twelve years from the age of eighteen. By 1939 the RAF was well into a major expansion, so that my entry, the Fortieth, rather than the more normal 3–400 strong, numbered over 1,200. Moreover, instead

of a three-year course, ours was to be compressed into twenty-plus months. Exigencies of the Service too, dictated that we began training, not at Halton, the well-established No. 1 School of Technical Training, but at the No. 2 School at RAF Cosford, near Wolverhampton.

Don Illsley, aircraft apprentice,
1939

At Cosford we set about learning our basic trade skills, filing metal shapes to within thousands of an inch, riveting, panel beating, and woodworking, occupations which roughened both our hands and vocabularies. The next phase, though, saw us working on an actual aeroplane, a Gloster Gauntlet!

It was not until March 1940 that we joined the main apprentice body at Halton, our incoming wing made distinctive by its red-and-blue-chequered hatband but sharing with those already in residence the 'wheel' armbadge – a four-bladed propeller, in fact – denoting boy service, as opposed to man service, regular airmen being loftily regarded by us as 'boggies'. Not that such cliquish prejudices were either malicious or one-sided, mature airmen holding that the two noisiest things in the RAF were Rolls Razors and aircraft apprentices.

All healthy give and take. The fact was, however, that the RAF apprentice scheme had long since forged an enviable record of achievement, with character moulding held as of prime importance; certainly, unlike school, the RAF saw no crime in left-handedness, so no more remedial heavy wooden rules across my 'leftie' knuckles!

We studied hydraulics, pneumatics, aero-carpentry, stressed-skin repairs, hulls and floats, fabric repairs, paintwork, machine-shop practice, heat treatment of metals and, of course, theory of flight. We also attended school, pursuing mathematics to calculus, and 'cultural' studies: English, geography, and the like. It was a demanding course, but fulfilling too, and although many fell by the wayside, the bulk of us passed out – as leading aircraftmen (LACs) – on 19 May 1941.

My initial posting was to No. 27 Operational Training Unit (OTU), RAF Lichfield, known then as RAF Fradley, after the nearest village. This OTU's particular role was to teach Commonwealth aircrews to operate Vickers Wellingtons, my job, as a fitter, being to keep the aircraft serviceable. Within days of arriving, though, I exercised my right as an ex-apprentice to apply for pilot training myself: the right being dependent upon having declared the intention before passing out.

Finding that I hadn't yet flown, my commanding officer, declared, 'We'll soon alter that,' and organised a three-hour flight for me. Suffice to say that on landing I was well and truly sold.

I reported for aircrew selection just five days before my eighteenth birthday, and initially all went swimmingly, even the critical interview by two group captains and an air commodore. Did I know, one asked me, what my station commander was famous for. This was easy.

'In 1933, sir,' I told my interlocutor, 'Group Captain Gayford flew a Fairey Monoplane from Cranwell to South Africa – to Walvis Bay –, and set the world long-distance record of 5,400 miles.'

Smiles all round, after which the result seemed a forgone conclusion. Until the eyesight test revealed that I was longsighted. They called in two specialists. But it was no good. And that was that.

I tempered my disappointment with the rationalisation that while the RAF might have lost a great pilot they had, in his place, a first-class airframe fitter. Mind you, I've always had a sneaking suspicion that had I been less valuable as a fitter I might have been called back a few months later as a flight engineer. It would be many a long month, though, before it dawned on me that my eyesight defect had probably saved my life, aircrew losses being what they turned out to be. And yet …

In September 1941, after a week's embarkation leave, I boarded His Majesty's Troopship SS *Strathaird* at Glasgow. We sailed in convoy, touching at Freetown, in Sierra Leone, then making a four-day stay at Cape

Town during which we were allowed ashore. After that, it was on to Durban, accompanied now by the battle cruiser HMS *Repulse*.

HMS Repulse

We knew that in 1917 *Repulse* had been the first capital ship to have an aircraft fly off her – a Sopwith Pup! the warship's first acquaintance with air power. Her last, sadly, was to be nowhere near so benign. But now, when the convoy turned north for Aden, she surged forwards, her crew lining the rails as she passed through the ranks before curving away towards the eastern horizon. A majestic sight! Yet poignant. For just weeks later she would be sunk by Japanese torpedo bombers off the east coast of Malaya, suffering the loss of over 500 of those who had so cheerily waved us farewell.

Our convoy duly arrived in Aden where I vainly applied for permission to visit the grave of my soldier-Uncle Jim, who had died there in 1924. Instead, it was off up the Red Sea to Port Suez, where we disembarked and where, reflecting on our nine-week trip, I could only observe that wartime troopers in no sense offered luxury cruising.

The Desert War: The Libyan Theatre

My posting, I learnt, was to No. 59 Repair and Salvage Unit (RSU), then forming at Amriyab, on the Mediterranean Coast, about twelve miles west of Alexandria. I learnt too, that America had joined us in the war.

While our unit got itself sorted out I was one of a party sent to No. 103 Maintenance Unit at nearby Aboukir to re-assemble some of No. 39 Squadron's Bristol Beaufort torpedo bombers which had had to be dismantled after bogging down on Lake Mariut airfield. We were billeted in vacated married quarters that had no electricity, no furniture and only straw-filled, bed-bug-infested mattresses. Here too, I suffered my first war wound, ducking beneath a Beaufort's flap and sustaining a cut that needed four stitches.

We finally joined No. 59 RSU in the new year, only to find them wallowing in a sea of mud. Fortunately, when one of our heaviest vehicles bogged down, we were able to beg a tow from, of all things, a passing Crusader tank.

Once fully equipped, No. 59 moved 150 miles west of Alexandria, first to Landing Ground 07 (LG-07), near Mersa Matruh, then backtracking thirty-five miles to LG-101, near Sidi Haneish.

On decamping from LG-07 we had left some lads to carry out an engine change on an Italian Caproni Tri-motor which had been captured, but had then forced-landed en route to the Canal Zone. Our commanding officer, learning that it had become serviceable, and knowing that Roy Manners – another Fortieth-Entry chap – and I had to travel to Ismailia for a course, came off the telephone and told us, 'Get tiffin, then pack. I'll take you over in the Caproni. ETD 1400. Hurry back.' And hurry we did. Better a quick flip any day than the dusty ride along the always crowded, always potentially hazardous, Desert Road.

We arrived back dead on time. Only to hear him on the phone again, his tone incredulous, 'He's done *what?*'

It transpired that the ferry pilot had over-primed the new engine, set alight the fabric-covered structure, and reduced the Caproni to embers.

With the three-week course over, and now familiarised with the American P-40 ground-attack Kittyhawk, Roy and I stole a nefarious overnight in the Cairo fleshpots, missed our train, and thumbed our way back on a Bedford petrol tanker. 'Where's all this traffic coming from?' we asked as the driver beat his way against the flow. 'Tobruk,' he allowed. 'There's a bit of a flap on.'

It was April 1942, and we had been well aware that when Rommel launched his new onslaught Sidi Haneish would become a prime target. Indeed, in anticipation, Flight Lieutenant 'King' Cole, a former chief petty officer, had ringed the perimeter with air-raid warning posts: fair enough suspending engine cylinders to raise the alarm but he had also insisted that sentry stints were marked off in 'bells', naval fashion!

Back with the unit, though, nobody seemed concerned with the situation. Just the same, Roy and I packed the rest of our kit. And sure enough next day our seventy-strong convoy joined the largely off-road, horizon-to-horizon trek eastwards – passing a nondescript rail halt called El Alamein without it even registering – to finish up back at Amriyah.

Once Rommel had been halted, No. 59 RSU moved westwards once more, leaving me with a stay-behind party to service a replacement pool of thirty Hurricanes. Though an airframes man, 'gyppo tummy' was so rife – I had only just recovered from a bout myself – that I was frequently the only fitter available to do the daily inspections, signing off engines, of course, but also electrics, radios, and armaments! Our fellow lodger unit was equally stretched, its thirty-six Kittyhawks supplying escort to succeeding waves of Boston bombers. Moreover, with the front being so close they were always back within twenty minutes, each Kittyhawk plaguing us with a periodically-renewed personal sandstorm.

Having missed several of No. 59's moves – moves which brought it the soubriquet, 'Ship o'the Desert'; albeit a seventy-vehicle ship! – we eventually rejoined the unit at Wadi Natrum, some sixty miles west of Alex, or as we had learnt to put it by then, about halfway to El Alamein. And here, as we supported the re-equipping of local Hurricane squadrons with Spitfires, life took on a certain stability. We even had a hangar! if only one. Though, in truth, there were few other amenities. Certainly there was the nearby Halfway House, a Thomas Cook hotel, but it was for officers only. What we got, conceivably in lieu, was a weekly 24-hour pass to Alex.

Then the Germans found us. After which they raided us night after night. And particularly heavily when a 'bombers moon' allowed the Junkers Ju88s to come in so low, bombing and strafing, that we could see their gunners.

Of all our casualties the one that affected me most was Taff Richardson, yet another Halton Fortieth-Entry chap. He'd taken cover in the slit trench beside mine when he was joined by a bomb which momentarily failed to explode. Taff was at full stretch springing out when it did go off. Paralysed, he would linger on until June 1945. On a more banal note, our sergeant needed shrapnel removing from his buttocks.

Casualties aside, twenty-one of the twenty-three fighters on the strip were destroyed. What intrigued us, however, was that two of the South African Air Force's very unpopular Martin Marylands, though distantly parked, had also burnt out, the general feeling being that the Yarpies themselves had torched them in order to get Blenheims as replacements.

More positively, the army moved in some Bofors anti-aircraft guns so that when the Germans raided us again they ran into such a barrage as to put them off bothering us for the rest of our stay.

In the next few weeks, and as reinforcements poured into the theatre, so No. 59 RSU was split in two, with me among those transferred to the new No. 3 Repair and Salvage Unit. Then came Montgomery's counter-offensive, after which the breakneck speed of the westward advance was such that just days later we paused overnight at Sidi Haneish. Indeed, we even found a Hurricane mainplane on the trestles where we had left it! And where it may well sit to this day, for we had learnt our lesson after a cook had moved an obviously obstructive stone slab, only to set off a booby-trap grenade.

A while later we moved from Egypt into Libya, to Martuba, an airstrip on an escarpment seventeen miles inland from Derna, where we diversified, running a small training flight to convert pilots onto night-fighters. Now, with our aircraft flying round the clock, sixteen-hour duties became the norm, with night guard coming around twice a week along with other airfield duties. As for days off, they fast became a memory. But nobody complained. Certainly not the conversion instructor, Flight Lieutenant 'Nipper' Joyce, of No. 73 Squadron, who, at the sound of bombing, tumbled from his bedroll beneath the wing of his Hurricane, got airborne, shot down a Ju88, had breakfast, then set about his day's work.

Additional jobs frequently fell to us non-warriors too. As when the Turley and Williams cookers on our field canteen became unserviceable and we got them going again; a feat that so delighted the sergeant cook that, from then on, he gave us of his best.

A westward move to Nufilia, on the Gulf of Sidra, some 300 miles further on, was noteworthy in being the shortest of our sojourns. And just as well, perhaps. Our vehicles had been parked and we had all milled around for two hours as the cooks awaited the broken-down water bowser they needed to prepare a meal. As it arrived, however, it exploded a mine and lost a wheel. How the device hadn't been set off beforehand, heaven knows: the question now being, how many others lurked!

We were still gingerly considering that when a United States Army Air Force Kittyhawk roared noisily overhead and crash-landed yet more noisily on the strip. Enough, surely? But before the long awaited water had even begun to steam we were ordered to get under way again, another 200-plus miles west, to Miserata, just sixty miles short of Tripoli.

At Miserata the unit converted pilots from Britain, Canada, America, New Zealand, and a noteworthy gent from Yugoslavia. The latter, a Sergeant Cenich, broke off from a training flight to harass some German bombers, only to run out of fuel and be forced to put down in the desert, damaging his valuable aircraft. Better, it was felt, to have contained his zeal until he was flying a machine with loaded guns.

Our next stopping-off place was Zuara, 50 miles beyond Tripoli – and just that much short of the Tunisian border. Zuara was a former Italian garrison town where we could relax on the beach, swimming out, and riding the waves back. Until one afternoon when amphibious tanks appeared and turned inshore. Friendlies, as they proved to be, on an exercise. But nobody had warned us!

I was equally surprised when a USAAF Kittyhawk dropped in one day. I jumped onto his wing root and as the canopy came back discovered a pilot both widely-grinning and coal-black. He was from the Tuskegee Fighter Group, it transpired, and therefore, one of the first black American combat pilots. Having become uncertain of his position he'd put down at the first airstrip he saw, and was soon on his way again, his grin even wider.

The training task here at Zuara was to convert forty South African Air Force (SAAF) pilots from Hurricanes to Kittyhawks. Though we were used to dealing with pilots' whims by now, these were far from easy to work with. 'They treat us like Kaffirs,' the lads complained. Indeed, a Lieutenant Van Diggelin snarled that he was only fighting the Germans because he disliked them fractionally more than he disliked the English.

Having finished the SAAF job, we again moved westwards, now into Tunisia, to Ben Gardane, an almost landlocked bay, south of Djerba, very salty, with many spectacularly large jellyfish. A pleasant enough interlude, especially when Tunis fell and we sent up a water bowser and, in a desert miracle of our own, filled it with red wine which we sold for a pound a jerrycan. Replete, and wealthy, we then moved back to Zuara, and began re-converting the SAAF contingent to the Spitfire 5B. That done, we folded our tents, and took ourselves eastwards down the entire length of the Desert Road, and so to the Canal Zone.

Initially we lodged with No. 107 Maintenance Unit, at Kasfareet, on the Great Bitter Lake. The plan was for us to re-equip, then move to the Greek island of Kos, except that the Germans invaded it before we could sail, and so we escaped becoming prisoners of war, or worse. Meanwhile we helped the 107 lads assemble some Kittyhawks which were then flown, via Syria, to our Russian Allies. As we noted though, they had no armour, no armament, and only hand-starters for the engines. Clearly someone had reservations about just how close we were to the Ruskies …

The highlight of that time, however, was a week's leave which three of us, Fred Long, Lofty Smith and I, spent in Tel Aviv, with trips to Jerusalem and Bethlehem, and a memorable visit to the Garden of Gethsemane. Towards the end of our stay, though, the Arabs blew up the railway line, condemning us to three weeks in the nearby Sarafand Transit Camp. And, by that stage, with not a penny between us!

Finally back in the fold, we found No. 3 RSU yet again under orders to move. The obvious destination was Italy, which the Allies had invaded on 3 September 1943. Instead, two weeks later HM Troopship SS *Mooltan* offloaded us in Bombay.

Not Italy, then, but India. And so we entrained across the sub-continent to Calcutta, where we lodged at Barrackpore Racecourse while awaiting our heavy equipment, a wait which left us free to celebrate Christmas 1943 in rip-roaring style: though still a lowly LAC I was made free of the sergeants' mess, acquiring a life-enduring taste for cigars.

Days later a few of us were detached to service some Hurricanes operating from the statue-lined, red-gravel drive of the Governor of Bengal's residence. We were well accommodated, in bamboo *bashas* – airy, native-style huts. More tellingly, merely crossing a park took us onto Calcutta's main street: after two years of the Western Desert we had cinemas, restaurants, shops, canteens and anything else – indeed everything else –, all within a five-minute walk!

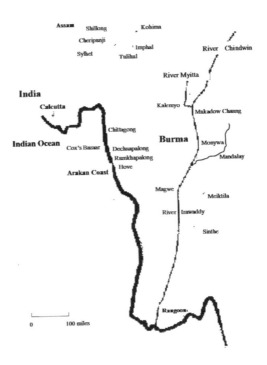

Map: The Burma Campaign

All too soon our heavy equipment arrived, with which we were rushed south-east down the Arakan Coast, to Cox's Bazaar. I became part of a twenty-four-man detachment sent further south still, first to Dechuapalong (in 2012 the largest refugee camp in Bangladesh), then to Rumkhapalong, where No. 607 Squadron was operating Spitfires. Our task, however, was to service the Hurricane 2Ds based alongside them, the tank-busting variety armed with two 40-mm Vickers 'S' cannon.

The airstrip was just off a jungle-fringed beach, our work station being beneath a tree so large that it provided shade for three Hurricanes. As constant attendants we had a troop of monkeys and swarms of multi-coloured woodpeckers, while only just around the hill we found elephant tracks. Daily though, we would encounter *kabaragoya* monitor lizards, three- to four-foot long dinosaurs, but harmless.

After a while, when No. 607 moved on, the natives turned to us as their patrons, asking us to deal with a troublesome tiger. Swiftly protesting that Sten guns were unsuitable for game shooting we cravenly opted out.

Conveniently enabling us to save face, we were then sent to support the tank-busting Hurricanes of No. 20 Squadron at the advanced landing ground at Hove, a low tide only airstrip at the head of the Mayu Peninsula. As the Japs didn't have many tanks left in that area, the pilots had free rein, a chalk board recording their destruction of one river steamer, one staff car, two bicycles, three canoes – and one elephant ...

With the onset of the 1944 monsoon we moved north to Chittagong to give assistance to No. 126 RSU with Spitfires and Hurricanes but also Vultee Vengeance dive-bombers. Here we had a semi-permanent camp with bamboo bashas, concrete runways with dispersal sites, and a town nearby: luxury living!

At very short notice, though, I was sent back to the Cox's Bazaar area as one of a small party ostensibly detailed to assist No. 131 RSU; in reality to sort out a reported work-quality problem: an unenviable duty, snooping on another unit, and one that, in my case, turned sour.

Early on I had to report that the propeller blades of one of their Hurricanes, signed off as fit to fly, had been negligently left loose on the hub; a potentially fatal oversight. This, predictably enough, went down very badly with the warrant officer and supervisory NCOs of 131. How badly, I quickly discovered.

Next morning a pilot – a Flight Lieutenant McGill, I remember – arrived to fly one of the Hurricanes I had just minutes before pre-flighted. Seeing him about to board, I ran back to the machine, got him strapped in, then jumped down ready for the start. Only to have him beckon me onto the wing again. His face grim, he pointed out that a cable, plugged into the gunsight, was looped around the control column in a way that seriously restricted its movement. I was, of course, aghast. As an airframes chap, checking that flying controls were 'full and free' was fundamental. I knew full well that when I'd completed the DI – the daily inspection – the cable had been coiled and safely tucked away, as per. Clearly it wasn't now. And had the pilot been in a hurry – on a panic scramble, say – and tried to get airborne without properly checking his controls …

There was nothing I could say. The cord fouling the control column told the tale. And there was my signature on the Form 700 – the maintenance log – certifying the aircraft's fitness to fly. I was duly charged by the unit's commanding officer and given seven days' 'jankers' – confined to camp, a minor Service punishment that meant, along with normal duties, reporting at intervals during off-duty hours and carrying out fatigues seen as demeaning.

In fact, it was rather nastier than that, because some of the squadron's NCOs had warned me that if I refused to accept their commanding officer's punishment it would mean a certain twenty-eight-days' detention, that is, Service prison. Now detention, unlike jankers (itself often an indication of independent spirit!), was a damning entry to have on one's record, especially as a career airman. In view of which I felt obliged to bite the bullet, and settle for serving out my seven days.

Of course, the whole thing was a put-up job by the warrant officer and NCOs, and the threat of a certain prison sentence deliberate scaremongering. Certainly that was my own CO's take on the incident for he not only deleted the punishment from my records but added a commendation.

All very well, but I wonder still what would have happened had Flight Lieutenant McGill not checked his controls, but allowed me to start him. Would one of the 131 crowd have coming arunning to put things right? And then have to admit to the heinous thing – life-threatening sabotage, no less – they'd done?

My overriding concern on arriving back at Chittagong, however, was an attack of tertian malaria. This put me in hospital with paroxysms for five days, but thankfully, has never again troubled me. Afterwards I was sent to a convalescent camp at Shillong, in Assam, some 250 miles to the north. This involved a train journey through Sylhet, with its tea plantations and orange and pineapple groves, then a truck ride up through the Khasi Hills past Cheripunji: reputedly the second wettest place in the world. But though the coolly-fresh Shillong, at 5,000 feet above sea level, was known as the 'Scotland of the East', convalescents at the camp were treated more like prisoners. The accommodation was poor and we were set to fatigues, with compulsory daily sport, and even parades. Moreover, it rained daily, and the town had little to offer. I can tell you, I pulled every string to get back to Chittagong for my twenty-first.

Regrettably, Aviation takes its toll, and regardless of our expertise. As it did on Battle of Britain Sunday in 1944. Being on duty crew I had carried out the daily inspection on a new Spitfire which, arriving in Burma in the normal way of things by sea, had been uncrated, reassembled, then ferried to us. Some time later I heard a prolonged steep dive, then a thud. It transpired that our test pilot, Flight Lieutenant Christison, had put the machine into a power dive as part of his acceptance check, only to have a wing break off as he pulled out.

The court of enquiry took note when I observed that this was the first Spitfire I'd seen which hadn't been painted on the inside, though whether this might have indicated too-hasty a re-build was never determined. Far more likely, though, that the pilot had simply overstressed the airframe.

Historical note: in 2013 an expedition to find a large number of crated Spitfires, believed to have been buried as surplus to requirements at the end of World War Two, was unsuccessful in excavations at Meiktila, Mingladon, and Myitkyina.

After the monsoon we moved up to Tulihul, in the Imphal–Kohima area where the Japanese advance was to be finally reversed and India saved. Getting there involved a week's circuitous journeying by ferry-boat, standard railway, and then narrow-gauge railway to the western end of the Imphal Valley, Tulihul proving to be an airstrip made all-weather by being surfaced with Bithess tar-coated hessian. Thankfully, as the strip was within range of the enemy's field artillery, we didn't stay long, merely time enough to sort out our baggage and have various injections. We then drew Stens which we were instructed to have ready at all times. And now, with eight full magazines, clad in jungle-green, with boots, gaiters, and terai – slouch-rimmed – hats, we were ready to see off the Japs.

Our destination was Kalemyo airstrip, three days away by what passed for a road over a soaring range of tree-clad heights. Throughout the journey we perched on our loaded wagons, Stens at the ready, always with a mountainous slope to one side and a steep gorge to the other, the depths liberally strewn with crashed and burnt-out trucks. Kalemyo, we discovered, lay on the River Myittha, to the west of its confluence with the River Chindwin. We discovered too that no provision had been made for our unit, our first task being to cut back enough only too healthily-profuse, secondary-jungle growth in order to set up tents.

Besides establishing No. 3 RSU headquarters we were required to service a fighter wing operating both Spitfires and Hurricanes, the constant sorties – and the jungle-clearance work – keeping us so busy that we really appreciated after-duty cooling off in the Myittha. Finally, after a week or so, with the preparatory work completed, the unit was split into four Mobile Repair Section teams (MRS), each located at a different airstrip.

My MRS was commanded by a Warrant Officer King who, early on, dispatched a party of us, under a Sergeant Shepherd, to salvage a Spitfire at a spot called Mukadaw Chaung. We took with us a Ford 6-by-2 'Wrecker' road recovery vehicle; a Bedford 4-by-2 high loader articulated vehicle; and a 4-by-4 Dodge fifteen hundredweight truck. Having reached the chaung – dried river bed –, we then had to drive five miles up it to where soldiers were guarding the downed aircraft.

A GM 6 towing vehicle

Dismantling and loading the Spitfire took several days in itself. But only then did our problems really start. For the articulated Bedford was only single-axle drive and had to be winched the whole five miles down the rock-strewn river bed to the road: a full day's enterprise.

As for the salvage task, that proliferated. We spotted another Spitfire in a paddy field, although only its Merlin engine was worth saving. Then, alongside the Chindwin military ferry, we saw a Tiger Moth biplane on a mid-river sand bank.

Having begged the use of a collapsible dinghy, it took us two days to recover the engine and two undamaged mainplanes, only to find, with the last load, that the current had become too strong for our paddle power. Ingenuity being our stock in trade, three of us stripped off and got into the river to push, landing downstream, then emerging to play at dray horses.

Only to look up after a while and find ourselves, clad only in hats and boots, under the critical, and far from complimentary, scrutiny of a group of army nurses.

Our blushes having subsided, we were able to load our wagons on the ferry, at that time comprising two Bailey-Bridge sections towed by a DUKW amphibious vehicle, a combination capable of carrying heavy lorries and tanks, so by-passing ten miles of damaged, and presently unusable, road.

Back at Kalemyo there was little to do in what passed for off-duty time. For my part I chose to reconstruct an Auster – an army observation spotter – out of two damaged machines, working alone, except for getting in beefy types to help lift. Having proudly signed my creation off, I bridled just a little when the army pilot assigned to take delivery, asked, a little too doubtfully to my parental mind, 'Would *you* fly it?' Cheeky beggar!

Our next uprooting was to Monywa, some way downstream but on the eastern bank of the Chindwin. Initially though, I was again detailed as part of a stay-behind party at Kalemyo. A cushy number. Or so I thought. Until just before dawn.

'Off your pit.' It was Warrant Officer King. 'The jeep's outside. A Mossie's hit a water buffalo.'

I suppose in those days one assimilated such summonses without blinking. A Mosquito fighter-bomber, it seemed, had been taking off when a water buffalo – presumably kamikaze bent – had strayed across its path. The machine was a sad spectacle with its fuselage twisted and a prop and reduction gear sheared off. The buffalo was even sadder, strewn in not-that-neatly-butchered joints across the runway.

'Right, young Illsley!' rapped my mentor, 'Get rolling this clear.' And arguably even now not quite awake, I found myself, trundling at arms' length a 250-pound bomb which had spilled from the Mosquito's bomb rack. Realisation, though, brought instant awareness. So that a moment later I was yards away and accelerating rapidly towards the jungle fringe. Even the bellow, 'Come back, you silly bastard, it's been made safe,' slowing me only by degrees.

To rejoin the unit we drove overnight to Monywa with me positioned on the spare wheel with my Sten. At one point we saw a body on the road, but swerved around it without slackening speed. At another, a shot was fired, and again we drove on. Judiciously, it proved, for next day we learnt that a Japanese patrol had indeed been active in the area.

From Monywa we were soon moved some 170 winding miles down to Sinthe, a very active airfield, with parallel strips, on the Mandalay–Rangoon railway line. Our main customer here was No. 907 Wing with its Spitfire Mk 8s and 9s. My especial problem, though, as airframes, was that the retractable tailwheel of the Spit Mk 8 consistently caused damage to the rear fuselage.

In essence, the locking mechanism was badly designed. Further, no thought at all had been given to the poor chap who had to set it to rights, particularly using limited equipment in jungle humidity. For a start the repair called for removing fifty-two bolts, several flying control cables, and various electrical and hydraulic runs. Then the fuselage had to be placed on a stand – two oil drums – to facilitate the fitting of a modified tail lock. Before the lock would fit, however, the receiving structure had to be reshaped, after which both it and the renewed outer skin needed re-riveting. But then, before the new assembly could be tested, the tailplane had to be re-rigged. The snag being that if the new lock proved unsatisfactory, as by the law of Sod a substantial number did, the whole thing had to be done over. Eventually though, I made a time-and-labour-saving test rig from Hurricane and Spitfire components so that the function could be tried out before the refitting stage.

Dealing with a faulty design, of course, was additional to keeping the other machines flying. Further, on a unit like ours everyone pitched in when needed, as when a dismantled Spitfire was being loaded into a Dakota and a tropical storm struck. In an instant, several fighter aircraft were torn from their pickets and badly damaged. Seeing the loaders with their Spitfire half-in, half-out of the transport's fuselage, we rushed over and threw ourselves bodily across the Dakota's elevators. We could feel the transport heaving beneath us, but big as it was our combined weight was just sufficient to prevent the wind spilling it tail over apex. As for us, our shirtless backs were blasted raw by twigs and other jungle debris.

Although technically fulfilling, the stay at Sinthe, with poor accommodation, no fresh food, and only meagre army supplies, stands as the low point of my Service career. I was probably tired too when, once more a stay-behind, I came to recharge a Hurricane's compressed-air system and the 2,000-pounds-a-square-inch connector hose spat free of its jubilee clip and caught me in the eye. The medics had gone off with the main body, so I had no proper treatment, and that eye has remained weak ever since.

Even getting away from Sinthe was fraught, for the Chindwin ferry having been withdrawn due to bad weather, it looked as if we stay-behinds would have a lengthy trek. Only then, in the nick of time, a Dakota dropped in and took us out the easy way.

We would have welcomed anywhere after Sinthe, but Meiktila Thedaw, fifty miles north, up towards Mandalay, would have been hard to beat, set in a picturesque grove of palms and being a headquarters, with facilities to match. The job was unchanging though, repairing crashed fighters, and dismantling others for transportation to maintenance units in India.

Servicing a Hurricane in Burma

On 8 May 1945, back in Europe, they celebrated Victory in Europe Day. In Burma, of course, it was business as usual. Early in June, however, there was a break in routine when two of us, me, and a friend named Johnny Martin, were sent down to newly-liberated Rangoon to participate in a capital-city victory parade. With our own contingent taking two hours to reach the saluting base it was a real spectacular. Sadly, the rainstorm which persisted throughout was even more spectacular. Yet the reviewing officer, Commodore (acting Admiral) Lord Louis Mountbatten, GCVO, KCB, DSO, the Supreme Commander, stuck to his post until the end, standing there, at the salute, with the water simply pouring off him.

Rangoon liberated

The Japanese war, though, was far from over, and back at Meiktila the P-47 Thunderbolts ceaselessly harrying the enemy kept us busy. On 3 August 1945, however, my twenty-second birthday, I was posted home. And on 15 August 1945, as our homebound contingent passed through the Suez Canal, the Japs packed it in too. So it was that on Sunday, 31 August 1945, when we docked in Liverpool, I was far from alone in anticipating very great things after four years away.

Expectations were dashed, however, when we realised that we were not to be sent straight off on leave. Instead, despite protests, we were entrained for Hornchurch, in Essex, with me being particularly aggrieved when the train actually halted in Derby! To make things worse we found the Hornchurch staff so offhand that after a day or two we staged a bolshy demonstration. At which someone in authority saw sense, for suddenly leave passes were forthcoming for all. At best, though, it was a sadly dispiriting welcome home.

My first peacetime posting was to No. 58 Maintenance Unit at Newark, Nottinghamshire, where I joined a salvage party consisting of a sergeant, a corporal, and six airmen, the task being to recover crashed and unwanted aircraft from Lincolnshire, Nottinghamshire, and Leicestershire. By February 1946, however, both NCOs had been demobbed, and now a corporal myself, I was commanding the detachment.

Making my own, largely unsupervised decisions obtained for a gratifying twelve months, but in 1947 I was posted to the Central Signals Establishment at Watton, in Norfolk.

This was a unit veined throughout with secrecy, though my everyday role was the mundane servicing of Lancaster and Lincoln bombers. But odd 'cloak and dagger' tasks came up. As in May 1948 when I had to modify the chute on a Lincoln through which the metallic strips – 'Window' – were dumped to disrupt hostile radars. At the same time other erks painted out every identifying mark to leave the aircraft night black. Then, in the June, the Berlin Airlift began. Though what part Lincoln RF398 played, who knows! I next saw it, however, in the Cosford air museum.

Lincoln RF398 at Cosford

All very satisfying. But with the war over, the Service was undeniably changing. In the technical field Routine Maintenance was the word, each task time-listed and card indexed, and with jobs unfinished at shift's end to be passed on. This robotic procedure became unbearably boring, especially as the Service was flush with Fitters (airframe) like me. Routine Orders, however, showed that there was a great demand for Fitters (motor-transport: MT). I volunteered to remuster, and was accepted, and spent from September 1948 until March 1949 at RAF Weeton, near Blackpool, learning my new trade.

Having become a qualified MT fitter, and a sergeant, I was posted to RAF Shepherds Grove, near Bury St Edmunds, where I spent three satisfyingly productive months in charge of the MT Repair and Maintenance Section. After that I was posted to Germany, to No. 5 MT Base Depot, in Hamburg; same responsibilities, but this time supervising German staff.

This was a posting that became truly memorable when I was brusquely told by a canteen waitress, 'You are too late for dinner.' Her name, it transpired, was Helena Kluknavsky, a Czech-born German. Hardly a propitious introduction. But it heralded in a lifetime's friendship and 41 happy years of marriage.

As our officially-beset relationship developed – political complications abounded –, I became a corporal technician, taking as a specialization Fourth Line (very deep) MT Servicing, the only individual, I was told, ever to do so. And at times there were still echoes of the RAF I had known: serving, for example, under Group Captain A.E. Donaldson, who had broken the world speed record in 1946 in a Gloster Meteor twin jet, and under his second in command, another notable, Acting Wing Commander 'Johnny' Johnson, the Allies' highest-scoring fighter ace. Both these pilots still flew like teenagers.

On returning to UK in 1952 I was posted to the RAF College Cranwell, in Lincolnshire. Not a happy sojourn. Indeed, as all my non-commissioned superiors were drivers, as opposed to fitters, and had little idea of technical matters, it smacked of that trouble-locating job in Burma. Certainly the disparity in quality between jobs I had signed off and those signed off by others did not go unnoticed.

'Why is this, Illsley?' my frustrated commanding officer asked finally.

'Standards, sir, I suppose,' I told him. 'Being ex-Halton, and all that.'

Disillusionment, however, had long set in, and 1 September 1953, after fourteen years in the Service, I returned to a civilian world I had barely experienced.

In fact, this new world was to see me embrace the Derbyshire Fire Service and rise to sub-officer in a brand-new and utterly fulfilling career. Between the two, then, the RAF and the Fire Service, mine, I maintain, was truly a life worth living.

Don Illsley, early 2000

3. Lots Of Luck, But Nous Too

Leading Aircraftman Peter McArthur, engine mechanic

In 1936, at the age of fourteen, I left school in Stirling and got a job in a cast-iron foundry, a place of clamour and dirt, and of unguarded driving bands, one of which left me with a deformed finger. Even so, by the time war was declared the works had given me a good grounding not only in engineering but in nous – what would now be called 'street-wisdom' – both of which were to stand me in good stead.

Stirlingshire was the recruiting area for the Argyll and Sutherland Highlanders but although four family members had served with the Black Watch and come unscathed through Ypres (Wipers, as they had it), the Somme, and Passendale, I determined from the outset that the army was not for me. My mother, like all her generation, was well versed in the way the army warred and backed my application to join the Fleet Air Arm. I was found 'very acceptable', except that as the weeks dragged on, nothing happened. Realising that if something had gone astray I'd be at the mercy of the Argylls, I began to consider the RAF.

Even so I was delighted when the Navy's official acceptance letter arrived. Until, that is, my eye fell on the initials *RM*: not an invitation to join the Fleet Air Arm then, but the Royal Marines! At which I realised there were even worse things than the Argylls!

'Did you sign anything?' Dad asked. His advice on life would always be to accept luck, but back it with common sense – nous. And here, of course, my not having signed anything totally binding was key. Fortunately, there was an RAF recruiting office in Stirling, so I applied, sat tests, and was accepted on the spot. As with the Navy I was told to go home and wait: in this case, await a rail warrant to Blackpool where I was to do my basic training. Only here the nous came in.

'I've come prepared,' I told them, 'so can't I get this evening's Blackpool train?'

They agreed, so I nipped home, said my goodbyes, and duly arrived in Blackpool.

In the course of time an official arrived to collar me for the Royal Marines, only to be told I'd been in the RAF for months.

Peter McArthur during recruit training at Morecombe, 1941

We drilled on the front at Morecombe and though many former airmen look back on square-bashing with mixed feelings, to me it was a welcome escape. If I had any doubts, these were dispelled during the subsequent three months I spent at No 10 School of Technical Training at RAF Kirkham, near Preston. No noisily clanking belts, no filth and dirt, and no hubbub, but engineering as it should be! As a trade I'd chosen engine mechanic, with rigging (airframes) thrown in, and in mid 1941, on passing out as an aircraftman grade two (AC2), I was posted to No. 614 Squadron.

This was an Auxiliary Air Force unit tasked with army co-operation duties but equipped with sadly second-hand Bristol Blenheim Mark Fours. It was stationed, I found, at RAF Macmerry, a grass airfield, some nine miles east of Edinburgh, and therefore virtually on our doorstep. Certainly my proximity to home was noted by one Flight Sergeant Foy, who greeted me morosely with, 'So, a fireside airman?' Then, with the same breath, 'Get over there to 'A' Apple and sort out its engines.'

Bristol Blenheim Mark Four

I started with the plugs, taking them out and sand-blasting them. Then, over the next two days, I really went to town, so that when I ran them up both engines were as good as they were ever going to be.

Not that this show of technical ability cut any ice with Foy, for some days later, when the electricians supplied us with a flat trolley accumulator and I couldn't get an aircraft's engines check-run on time for a detail – I suspected the plugs had oiled up –, the waiting pilot complained. Foy rushed out – he never normally left his office! – got into the cockpit and began grinding the starter motor using the aircraft's batteries. Realising that he was simply flattening these too, I got beneath the engine and, using the priming pump, began pulsing through additional fuel to supplement his futile use of the starter. It worked, and within moments the engine bellowed into life. No thanks for yours truly, though, for Foy had borne the brunt of the pilot's displeasure and now took it out on me, charging me with incompetence and landing me with seven days' jankers.

No matter that when a corporal and I stripped the engines down we found the cylinder scraper rings so worn as to be useless, allowing oil to foul the plugs, my seven days still stood. What really upset me, though – and thoroughly amused my mates –, was being marched into the cookhouse at mealtimes with the escort bawling, 'Make way for the defaulter.' And defaulter singular it was, because I was the only one. That I didn't have to queue, as the rest of my section laughingly pointed out, did nothing at all to salve my hurt pride.

Clambering up beside the pilots to put things right soon got to be commonplace. Invariably it was to find they'd flooded the engine. Of course, most of them were hardly any older than I was, but if many were from wealthy backgrounds and had la-de-da accents they were, for the most part, nice with it. In all honesty, though, some of them could be as thick as puddings.

For instance, I was flying with one when he decided to stop an engine in the air. However, he then left it so late to restart that, when it wouldn't fire up, there was too little power in hand to recover the situation. Though I was sitting beside him there was nothing useful I could do, bar lift my feet onto the instrument panel. He had to keep his feet on the rudder pedals, of course. As it was, he thumped the aircraft down so hard that a wheel collapsed and we careered sideways through a blackthorn hedge.

'Now we've done it,' he said, massaging his battered ankles.

'No *we* about it, Sir,' I told him, 'nothing to do with me.'

In fact, flying became my regular practice. The first time had taken me rather by surprise, for I'd never flown before; never really thought about it. But I'd worked on this Blenheim overnight, rectifying an engine fault, had duly signed the Form 700 – the RAF's aircraft-maintenance record –, and was back on duty when the pilot turned up on his bike to air-test it. And I say bike advisedly, for at that time there was little motor transport available and bikes were the order of the day.

'You've signed it out, Mac,' he grinned as he finished his walk-around inspection, 'so grab yourself a parachute and let's see if you trust your workmanship.'

I knew he was joking, or at least, half-joking. There was no real requirement to put my skill to such a test. I was aware too, that to get a parachute and lug it back to the aircraft from the parachute section would delay the flight. Indeed, one of the priority tasks of our limited transport pool was to stow crew parachutes aboard any aircraft scheduled to fly, chutes being such awkward things to carry on a bike!

'With my signature on the 700,' I told him breezily, 'who needs a parachute?'

And so I did my first flight. And thoroughly enjoyed it.

On that occasion, as it happened, it had been quite a while before the tower had given us take-off clearance. Seeing the cylinder-head temperatures rising, therefore, I had leant over to eye the angle at which my driver-to-be had set the gills – the cooling shutters. He might well have taken umbrage, instead, he had nodded approvingly. The same just after take-off when it came to closing the shutters: they had been that much easier for me to reach. Certainly, after we landed the pilot must have commended my competence, for just days later I was promoted directly to leading aircraftman (LAC), so saving me months of dwelling as an AC1 (aircraftman first class), and raising my pay from 3/9d a day to 4/6d [45p to 54p].

A trip that stands out was the first I was actually detailed to fly on as travelling groundcrew. Nobody thought to tell me beforehand where we were bound for, but it turned out to be Middleton St George, near Darlington, down in Teesside. All seemed to go well until the visibility deteriorated markedly and the pilot confessed, 'I'm lost.' Not something I really wanted to hear. Then, of all things, he asked, 'Any ideas?'

I looked out at a landscape now become as blank as I felt.

'Why not,' I suggested, 'get lower and follow the railway line?' And that's what we did. Until suddenly chummy let out a yelp, and pulled back hard, only just clearing a train steaming headlong towards us!

That mishap notwithstanding, we duly landed to find Middleton preparing to receive squadrons from the Royal Canadian Air Force. Indeed, some of their newly-arrived aircrew came aboard to look over what was their first Blenheim. I'm not sure how impressed they were initially, but when one of them got to mid fuselage it became very evident.

'It's been repaired,' he announced in awed tones, 'with a McVitie's biscuit tin.' Which seemed to strike them as odd. As I said, though, all our aircraft were very much second-hand.

In fact, because Macmerry was something of a backwater, I was able to get flights in such outmoded types as the Sparrow – a variant of the already vintage Handley Page Harrow – and the Virginia, as well as the normal Ansons and Tiger Moths. Hardly surprising, my willingness to get airborne soon drew notice. In fact, one of the flight sergeants – not Foy – took me aside and asked why I didn't volunteer for aircrew. 'I know its pretty dangerous,' he said, 'but this flight-engineer business on the new heavies means an immediate three tapes, which, as an engine man, would take you years to get otherwise.' He made me think, I must say. But while flying had its attractions I'd already realised that it meant merely managing fuel gauges and opening and closing cooling flaps, that becoming aircrew would disbar me from what I loved doing, from diagnosing some elusive fault, locating the defective component, and setting the sickly engine to rights.

True, I might well have considered it had I joined just a year or two back, for at that time technicians who elected to fly got a winged-bullet gunner's badge, got flying pay whenever they flew, and on landing reverted to their trades. Now, though, 'aircrew' had come in as a separate breed from what was now 'groundcrew'. And so I decided against applying. As for the danger. Well, who was to say what life had in store, whatever choice one made?

To illustrate this, while travelling home by bus I fell into company with another airman, Peter, as I knew him, from Falkirk, a lad who never sought out danger yet, sadly, was to meet a tragic end. The fact was, I was young, thrived on delving into engines, and was good at my job, so work was fun. Then again I liked cycling and was a keen footballer, and the RAF always loved sportsmen. I was also a keen dancer, and even outside the Glasgow- and Edinburgh-Fair fortnights, girls abounded. So I was having a great time, and was perfectly content.

Our section, with a Blenheim

Most of our aircrews – pilots, air gunners, and navigators – first saw action at the very end of May 1942 when eight Blenheims were sent down to West Raynham, in Norfolk, to support a raid on Cologne, the first ever one-thousand-bomber raid. No. 614 Squadron's part was to help disrupt German night-fighter response by carrying out intruder raids on their airfields. I wasn't sent on this detachment, however, instead I stayed to help the rest of the squadron enliven the battle training of the Argylls – the very ones I had eluded! – by having our Blenheims bombard them with bags of soot.

Halfway into August 1942, however, we all moved down to West Raynham where we loaded smoke bombs which were dropped to screen the Commando raid on Dieppe. It was during this detachment that I first came upon Hugh Malcolm, a fine officer but one whose dauntless courage was destined to have such a significant effect on my life. As for the Dieppe raid itself, hard to know what to think about it, but just months later, in North Africa, we were to hope that the lessons learnt might, at least, have taught higher command something about seaborne landings.

The Sad aftermath of the Dieppe Raid

With the Dieppe debacle over we returned to Macmerry. But late in September 1942 the squadron was moved south to Odiham, in Hampshire, where we took delivery of Blenheim Mark Fives, Bisleys. These had the improved Mercury Mark Thirty engines and, fitted with an additional four Browning machine guns in the nose, were especially intended for army co-operation close-support operations. In the end they were to prove a let-down but at the time we thought they were the bee's knees.

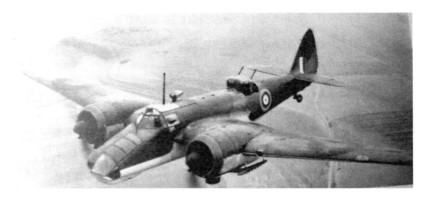

The Bisley (Blenheim Mark Five)

It was during this re-equipping that I came together with the pilot I was to regard as mine. He was an officer, but totally without side, red-headed, very keen, and very competent, Flying Officer Cyril Georges, from Newcastle.

'You take the left engine, Mac,' he said lightly, 'and you, Cookie, take the right.'

And, of course, I should say a word or two about Cookie. He was a big lad, six foot plus, and sturdy, and a great chap to have by your side when things got sticky. Before the war he'd been an engine man at Vauxhalls and was, therefore, able to teach me an enormous amount. His particular talent, and great love, however, was singing! A great comrade, and it is to my eternal regret that I allowed us to lose touch after the war.

Me, Cookie (centre), as always, refusing to wear tropical uniform, and an American friend, 1943

At Odiham it became clear that something big was in the offing when we found ourselves formed into a wing in company with three other Bisley squadrons, No. 18, No. 13, and No. 114. All four squadrons were kept busy working up ground-support tactics, but where they were to exercise these skills nobody knew. It seemed to become clearer when we were issued with winter clothing, for that suggested supporting our hard-pressed Russian Allies. And I, for one, wrote home advising mum and dad accordingly. I never did check whether they got the message or whether, as should have happened, our officer had black-pencilled out my indiscretion.

Speculation over a Russian venture died a death when the winter gear was withdrawn and we were issued instead with tropical kit. No doubt now, then, clearly we were to reinforce the desert air force in Libya! So clear, indeed, that one of my section wrote home to that effect. In his case though, things went awry. The wing commander harangued the hapless lad before the paraded personnel of all four squadrons.

'This airman,' he told us all, 'thinks that "Careless Talk Costs Lives!" doesn't apply to him. But whether we're off round the Cape to Suez, and Libya, or direct to Murmansk, it's you he's put at risk.'

Knowing that the message had gone home, he took no further action.

Contemporary poster: **Careless Talk Costs Lives!**

Only days later, having waved our Bisleys away from Odiham, destination unknown, we groundcrews found ourselves boarding RMS *Strathaird* at

Clydeside and sailing in convoy for our own yet-undisclosed destination. Even the tropical kit no longer gave a clue, for it was bundled up and stowed as 'not wanted on voyage'.

As we gradually moved south the convoy was joined by more and more warships, at least two aircraft carriers, some cruisers, and scuds more destroyers. It was not a comfortable voyage, indeed to this day my mind's eye sees a destroyer being completely swallowed by the waves, only to reappear again an interminable time later, making me more thankful than ever that I hadn't let the navy take me. Then came a dawn when we awoke to find ourselves stationary amidst a vast flotilla, and realised that we had crept past Gibraltar in the night, and had anchored in some Mediterranean bay!

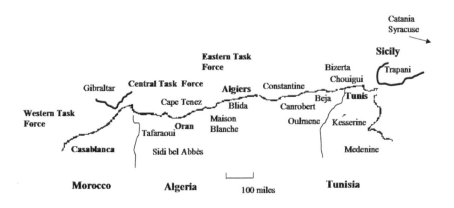

The North-West African Campaign (Operation Torch)

What we were part of, we were to learn, was Operation Torch, an Anglo-American enterprise aimed at establishing a second desert front in Vichy French Africa to drive the Axis forces eastwards against Montgomery's Eighth Army advancing westwards from Libya. Our convoy had been just one of many starting from both Britain and the United States and variously bound for Casablanca, Oran, and Algiers. Our own assembly was part of the Eastern Task Force and had proceeded, as scheduled, to Algiers.

The assault troops were already ashore, and we could see flashes as they fought it out with the Vichy French. Then came news that a political agreement had been reached. At which the fighting stopped, and the support elements began to land. As they did so, however, in came German and Italian bombers and proceeded to subject Algiers Bay to three days and nights of nerve-shredding aerial bombardment. *Strathaird* wasn't touched but beside us the *Strathallan*, from the same stables, was sunk, though with only a dozen or so fatalities out of the 5,000 personnel aboard.

Eventually our contingent was ordered to land, but with the situation still uncertain we were issued with Sten machine guns: far from the trustiest of weapons, but even so a step up on the cudgel crowned with barbed-wire I'd been given for sentry-go during basic training! Once ashore we were rushed through the suburbs of Algiers City to Blida Airfield, which along with that at Maison Blanche, was now in Allied hands and where, a matter of hours later, we were joined by our Bisleys. They had left Odiham, we discovered, for Portreath, in Cornwall. Then, when the time was ripe, they had positioned to Gibraltar and, once we were ready to receive them, on to Blida.

As ground-attack aircraft they were to be on permanent emergency call to the army, but their bread and butter task was to be night-intruder raids on enemy airfields. From the start though, things went askew. A night or so later we'd just finished the post-flight checks after our section had flown the first sortie, when a second wave taxied past us for the airstrip.

'Hey, Cookie,' I called over the din, 'the flares are angled a different way now: yet there's a house back there.'

'Maybe the wind's changed,' he suggested. But there was no wind.

Moments later the first Bisley got airborne, then the second. But just after the third lifted off there was a sun-bright flash and a thunderous roar, and both aircraft and crew, and the Arab house, were gone. Why the flare path had been re-aligned we never were to discover.

The bitter truth was that cock-ups were far too frequent in those early weeks. For example, at the beginning of December 1942, having moved to Canrobert, some forty miles south-east of Constantine, we found that the engineers had sited our tent lines right by the landing strip instead of where we'd have put them, back among the sheltering hillocks – later, in Sicily, we'd conceal them deep among the olive groves! Hearing aircraft approaching, and knowing ours weren't due back yet, we assumed they were American. Until we saw the black crosses! No bombs were dropped but they thoroughly strafed the tent lines, their only opposition being the odd burst of Sten fire some of us pointed their way, for although there was an anti-aircraft gun on the field – just one! – there was nobody around to man it.

There was no element of cock-up, however, when Cookie and I were faced with a Bisley whose left engine proved reluctant to start.

'I'll get up in the cockpit,' I told him, 'while you toggle the priming pump.' It was the wrinkle I'd used with Foy, and moments later the engine was giving full power. Before starting, I'd taken the usual precaution of hugging the stick back to my chest (to keep the elevator up, and the tail from lifting), only to realise that said stick had suddenly begun buffeting me. Glaring out, I saw Cookie, standing clear now but frantically giving me the edge-of-hand-across-throat 'Cut-engine' sign: unable to attract my attention otherwise he'd been waggling an aileron – and so, the stick. Now he pointed upwards, where I saw a still high, but purposefully circling, Jerry bomber.

'He's seen the sand plume,' Cookie bawled as the engine died.

Hurriedly vacating the cockpit it was to find Cookie making off towards the nearest slit trench, 'Come on,' he yelled.

I was watching the bomber, though, now in a steep dive. 'No,' I barked. 'Wait.' Moments later it pulled out and swept overhead, leaving in its wake four ominously arcing bombs. '*This* way,' I yelled. And shoulder to shoulder we sprinted for some slit trenches in the opposite direction from those Cookie had been heading for. We made it, but only just. Even so we were covered in sand.

'You saved my life, Mac,' Cookie told me, visibly shocked as he craned towards the now blazing Bisley. Apart from which, nothing more was said. Another Bisley was flown in, and that was that.

As I say, that was no cock-up, just one of those things. And we were only too well aware that it might have been worse. Indeed, we might have ended up like the mechanic who, caught in similar circumstances, hurled himself into cover, only to choose a latrine trench and find himself safe from blast and shrapnel but up to his neck in excrement!

In later years I learnt that one of the problems with Torch had been that initial pussyfooting to keep the French on-side had delayed the vital eastwards push. Then the weather had turned fouler than expected, and although this affected the Axis forces too, they were battle hardened and superbly commanded – by Rommel – whereas on our side both the troops and their commanders were inexperienced; especially, it seems, the commanders of the Allied air forces. Even now I find it painful to talk about how this affected us, but I might as well get it over with.

It was early December 1942, we had moved a little further south and east, to Oulmene, and to desert strips, on this occasion to one named Sloane Square. At about midday on 4 December, a call came in from the army requiring an immediate strike on an airfield near Bizerta: as we heard it, there was slim chance of any fighter escort: so, an unescorted raid! Although No. 614 was not initially involved, Cookie and I, and the rest, turned out to give a hand. I was surprised, therefore, when Georges and his crew, with two other 614 crews, all in flying kit, made their way towards where our squadron's aircraft were parked.

'Is she all prepped?' Georges asked, as we panted up to our Blenheim.

She was, of course. Only, I was aghast. Unescorted! 'But, Sir, this is Eighteen's show, surely?'

'They're short of kites,' he explained, 'so three of ours are going along, as volunteers. Besides, Mac,' he grinned, and suddenly, he looked the age he was, hardly older than Cookie, 'I'm told there's a gong in it.'

There was little I could say after that, but what I could say I did. Given notice, of course, I could have brought his jaunt to a stop right there; just a plug lead surreptitiously tugged loose would have sufficed … After which I could have happily let his curses pass over my ostensibly puzzled head as the other ten Bisleys lifted into the air. But I wasn't given the moments I would have needed, so Fate had its way.

Suffice to say Wing Commander Hugh Malcolm (from the Dieppe-Raid days), CO of No. 18 Squadron, got airborne and in accordance with his orders duly laid waste Robb airstrip, near Chouigui, Bizerta, only to have his unescorted Bisleys set upon by Messerschmits, with not one of them surviving. He would indeed, get a gong; a posthumous Victoria Cross. And later be commemorated by the Malcolm Club chain of Service canteens. But no commemoration for Pilot Officer Cyril Hollingsworth Georges. Just a headstone in Beja Military Cemetery. And certainly, no gong.

Beja Military Cemetery

I cannot adequately express how this utterly pointless waste affected me. I'm convinced though that it was at this juncture that my street-wisdom – my nous – received its final, and now provenly-indestructible shell.

More Bisleys were flown in, but by then it had become clear that they were far too vulnerable to be employed on even escorted daytime operations, that role passing to the far more effective Bostons, Mitchells, and Marauders.

Losses were, of course, an everyday event on operational squadrons but Life's uncertainties suddenly seemed even more prevalent. As an instance, shortly afterwards we were moved westwards, back to Tafaraoui, near Oran, and within hitching distance of 'Sidi-Bel', as we called Sidi bel Abbès, the French Foreign Legion garrison town made familiar by P.C. Wren's *Beau*

Geste. Our section had visited it several times, noting that the high walls surrounding the Legion barracks offered no hope for any reluctant five-year-term recruit wishing to opt out! But among Sidi-Bel's attractions was a brothel run by the Americans.

Peter, the Falkirk lad I'd met on the homebound bus, decided he needed to visit this facility and asked if I would come with him. When I'd declined, he hitched in with another couple of chaps. On the way back, however, an oncoming vehicle sideswiped their soft-topped truck, killing all those on Peter's bench seat. I attended the ceremony. Saw the roadside mounds; the steel helmets atop the inverted rifles; heard last-post sounded …

Months later I would see similar mounds in war-torn Sicily, 150 of them, only topped with scuttle-shaped helmets bearing black crosses. Except that the Sicilian field was altogether too convenient to our tent site, and within days had become a featureless football pitch.

The weather had been awful for months, but when the desert reasserted itself things got worse. The main trouble was that sand insinuated itself everywhere and particularly into our engine filters. Cleaning them took three hours, but the job had to be repeated every five flying hours. Fitting a spare would have been a thirty-minute job. Had there been any spares. But sand aside, even the airframe lads were affected, for the high temperatures distorted panels and cracked perspex components, often beyond the limits of ingenuity to repair.

Then again the heat brought unexpected hazards, like the mirage that materialised on the airstrip at Tafaraoui as a flight of replacement Spitfires winged in from Gibraltar. What they saw, evidently, was an unlimited landing area running on into a watery haze. What they didn't see was the one hundred foot drop beyond the end of the only too restricted cleared strip.

Cookie and I watched the first Spitfire approach, exclaiming as it touched down so far into the runway: the mirage being only partially evident to us. To our horror, though, we saw him run off the end, plunge down, and explode, with numbers two and three following seconds later, each ending in a ball of flame. Only then did Very-cartridges soar skywards to warn off the remaining aircraft and have them divert.

It was never all doom and gloom, however. As when Cookie and I were airlifted back to Algiers to sort out an unserviceable Bisley. We set to work and in a short while were able to give the crew the thumbs up. Only to find them less than grateful. It took some time for me to catch on.

'I haven't actually signed the 700 yet,' I told the pilot. And when his face brightened, added, 'Some of these ignition-harness snags can take some time.'

'Until tomorrow morning?' he suggested.

'Certainly that long,' I agreed.

With which we all had a great night out in Algiers, the Form 700 got signed at a reasonable time next morning, and the Bisley arrived back at Tafaraoui with nobody there, or anywhere else, turning a hair.

We made more conventional visits to various towns, of course, and were suitably intrigued by their outlandishness. Although an early experience, differently handled, might well have led me too, to adopt the average airman's attitude to Arabs. We'd been pestered by traders in the normal way, only as time went by and most had left to seek easier pickings, I noticed one,

with a tray of jewellery, who continued his haranguing. Eventually, instead of shooing him off, I gave him a moment, and found that he was complaining. Then it all became clear!

'Lads,' I called, 'who pinched this chap's ring?' Well, the Arab got his ring back, and something for his trouble. But after that how could I go along with anyone blithely mouthing off about thieving wogs?

Our section, with Arab supporters

I also developed a lot of time for the Americans, although they could initially give the impression of being insular, as Cookie and I found when first venturing into one of the cabaret-bars in their area. Nobody spoke to us, so after a while I nudged Cookie, 'What about a song?' Nothing loth – he loved to perform! –, he had a word with the band, then launched into '*Begin the Beguine*', and immediately had everyone wowed. After that nothing was too good for 'our Limey friends'. And generous! they'd never give you a cigarette, it had to be a carton of 200. Certainly, from that day on, while most of the lads slept on groundsheets, I slumbered on a natty, fold-small American camp bed.

Despite the good times, there were others when tensions in the theatre ran high, often without us knowing why. So it was that, in early February 1943, when Cookie and I were ordered to dig a two-man slit trench on the far side of the airstrip, we didn't question it. And just before nightfall, when a flight sergeant called on his rounds, all he could tell us was to stay in the trench, and to keep on the qui-vive. As the hours went by, though, it suddenly struck me that everything was oddly quiet. Had everyone else forgotten us, and gone? Cookie had a rifle, I had my Sten. And that was it. So if the threat was, as I'd begun to suspect, from the *Afrika Korps*, we weren't all that well placed.

'Tell you what,' I decided in the end, indicating the nearest aircraft. 'Come first light, if we find something's happened, I reckon I can fly that Bisley to the coast and get us clear.'

My unease was not too far out. The *Afrika Korps* had indeed attacked, and not that far to the east, utterly routing the predominantly-American troops in the Kesserine Pass. Opposite our particular sector, we would learn, only the Grenadier Guards had held Rommel's men from breaking through!

But we also shared a totally bizarre escapade, Cookie and I, one well worthy of Gunner Spike Milligan, who also recorded his experiences on Torch. We'd been to most places on off-duty jaunts, and planning to visit Constantine, found a taxi driver, if pidgin-speaking, and one-armed, willing to take us. Having travelled for some way, however, we found ourselves threading past scores of vehicles halted by the roadside, jeeps, trucks, transporters, guns, and tanks, with masses of equipment-festooned infantry cheerily waving us on. Until, having won through them all, we were flagged down by an American military policeman.

'On a day trip?' he repeated incredulously, 'Buddy, you've driven over the start line of a counter-offensive.' At which – and without a word from us – our suddenly-fluent-in-English, one-armed taxi driver did a hurried turnabout.

Over the next month or so it became clear that Torch's commanders had finally learnt their jobs, so that in mid-May 1943 our First Army met up with Montgomery's Eighth Army and the Germans in North Africa capitulated. At virtually the same time higher authority withdrew No. 614 Squadron from its army co-operation role and reassigned it to maritime duties.

The North-African war was over. And that might well have been the end of my own overseas warring, for in July 1943, as I was changing after an inter-unit soccer game, a physical training instructor pointed to a varicose vein below my knee. 'They'd have to send you home to get that fixed,' he declared. So, ever the opportunist, I duly reported sick. Except that, with fewer wounded coming in, space and specialists were available in the military hospital in Oran. And instead of an early return to Blighty I got three weeks of 1940's Service-hospital discipline! Nous is not invariably trustworthy!

Despite the dwindling number of wounded I was honoured to shake hands with a convalescent Grenadier, one of those whose refusal to give way had kept the *Afrika Korps* from joining Cookie and me in our slit trench. What I found less inspiring was to discover a compound packed with hundreds, if not thousands, of patients – both American and British – wearing hospital-tops emblazoned on the back with the initials VD!

For my part I soon began fretting, and the moment I could, had myself discharged. I knew the squadron had moved to Sicily during my absence but that was no problem, for hitching had become a way of life.

Oran airport was packed with transports so I had no difficulty in finding an American Dakota pilot who agreed to take me to Syracuse, on the eastern coast of Sicily. Shifting his cigar to one side, he nodded at my Sten. 'If we meet any trouble, shove that thing outwards and get blasting.'

Fortunately, the flight was non-eventful, but having landed I discovered that the squadron was, in fact, at Trapani, back at the western end of Sicily. Nobody hindered my collecting meals in the airfield's cookhouse, but there were no flights going west. There was though, a Bisley, parked remotely, and all locked up. Seeing no other option, I camped beneath its wing each night until on the third morning a pilot turned up who was indeed going to Trapani. He ignored my Sten, but pointed to the turret. 'Can you fire the Brownings?' I didn't hesitate. 'No problem.' Not that I'd ever fired one in my life! However, shortly after we got airborne he advised, 'OK to test fire.' And after a few moments of pulling and squeezing, the things began stuttering merrily. Fortunately, nothing more was needed of them!

If I'd expected any recognition for my initiative in getting myself back to No. 614 I would have been disappointed. Even Cookie merely grunted, 'Hospital? Lead-swinging, more like.' With which it was back to the old routine, him on the right engine, me on the left.

But not for long, for out of the blue I received orders home, and after travelling across to Catania, on Sicily's east coast, I boarded RMS *Strathnaver*, for Liverpool.

After my disembarkation leave I reported to RAF Rhu, at Helensborough, on the Firth of Clyde, a Marine Aircraft Experimental Establishment, indeed an extension of Boscombe Down. Being a hush-hush unit there were things I wasn't expected to know about. Like the large, but less-than-full-sized float-aircraft various boffins spent their time fiddling with. At one time they were joined by Frank Whittle, of jet-engine fame, so I can only suppose they were trying to develop some amphibian jet plane. Judging by the number of failed attempts I saw they weren't getting on too well. But work, I knew, had been done there a year or so before on a certain bouncing bomb …

My responsibilities were Sunderland, Walrus, and Catalina flying boats, and a seaplane Spitfire. As always, I managed to get a fair amount of flying in, mostly quite uneventful, though there were moments. Like looking up as we lifted off in the Walrus to find a landing Sunderland filling the windscreen above us: concentrating on his take-off my pilot simply hadn't seen it, fortunately, my yell gave him time to take avoiding action.

The job was fine, but native though I was, the Scottish weather eventually got me down, and having successfully applied for a transfer I was sent to Wigsley, near Newark, in Nottinghamshire, on Stirlings. Now engines are engines, but I was never to feel comfortable working on them reared up at twenty-two feet off the tarmac as the Stirling's were! As for the Stirling itself, though dropped months since from Bomber-Command's main force, it enjoyed a brief flowering during Operation Market Garden, the airborne assault on Arnhem in September 1944, but then it went, and the Lancasters came. And life was suddenly sweet.

The Stirling engines, twenty-two feet above the tarmac …

*And the Lancasters came ... Me in the centre, being cuddled
by young lady*

I was still at Wigsley when the war finished, after which I was posted to Full
Sutton, near York, where I continued to service Lancasters, though silver
ones now, being on VIP transport duties.

What was to be my final posting was to Oakington, in Cambridgeshire,
where I worked on both Liberator and York transports. I was content enough
here, for I'd not yet fixed upon what I wanted to do in Civvy Street. If, that
is, I decided to leave. In fact, I'd actually held off demob while weighing the
incentive payment of a hundred pounds on offer to engine mechanics who
signed on for an extra year.

While I was yet pondering, however, I was detailed to do an inspection
on an Avro York. Having changed the plugs in the port engines I was just
setting up to start on the other side when a WAAF corporal banged on the
steps. 'Stop wasting time, Airman,' she called up, 'you know the plugs have
been signed off.' I didn't like her tone. So there was no way I would deign to
tell her that whoever'd signed off the job had skimped it, and hadn't actually
done the plugs. Not the first sign of such slackness I'd come upon, with so

many tradesmen leaving. Instead, I ignored her, finished the job properly, then reported to the orderly room, waived the one hundred pounds, and duly took my demob.

Any regrets? Even for finally chucking it, in what may have appeared a simple fit of pique? Actually, of course, it was deeper than that. Far more to do with realising that I didn't like the way the Service was changing.

Initially I returned to the Scottish foundry, then to another down in Nottingham, predominantly working on cookers. Both concerns having given me a good grounding in cookers of all sorts, I then secured a sales post in 'The Harrods of Nottingham', making countless good friends of customers and eventually retiring after some thirty-five very gratifying years.

So, looking around me, eagerly anticipating my annual trip north for the salmon fishing, I have to confess, no – not a single regret. Except, perhaps, that I didn't keep contact with good old Cookie.

Peter McArthur, 2012

4. My Hansome Corageous Brother

**Barbara Tyas, schoolgirl, later Mrs Morris.
Sergeant Nikodem Płotek, pilot,
Polish Air Force under British Command**

Pilot Trainee, Leading Aircraftman Nikodem Płotek, 1941

On the afternoon of 3 July 1941 a Blenheim Mk 4 on a ferry flight was descended through low cloud and crashed on Derbyshire's Kinderscout, all four occupants, including the Polish pilot, Sergeant Nikodem Płotek, being killed. This tribute to the members of an English family who befriended the Polish flier and thereby eased his life in exile – their support keeping him flying in a very real sense – is derived from the letters retained, and the diary entries made, by then-schoolgirl Barbara Tyas (later Mrs Barbara Morris) after Sergeant Płotek had been billeted on her family.

To set the scene, on 1 September 1939 German forces launched a blitzkrieg attack on Poland from the west. Sixteen days later Russia invaded without warning from the east. The Poles resisted fiercely on both fronts, only capitulating on 6 October 1939. Even then, many of their servicemen made their way to France, and when France fell, to Britain.

Sergeant Płotek's record shows that before the September Campaign (*Kampania Wrześniowa*), alternatively the 1939 Defensive War (*Wojna Obronna*), the twenty-four-year-old had served with the Third Polish Air Regiment, logging nearly four hundred hours. Prior to the German invasion he had been transferred to the hurriedly-formed Bomber Brigade (*Brygada Bombowa*) which suffered grievously while attacking the enemy's armoured columns. Certainly, his wish was that once the RAF made him operational it would post him to fighters.

'Then,' he told the Tyas family, his billeted hosts, 'I can kill Germans and if I have to die it will be alone, and no longer responsible for other people.'

On arriving in Britain on 9 February 1940, Nikodem Płotek had been accepted into the RAF Volunteer Reserve (RAFVR) at Eastchurch, on the Isle of Sheppey, and given the rank of aircraftman class two (AC2), remustering next day from general aircrafthand to U/T (under training) pilot.

This reflects the stance the British took when envisaging Polish airmen coming to Britain. All were to be inducted into the RAFVR, commissioned Polish pilots becoming pilot officers, warrant officer pilots downwards becoming AC2s; further, no credit was given for any operational or other flying experience before arriving in Britain.

These rules were originally based upon the premise that Poles would be suffering from low morale after their defeat in Poland, a canker that might infect any British units they served alongside, also that the language barrier might prove insurmountable in air operations. Only after a while, on reflecting upon the mettle shown by Polish units when under French Command in France, did the British – in their own extremity! – realise that, among the Polish fliers, they had seventy experienced and highly motivated fighter pilots who could aid in the operations that, evidently decisive, would become known as the Battle of Britain. An agreement was reached as early as 4 June 1940, after which the British attitude became ever more relaxed regarding the Polish forces.

Not being a fighter pilot, AC2 Płotek had basically been 'refreshed', successively passing through No. 3 (Polish) Wing at Blackpool – his introduction to both the English language and RAF techniques –, No. 15 Elementary Training School at Dumfries, and No. 18 Operational Training Unit at Hucknall, Nottingham.

Sergeant Nikodem Płotek, 1941

Appointed acting sergeant, and with his experience on twin-engined aircraft acknowledged, he was ideal material for one of the newly-formed Polish bomber squadrons. When he became available, however, these were fully manned, so he was sent instead to mark time flying Blenheims for Anti-Aircraft Cooperation Units (AACU) and attached in turn to No. 110 AACU at Manchester's Ringway, No. 6 AACU at Kirton in Lindsey and then, on 29 May 1941, to No. 12 AACU at RAF Digby.

Back on 6 August 1940, having been formally discharged from the RAFVR, he had become a member of the Polish Air Force under British

Command, a formation hastily legalised by parliament. He had also been billeted in various British homes, notably, that of the Tyas family, as the former Barbara Tyas remembers:

'I would have been about eleven when Nik came. Despite his marked – intriguing – accent, I thought his English was very good but he was never without his Polish-English dictionary, even using it as a wallet. Mother offered to open a bank account for him but he wouldn't let her, saying that banks crash in Poland. Mother tried to assure him that they didn't in England, but he merely told her that if anything happened to him she should claim the money in his dictionary.

To me, Nik was a magical figure, a very real big brother, and he, in turn, treated me as his young and much loved sister, calling me 'Bacia'. He was a romantic figure too, for having fought the Nazis in the air, he had then escaped all the way from Poland. He was posted several times after being billeted upon us but whenever he could he would visit us in the battered 1938 Opel dad had obtained and vetted for him. In fact, Dad taught him to drive. Strange, isn't it? Nik could fly a plane but couldn't drive a car!

He was so good looking, and he attracted all the girls, speaking warmly of those he had known in Blackpool and other places. He could be very emotional. But how he hated the Germans! He also went quiet whenever Jews were mentioned.

What he really loved, though, was flying. He would come over our house, turn steeply, circle low, and ask later if we had realised that it had been him. In fact, eventually neighbours complained to the RAF. He particularly loved aerobatics, and once came home gleeful because he had caused two officer passengers to be sick by throwing them about. But he especially liked to catch Mother when she was hanging out the Monday wash!'

LEAVE OR DUTY RATION CARD

(14 Days)

NAVY, ARMY AND AIR FORCE

IF FOUND RETURN TO ANY FOOD OFFICE

1. Holder's Name ...... *PLOTEK.* ......

   Rank...... *SGT.* ...... No. ...... —

2. Unit or Ship ...... *No. 6. A.A.G.U.* ......

3. Leave or Duty { Beginning...... *23/12/40* ......
                  { Ending ...... *5/1/41* ......

4. Signature and Rank } ......
   of Officer Issuing }

5. Unit or Ship of } ...... *RINGWAY* ......
   Officer Issuing }

Serial No. **WB** 248808

R.B. 8.
(51776-1) 10,000m

Ration card held by Mrs. Tyas

In the same way that Mrs Morris evokes a past in which Monday was fixedly laundry day so the entries from the diary she kept as an eleven-year-old conjure up the essence of wartime 1941 in the Manchester area. In order to preserve their freshness, the extracts are faithfully reproduced:

Sunday 5 January [1941]. Went to see Hutch [famous cabaret star] at a concert.

Thursday 9 January. Had raid at 8 p.m. planes over every minute went in the shelter all clear 1 a.m. Time bomb outside and HE [high explosive] behind. Did no damage.

Wednesday 8 January. Nik came home very ill with a touch of flu.

Friday 17 January. Bomb went off at 11.45 a.m. Nick came home 8.45.

Saturday 18 January. Went to the pictures. Then I had a surprise because Tadek Król came in, Nick's friend [A fellow pre-war Polish pilot.] June is mad for Nik. [June, a friend, a year older than Barbara]

Friday 31 January. Saw *Convoy* with Nik [sea-war film 1940]. Was out of friends with him.

Sunday 2 February. Went to meet Nik at the station. He didnt come.

Tuesday 4 February. Received autograph book back from RAF station from Nik. Raid 8.30 to 11.30.

Thursday 6 February. Tadek says Nik has gone to Church Fenton.

Saturday 19 April. Nik came home from Wittering.

Friday 23 May. Air raid alarm. Nik came home again. Rained.

Saturday 24 May. Nik's friend, Tolek [a fitter], came with car.

Saturday 31 May. Out in Nik's car had puncture walked home.

Monday 9 June. Tolek went back to Swinderby.

Thursday 3 July. [filled in retrospectively] *Nik was killed airoplane accident Kinder Scout bad visibility crashed hill side. Four in crew.*

Saturday 5 July. Heard Nik was killed.

Sunday 6 July. Mum Dad and Uncle went to see about Nik at Digby. Nik my hansome corageous brother I will all ways have sweet memmories of him.

Monday 7 July. Two officers came to see Mum about Nik

Tuesday 8 July. Nik's funeral He's buried at Southern Cemetery

Sunday 13 July. to Nik grave.

Sunday 19 July. Went to Nik grave with June and Mum took flowers.

Sunday 27 July. Took flowers to Niks grave.

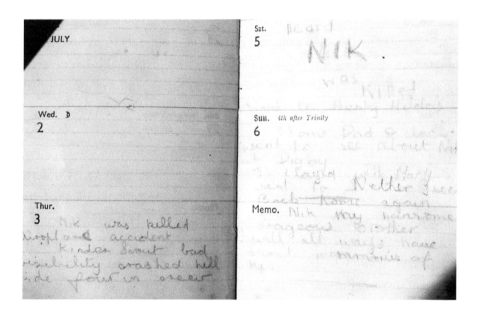

Barbara's diary entry of Płotek's death

Setting the diary aside, Mrs Morris goes on:

'Nik felt so close to our family that he made dad and mum beneficiaries of his will; in effect, his next-of-kin. He had loved flying so much that when the news came of his accident we were devastated. Dad immediately arranged to drive to Lincolnshire to find out what he could. By the time he arrived, just three days after the crash, Nik's things had long been packed up and put aside for him. Dad was also given a slip of paper by Nik's officer, detailing where the crash had occurred. My diary records the outlines of Nik's time with us, but it is in his letters, and our memories, that he lives on.'

As a schoolgirl Barbara regarded Sergeant Płotek's English as well up to standard, but he was, after all, a young Pole who was still feeling his largely untaught way in a foreign tongue. The following extracts from his letters – and from those of his relatives and colleagues – are, as with the diary entries, quoted as written, certainly not to evoke quaintness, but to preserve their freshness and vitality, and to reflect, as they do, the flavour of the times.

On 4 April 1941, Sergeant Płotek wrote from RAF Wittering.

'My dear Mr and Mrs Tyas, and Barbara. I spent Eastertide at Swinderby so I was very glad to hear some gen from you … and thanks for the letter enclosed. It was from a friend of mine, a sailor in a Polish destroyer … I really have pukka gen for you. At the end of this week I will come home for a few days … hope to see you soon after you have got this letter received. … no more punctures recently … I am dying to see your super-fashonable new coat, will you still speak with me having it on? … So long, … Nik.'

He wrote again on 28 April 1941, from RAF Duxford.

'I have come to Duxford again. Last week I was in Coltishall which is a desert indeed, but Sgt's mess is excellently good. I haven't seen no where else better food, by the way, here it isn't too bad either. I left Ringway last Sunday about 11.30 and came over you, but as it was raining very heavily I couldn't fly over lower and longer. I hardly could see my own nose, it was so dark in the rain. I went to fly over the quarry but unfortunately they haven't worked that Sunday. [Mr Tyas was a weigh-bridge inspector, and did duty at the quarry.] I hope next week I am home again and <u>probably</u> I shall get a few days' leave (7 or 8 days) … How is my moto car? I am going to make a long trip with my car during my leave. Sorry, I have asked about how is my car instead of to ask first how you are. I hope you are quite all right (much better than my car). I am OK either. Nik.'

On 22 May 1941, his letter came from Coltishall.
'I would like to get leave on 27 May as Tolek [his friend, Leading Aircraftman Antoni Ibron, a fitter on No. 301 (Polish) Bomber Squadron] will have some leave and is going to come to see me at home, will that be all right? The weather during the last few days is very lousy and that is the reason I shall be home on Monday instead of tomorrow. By the way my coming to home on Monday is still up to the weather … I caught a very bad cold last Sunday, having a sun-bath, but am not dying yet of that … Nik.'

His next letter came from Kirton in Lindsey on 31 May 1941.
'It was quite a nice day when I was leaving home but as you said, Mrs Tyas, I may find very bad weather on the top of the hills and so that was. It was not raining but such a thick fog that I couldn't drive more than 20 mph. Visibility was there no more than 80 yards. [*Ironically, Sergeant Płotek was transiting pretty well the area of Derbyshire's high ground, and in the same weather conditions, that would catch him out on his fatal flight*] I came here to Kirton but nobody knows what for and I don't know what I shall do. At the present I don't work at all. I am waiting again but this time not in the queue. Waiting in the queue was very popular in the Polish Air Force and in these days it is very popular in England too. … I asked if I could go away from the station till Monday morning, no was the answer, wait till we see what to do with you. "Once was a peacock waiting for Sunday but on Saturday they cut its head off". [He repeats the proverbial saying in Polish]. To know how to wait is the biggest airmen's virtue. France lost this war as the soldiers were fed up of the waiting for German troops. … Nik.'

He was still at Kirton on 17 June 1941 but expecting to move to RAF Digby the next day.

'Mr and Mrs Tyas, and Babs, Tomorrow, Wednesday, my flight will move to Digby what I don't like at all as from Digby is much farther to home. I would like to be sent to Church Fenton as I think this more convenient from there to get to the wide world. Tolek wrote me. But because I did not answer he wrote two letters more and was a bit exited [excited] what could happen with me and of course, had written to Marguerite [a lady friend of Płotek's from Blackpool] that I am not answering him and she wrote to me a funny letter which I am enclosing with this (as Mrs Tyas likes to read my letters from girls) (also a letter from Irene) [Another of his lady friends]. Do not send them back to me, burn them.

I stopped myself in the Sergeant's Mess … there was a "social party" but I think I'd better to call that "drinking party". Last night I was at Scunthorpe for dancing but I did not dance as a Sgt brought two girls but one of them does not dance at all, she supposed to be my partner. Never mind by chance a very bad dancer met a hopeless one. I did not get any of those letters you sent to me at Wittering. I think they are still on the road to me only not going towards me. … with love, yours, Nik.'

Regarding Sergeant Płotek's lady friends, Mrs Morris smiles, confiding, 'He did not feel serious about any of his girls as he used to joke about them to my mother. In particular, Marguerite. He felt that she was too serious, which made him rather afraid of her. In retrospect, I wonder if he was a little in love with my Mother – and she perhaps with him!'

Sergeant Płotek's final letter, written on Wednesday 2 July 1941, was headed, Heath House, Nocton, near Lincoln. It reads:

'My dear Mr and Mrs Tyas and Barbara, It has been so hot lately and beautiful days indeed we have had that I was not inclined to write even the very short letter before, for what I am very sorry. I do know you are awaiting for my letter (as sometimes I was too but that was not your fault). Aren't you surprised I have written such a lovely address of mine on the top of this letter?

Last Wednesday my flight had moved from Digby to Coleby aerodrome. [Coleby Grange, Digby's satellite airfield, just to the north-west of Digby] At Coleby there is only aerodrome and there is no station of the RAF so we [pilots] live in a very nice manorhouse, what makes us think we are lords. The owner of this manor house has moved somewhere and the RAF is now looking after the building.

I will not write much gen as I intend to see you at the weekend but that is only duff gen. It is up to the duty. If I am not at home at the weekend I will write a very long and newsy letter OK? With love, yours, Nik.

3 July 41 PS. I finished writing last night but as I did not write everything what I should write this time I am writing some more. I did receive your letters for which I thank you very much. I will not answer Barbara separately as I should write her the same news.'

Sergeant Płotek then appended a second PS, timing it at '9.20 a.m.' His flight commander's note to Mr Tyas affirmed that the crash occurred at, *'about 3pm Thursday 3 7 41.'* That is, Sergeant Płotek died just hours after writing the second PS. It read:

'I was just told I've got 7 days leave, it means that on Saturday night I'll be at home. I am afraid it is a bit late and Mr Tyas will not manage to get any holydays. Next leave after this one I shall get in the next month. I'll finish wishing you all the very best, yours, Nik.'

Among the early letters of condolence was one from Bessie Hope, a friend of the Tyas family.

'To you both and Barbara … We have so often watched you when Nick has come home. You were such a happy family and it was good indeed to see you make him so happy which he obviously was.'

As Mr and Mrs Tyas had been appointed Sergeant Płotek's next of kin, there was a more formal communication from RAF Record Office, Gloucester, dated 8 July 1941.

'Mr Tyas: It is my painful duty to confirm the death of No. 780497 Sergeant Płotek of No.12 Group Flight, Royal Air Force Station, Digby, who was killed in a flying accident on the 3rd July 1941. The Air Council desire me to express their sympathy and deep regret at this airman's death in the service of the Allies.'

Then, on 30 July 1941, came a poignant letter from Blackpool, from Marguerite [surname suppressed], addressed to Barbara's mother: a reminder in itself, of how wide a circle even one 'wartime statistic' affected.

'I think you will be very surprised to receive this letter – we are very great friends of Nikodem Płotek and we are all heartbroken to have heard that he was killed. I wondered if he had left any little personal things with you, if you could send me anything? I cannot explain to you what it would mean to me if you could. … I think that his watch would be with him, also his little red white and blue flower mascot which we gave him. Anything of his at all would mean so much to me. Please could you help me? Could you tell me anything about him? When did you last see him? Was he very happy?

Do excuse these questions, but it is so terrible – he is dead. I do hope you will reply soon, and do tell me if you think he was happy [double underlined] – that is most important. Yours, very sincerely, Marguerite: on his snaps, and in any of his letters, my name was "Margi".'

Marguerite then continued, 'He was in Blackpool last summer and he … practically lived here. Then he left Blackpool and whenever he could he came home to see us. About Christmas he and I had a misunderstanding. About six weeks ago he was going to come to see me to explain everything. Then on the very day his station was changed and he telephoned me to say he could not come but that he would come when he had leave in July. He never had this leave and so he never saw me to talk to.

Please give my wishes to your little girl "Bacia" – I know that he loved her. Thank you. Yours most sincerely, and I do hope you will reply soon, Marguerite.'

Whether Vera, 'Bacia's' [Barbara's] mother, was able to lessen the distraught young woman's grief is not known, but she was able to give expression to her own feelings in a letter she sent in late August 1941 to the leader of the Polish forces, General Sikorsky.

'We should have been very proud should he have lived to see things through, for he was a born leader and could he have returned to his own dear country he would have risen to some prominent position, he had ambition and ability for your cause and spoke freely of his admiration for you.

Although we who say this are only plain British people … he was a hero, a fine example of manhood, good, honest, truthful, and kind … He came from Poznan, had a brother in the Excise department of the port of Gdynia and seven or eight others in the family. If only we had been able to preserve him for them!

He won every heart while at the same time holding in reserve his own sorrowful feelings for his home and country. … He came to be so joined in our little family circle, the emptiness is too great now he is not present. Many times he said he would like to earn distinctions in England for the benefit of Poland and his flying accident has come as a severe shock.

He was not vain, but rather loved seclusion, and at the same time he had a secret admiration for great people … we talk of the Poles as a great and lovable people … May you rise in all your glory for we shall win. May I ask you to put this pilot on record for devotion to duty. RIP from his English Home.'

Just a week later an acknowledgement arrived from Brigadier General Ujejski [British substantive rank air commodore but at that time acting air vice-marshal].

'I thank you very much for your kind letter. Sgt Płotek, like unfortunately many others are now paying the noble sacrifice for our struggle for freedom of our beloved country and the freedom of the whole world. It is a great pleasure for me to hear whenever one of our boys makes friends with the English, it is a great help for us today and I sincerely hope that it will be a foundation for many years of collaboration in the better days to come.'

At about the same time Leading Aircraftman Tadeusz (Taddy) Petrus, a stonemason in civil life in Poland, then serving as an instrument mechanic, wrote from RAF Henlow. [The letter is beautifully handwritten and the notepaper is imprinted with the Polish Air Force and Royal Air Force devices interlinked.]

'Dear Mr and Mrs Tyas, As I had received no reply to last two letters which I sent to Nikodem Płotek I called the Polish Headquarters in Blackpool and was grieved to learn that he had been killed. I should very much like to meet you, to thank you for the kindness which you gave to my friend. I would greatly appreciate it if you could let me know where he is buried, so that I, being a sculptor, could make and place there something as a memorial … I should be grateful for any details which you could give me as to the cause of his death.'

After Sergeant Płotek's death, his friends, pilot Tadek Król and fitter Tolek Ibron, maintained contact with the Tyas household. But writing on 20 March 1942 from RAF Hemswell, Tolek, aged twenty-seven and a married man, had yet more dire news.

'My Dearest Family, I was expecting some letter from my dear little Babs, yet she must be still very busy and of course I do understand. Barbara do you not believe me that I eagerly await each of your letters. Yes, do believe me, because I do like very much to read your nice and very joyful letters. It is true my "young lady", as she is not a baby now.

And now, my dear family, to tell you the bad news that Tadek has been killed in a flying accident. I got this news from Blackpool in this week. He was buried last week at Barrow.

We were joking with Nik sometimes who will be the first one [to die] him or Tadek and now they both are together. I do not know what to think about Tadek's accident, but I wonder he was also a bit too sure [the 'also' implying, *like Nik, letting blindly down through cloud*!]. Many times, I used to say to Nik and Tadek too don't forget that "the circumspection should be a companion of the courage". They said yes, it is truth, but they both could have forgotten about it, I think. … Tolek.'

Tadek, Sergeant Pilot Tadeuszk Król, had been inducted into the RAFVR alongside Sergeant Płotek and had been with him at Blackpool and at Dumfries. After that, however, their paths had separated, with Sergeant Król refreshing at No. 8 Elementary Flying Training School and then at No. 10 Air Gunnery School at Barrow-in-Furness. On the 8 March 1942, at Barrow, he stalled a Defiant and was killed.

Tolek wrote again just nine days later, on 29 March 1942, evidently in response to the Tyas' reply.
'It was lovely to read your nice words about Tadek, and to know your view on the world and life … Oh, how very much I would like to be now like our dear little Barbara. She does not know anything about troubles and everything she wants she can get it from her noble parents. It is most wonderful thing for the child to live in that free Country and to have a good parents.'

Tolek, now a corporal, busy servicing No. 301 Squadron's Wellingtons at RAF Hemswell, wrote again on 20 June 1942, clearly feeling the strain.
'I can't sleep at nights and I feel myself very dejected. I think some influence on it have a very bad news from Poland, what we know about it and we can hear of it from the wireless, very often. All the murders which Germany are doing in masses now, in our country are making us very sad. It's terrible but we cannot help it now. We must wait and see.

My dears … It's really very sad but we also have the same tragedies in here. My plein [plane, the Wellington he was responsible for] was also over Cologne that night and … I think it was a marvellous raid on Germany and now at last the German people will begin to be frightened. A few nights after that the plein was lost over Essen. I was ever so sorry because the crew was very nice.

I was glad reading about our Nik … How could we forget him? Never! Love to little sister Babs, Tolek.'

Tolek wrote directly to Barbara on 24 July 1942, again from Hemswell.
'I would like to take a snap with you and with Mum and Dad too. Do you think will it be possible. … It would be nice if we could take some snap by Nik's grave …'

Some months later, on 25 January 1943, Tolek again wrote from RAF Hemswell, but in a different vein.
'Now my Dears, I am going to tell you something what you could never guess. Last week I received a good news from Poland from my wife Eleonora. This little message made me ever so happy because at last after nearly three years I have got a few words saying that they are alright and at the same place (Piotrków) as I left them before the war. You can imagine how very happy I was reading that wonderful news. It came through the Red Cross from Genève.'

He kept in contact throughout a squadron detachment to the Middle East, and after VE Day, when he returned. On 31 July 1945, just a fortnight before the war ended altogether, he wrote from RAF North Weald.

'My Dearests, do you realise that during my next leave I shall be with you for the first time after the war. I mean in Peacetime. No blackout at all. Isn't it strange that I am still in England. Two or three years ago I could never think that after so many months I shall be so far away from Poland.'

The war had been over for some time before the Tyas family found that it was possible to communicate with Poland. Indeed, it was 1946 before replies began to arrive from Sergeant Płotek's family. Once they did, it became clear that the Płoteks had been unaware of Nikodem's death until the arrival of the Tyas' letter. A brother wrote:

'Dear Lady, It was a very painful news for us because we never thought that we shall see no more our dear Nikodem. We always had hope and we believed that he will come back to his Country and his family. But alas the decree of God has changed our wishes. It was not given to Nikodem to live to see that moment when he could return to his people. He had lost his life far from his country and his grave is very far from grave of his father, who died in 1943. The only one relief is that there in England are his friends that will remember and look after the grave of our beloved Nik … How much we would give if we could have his body with us in our country … Perhaps you could tell where and in what circumstances he has lost his life.'

Another brother, Franciszek, an interpreter in the Excise, wrote a little later, dating his letter 29 April 1946.
'Dear Friends, I received to-day your letter you sent to my mother and announcing us these bad news about our dear brother. Though sorrowful it is I am very thankful to you because we have been waiting so long for news from him. We were always hoping the best, the more I always received answers to my letters written during the war to the Red Cross in Genève that his name was not to be found on lists of the killed.

And when we, his brothers, who were kept during the whole war in German camps and one of us had to hide himself lest the Germans would kill him, returned home, we were sure that Niku, who was in the best situation must return too … But there was not anyone returning from England who could tell us something about him. We told mother he might be in the Middle East, or Italy, and that his letters were lost.

He was in our thoughts during the whole war. Every time Allied bombers were over us we were supposing Nikodem is there, paying us visits. Parents expected the whole time to see us again home, and especially him, from whom there were no news. Father when dying (June 1943) didn't suspect that his loved son and our best brother is dead. For nearly five years he was alive for us until today and we shall never forget him with his childish smile.'

Franciszek wrote again on 10 March 1947.

'Dear Friends, Thank you for [all the details you sent] about our dear Nikus. I had to do translations of it to all members of our family. We always looked forward to the time he would return and tell us his story after his leaving Poland in 1939 ... now we can imagine a little of his life with you in England. We could hardly believe he lives no more, and in spite of your letters we always hoped he would return and that there is only a mistake as to his person. But after having received your last letter we got some others [from various organisations]. From all these letters we have unfortunately seen that our beloved Nikus is really dead and will return no more. ... The worst is mother who can't forget him. We are still living four brother and sisters but she always expects the fifth one. She can't say his name without tears.'

It was only in January 1948 that the Office of the Curator of Polish Estates was able to make over to Mrs Vera Tyas the estate of Sergeant Płotek. It amounted to £99/8s/8d together with 'some effects of sentimental value'. Even then it was March before the Anglo-Polish Society confirmed that money could now be sent to Poland. In a series of letters the two families discussed the matter, and finally, and in view of the restrictions and the sheer expense of sending money to Poland, the Płoteks decided that best value lay in having the Tyas family send a knitting machine. They also requested parachute material for dressmaking, although whether this request could be met, is not known.

Seven years earlier, in a letter dated 1 August 1941, Major [Squadron Leader] Robert Hirszbandt, of the Polish Forces in England, had written of

Sergeant Płotek's loss, inscribing the envelope, 'To the family and nearest relatives of Nik'. His letter reads:

'I would like to write something in memory of Nik. Nik was eight months in England during which time I got to know him as an excellent pilot, a sound military colleague, and a man who conquered all hearts. … Although Nik was living in England … everything he did was for Poland, and for the Freedom of Poland. Nik … matched his words with his actions. He should never be forgotten.

The sorry truth is that flying is not always safe, anything can happen. As it happened to Nik. I was the last one who saw him alive at about two o'clock on 3 July 1941. I was talking to him as he went to his plane. He took off, but didn't return. It was a thick fog which led to the catastrophe that killed him. And three more with him, English people.

I do not know if God will spare me to return to a free Poland …' The envelope then bears the emotive, *W Police Niepodlegtej*, which might be rendered as 'If Poland were only free!'

The final Polish tragedy, of course, was that post-war Poland was not free. Nor were the returning 'western-tainted' former servicemen welcomed by the now-Communist authorities.

In that context, back in 1947, on 9 January, Corporal Tolek had already discovered that the so-longed-for peace had raised not only new problems but new heartaches for him. He had written from RAF East Wretham, a resettlement camp near Thetford, Norfolk.

'My Dearests, I do not know when they will demob us. I have been trying all I could to get my wife over to England and to obtain British naturalisation … in the end I did not succeed. … I had at last to take a final decision and I did it. I declared to return to Poland and I expect to leave England next month. I know it is not the best way out but in my situation I could not do anything else. Naturally I could not sign on in the Polish Resettlement Corps, having my wife in Poland.'

[Signing on with the Polish Resettlement Corps for a two-year trade-training course would have allowed him to stay in England, an option taken up by many unattached Poles who chose not to risk returning to newly-Communist Poland].

Tragically, once Tolek Ibron had left England, hoping to be reunited with his wife, neither the Tyas family nor Air Ministry's Polish Section heard anything more of him.

For completeness, the broad circumstances of Sergeant Płotek's crash show that on the afternoon of 3 July 1941, Blenheim Mk4 Z5870 was being ferried from Digby to Ringway when it was descended through low cloud and crashed below Crowden Tower on Derbyshire's Kinderscout.

Crowden Tower, Kinderscout. Sergeant Płotek crashed where the photographer is standing, 400 yards below the crag

Although the aircraft impacted in a slide across a grassy slope and was virtually intact when found, all four occupants died: three airman passengers – two RAF and one Royal Canadian Air Force –, and Sergeant Płotek. By then Sergeant Płotek had logged 542 flying hours – above average for the time –, 147 being on RAF Blenheims.

Because the aircraft had suffered so little damage, and as air-crash enthusiasts in the 1960s had removed what wreckage there was from the spine below Crowden Tower, the dearth of evidence has led to various locations being proposed for the crash site. All doubts, however, were dispelled by Mrs. Morris' production of the slip of paper given to Mr Tyas by Sergeant Płotek's commanding officer just three days after the event, specifying, as it did: *Location, 400 yards South from Crowden Tower, N of Lee Farm, Edale* (that is, at SK 09435 87112).

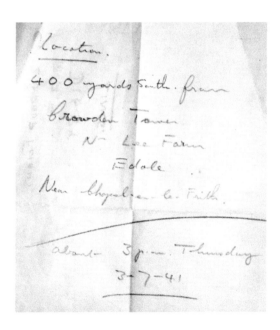

The crash-site location given three days after the event

Merely for the record, in November 2007 a three-party metal-detector search turned up nothing on the spine site, where debris is known to have existed until the 1960s.

Acting Corporal Charles Roose, radar operator/mechanic

Aircrew Cadet Charles Roose, 1943

I was born in Beeley, one of the Chatsworth Estate villages, in January 1926, and on leaving school at fourteen joined the Estate as a boy estate-clerk – the Estate, that is, as opposed to the House, which at that time was a separate entity: we make the money, we'd say, they spend it. Thereafter, sitting at a large brass-adorned, two-seater wooden desk, I began to learn all aspects of agriculture and estate management under the strict tutelage of Mr Lou Bond, the chief clerk. I have to say that, from the outset I found the work fascinating, and as figures came easily to me I felt my progression assured.

Out of office hours, however, it was Aviation that held my interest and in February 1941, when the Air Training Corps (ATC) was formed, I was among its first recruits, joining No. 1025 (Hope Valley) Squadron. We studied aviation subjects, particularly aircraft recognition and morse code, and, of course, drilled. At 15, I was far too young to join up, but the moment I could I also joined the Home Guard, and so took on a double ration of drill. What I really wanted to do, though, was fly, which meant, naturally, to fly Spitfires. And why not? I seemed healthy, was provenly good with figures, and certainly knew my foot drill.

A further concern I looked at, thanks to another Estate lad, Fred Bater, from Baslow, was the Royal Observer Corps (the Corps had just gained royal status!). The people Fred introduced me to who manned the Baslow post tended to be well-to-do and very dedicated. But though I found their dedication compelling, my eyes were firmly set on Spitfires.

What might have put me off – but didn't! – was that on 11 June 1943, just after I'd turned the magical seventeen and a quarter and was waiting to be called forward by the RAF, a Wellington bomber crashed in the Park beside the public road at Lindup Low. It was on a training sortie from RAF Cottesmore, near Oakham, in Rutland, and when both engines began to splutter the pupil pilot decided to set it down. All three crew members survived, although when I got there, just moments later, one had an impressively bloody face! The aircraft, however, was a total write-off. The site was quickly cleared, even so an Estate-authorised search in 2005 would reveal scraps of debris and even corroded ammunition where scores of people must have picnicked over the succeeding years. It would be as late as that too before I discovered that the pilot, Australian Leo Patkin, had got his wings and joined No. 467 Squadron, only to be killed six months after his Chatsworth crash, on 1 January 1944, when his Lancaster was shot down near Celle while raiding Berlin.

Left: Chatsworth Head Park Keeper David Robinson with a fragment of Wellington fuel line, 2005

Below: 0.303 inch calibre ammunition from Wellington DV678 unearthed in 2005

Not that the crash would ever have put me off, not with my fixation on flying; that and the fact that the alternative, waiting to be called up, might well have meant my being one of the ten per cent of conscripts drafted down the coal mines as a Bevin Boy!

When the call came I was sent to Birmingham for three days of aircrew selection comprising aptitude tests (fitting round pegs into square holes and the like), education papers, and a very thorough medical which included blowing up a column of mercury and holding it at a certain level for as long as possible. This was the test we dreaded most, for we'd all had friends pass through the procedure. Fortunately, in my case, it went well. In fact, I came away over the moon to have been accepted in the highest category there was, that of PNB, suitable for pilot, navigator, and bomb aimer; the grade automatically implying too, that I'd been assessed above those found suitable for wireless operator, flight engineer, and air gunner. Unsurprisingly, therefore, I returned to Chatsworth in a state of high glee: Spitfires, here I come!

Only to wait. To return to my heavy wooden desk, beneath the skylight, just down the corridor from my chief-clerk mentor. There was one significant difference, of course, for I had now been attested into the RAF Volunteer Reserve, and having served in the ATC, had received a Service number beginning with a three. In truth, therefore, the lad labouring on for months more at his accustomed Estate tasks was now '3050683 Aircrafthand-under-training Roose, Sir!'

As things turned out, it was to be December 1943, a full nine months after first applying, before I was summoned to report to No. 1 Aircrew Reception Centre (ACRC, or Arsey-Darcy) at Lord's Cricket Ground in St John's Wood, London. Here we aspirant fliers had kit thrown at us and were accommodated in what had formerly been luxury flats – the Abbey Lodge complex is still there – but were then bare of all but beds and lockers and the sheets and blankets we deposited therein. We also did drill. And at mealtimes we were marched to a dining hall situated alongside the monkey cage in London Zoo, eating under the interested and vociferous regard of the residents, one of the species that had not been moved away. After which we did more drill. Indeed, here we began our formal square-bashing.

They were long days. We had to fall in at 0600 and march to the zoo for breakfast, a good twenty-minute slog, the column tramping through the blacked-out streets like a crowd of itinerant Israelites, even to (in our case) the red lanterns fore and aft of us.

As I have said, most of us were familiar with the training pattern thanks to friends who were now with operational squadrons. We expected, therefore, to remain at Lord's for just a matter of days before being sent on to an Initial Training Wing (ITW) where we would begin to learn the rudiments of aviation, and – of course – complete our drilling. Except that our group found ourselves there for a full month. And even when we were posted, it was not to an ITW, but to Dowdswell Court, Cheltenham, where masters from Cheltenham College put us through a further six months' – *half a year*! – rigorous refresher course in maths, English, physics, and of all things, history! At course's end we were even presented with school certificates which, as most of us had left school at fourteen, was very gratifying. But puzzling. And certainly not a training qualification we'd heard about before.

Aircrew Cadets, Cheltenham, 1943

No ITW yet, then. But we knew we must pass through that stage before moving on to the next, that of grading school, where we would be given up to fifteen hours on Tiger Moths to see if we were really fitted for the flying life – and Spitfires. Thence onto flying-training proper, to elementary and then advanced flying schools, both as like as not overseas, where the weather was predictable and continuity could be guaranteed. After which, having gained our wings, would come the final training stage, the Operational Training Unit, where we would learn to use our aircraft in war; in my case the tactical use of the Spitfire. And so to our operational squadrons.

There was just the chance, of course, that some might be turned aside onto a bomber stream, but that was not to be seriously thought of. That was the sort of thing that happened to other people. And certainly not to someone who had hungered after Spitfires for as long as I had. First, though, the elusive Initial Training Wing.

Only instead of ITW – though now with school certificates in our knapsacks – we were sent off on leave. A rather irksome leave, in truth, at the end of which we were required to report, first to Lord's once more, and then to No. 14 Preliminary Aircrew Training Unit.

Hopeful though the latter sounded, all it meant was that we were set to fire-watching as London endured wave after wave of Doodlebugs – V-1 pulse-jet, pilotless missiles –, of which nearly 4,000 landed on the capital. While detailed for rooftop watch we could do little but eye the jet-flare and then, once the stuttering engine stopped and the dive began, telephone to control and report. When on street patrol, on the other hand, we swiftly learnt to hit the pavement face down when that ominous silence began, allowing our tin hats to take the brunt of the flying glass which could spread for a full half mile from the impact point. I should also mention that between times we were kept busy with yet more intensive foot drill.

Indeed, it was at this juncture that the drill corporals really seemed to irritate us. Probably a measure of our rising discontent, for in truth, they had been a fact of life for months now, with their razor-sharp creases and their screeching and bawling, ultimate thickies themselves, yet with a hackneyed repertoire of belittling personal comments to scream into their hapless victims' faces. And hapless, because we wanted to fly, not to end up in the guardhouse, and maybe classified 'ceased training', for venting our own spleen on some bully-with-two-stripes. In the nick of time, perhaps, we were posted, and finally, glory be! to an Initial Training Wing.

In our case this was to No. 13 ITW located, at that time, at Torquay. A special train was laid on which was all very fine, though our reception at the resort lives with me still. It was now late May 1944 and, as it happened, a blazing hot day. Denied transport, we were set to march to our accommodation, to the Hydro Hotel in Paignton (for me), at the very far end of the bay, wearing the obligatory greatcoat, strapped about with full webbing (back and side packs, water bottle, ammo pouches, and bayonet frog), and carrying our kitbags, eyeing ruefully, as we went, peeling posters carolling, Welcome to Torquay!

The saving grace was that here we finally got down to a purposeful six weeks of work on signals, navigation, airmanship, theory of flight, and lots of morse: all very arduous, but joyously so, and finally tending in the right direction. At last, we told each other, we were actually getting somewhere!

We should have known better. A directive arrived that all studies were to stop until we had been aptitude tested once again. This seemed unthreatening enough to those of us, like me, who were secure with PNB status, and therefore, suitable for all aircrew posts. So, rather like lambs to the slaughter …

Of the fifty of us on our course just ten emerged from this reselection as prospective aircrew, and those, to a man, were to switch from training as pilots, navigators, or bomb aimers, to training as air gunners: no wireless operators, no flight engineers. As to the rest, the choice was bleak, the army. Except for those few who – again like me – had numbers beginning with a three, indicative of Air Training Corps service, and we, at least, were permitted to stay in the RAF if we so wished, only not as prospective aircrew.

Best speak just for myself. I was shattered. In a stroke my aspirations had been dashed. I can re-live the feeling without effort. In fact, I still have the letter my mother wrote to me in response to mine pouring out my disappointment. Hers is consoling, suggesting that flying is not the be-all, and reminding me how much I enjoyed my job at the Estate. But perhaps, at this remove, many would find her letter surprising in that she does not express relief that I was not, after all, to engage in operational flying.

In fact, her apparent lack of concern reminds us that few of the populace knew of the losses RAF aircrews were suffering. John Snagge's imperturbable voice on the BBC might conclude, 'three of our aircraft are missing', but I cannot ever remember hearing him, or even Alvar Lidell, impassively announcing, 'eighty of our aircraft are missing – that makes something like 600 aircrew, folks', as must, on occasion, have been the reality. My mother's letter, therefore, resurrects a world in which the media had far less impact and in which security, perhaps, made life just a little more bearable.

Though the disruption of our ambitions came as a shock, yet the writing had long been on the wall. We all knew the rapidity with which friends had been sped through the training system and on to operations just months before. Today's reality was that the invasion was imminent. Which had to mean that the Allied commanders were satisfied that they had air superiority; that now their overwhelming requirement was for boots on the ground, and bayonets.

Anyway, for our lot, off came the proud white trainee-aircrew side-cap flashes. Gone, then, the glamour. Now we must work for a living. So what work to opt for? For another benefit of former ATC service was that we were offered our choice of trades. But with such a variety available, which to choose?

To assist us in making up our minds the Isle of Sheppey light railway deposited us at RAF Eastchurch, a revered flying station from the earliest days of aviation which had more recently played an illustrious part in the Battle of Britain. Now, though, as an Aircrew Disposal Unit, it had reached its nadir, the majority of men it dealt with being those who had been removed from flying duties under the stigma of LMF – lack of moral fibre. The battledress blouses of these unfortunates bore unfaded patches on sleeves and left breasts where stripes and brevets had been ripped away. No enlightened identification by higher authority of post-traumatic stress disorder back then, just the uncompromising initials LMF. The Eastchurch we experienced was a very depressing place.

In our case, though, it did the job of furnishing us with information regarding the trades on offer. There were all the mechanic-type ones you might associate with aircraft, but so many others that didn't naturally come to mind. There was clerk (accounting), of course, but I wanted a total change. For rather different reasons I discounted sanitary assistant, masseur, and pigeon keeper. The one I eventually opted for was that of radar operator; cushy, or so Fred Bater from Baslow had said, having opted it for it himself some months before: certainly better than clambering up ladders to mend aircraft engines on a winter's night in draughty Lincolnshire. Then again, radar had a special ring about it: by this time the term – standing for radio direction-finding and ranging – had emerged from under wraps and was openly spoken of.

Those of us who opted for radar were duly tested – it was all quite technical, I seem to remember –, and the successful ones sent to RAF Hartlebury, near Kidderminster, to await a course.

Hartlebury turned out to be No. 25 Maintenance Unit (MU), a vast repository for stores of every conceivable sort, spread over several sites. It didn't take us long to realise that we were merely here to kick our heels again, the truth being that if once-proud Eastchurch had gathered to it victims of LMF, Hartlebury had done the same for dodgers. Nowhere could one have found such a gathering of lead-swingers, indeed, I'll swear there were warrant officers there who had carved out their niches in the Great War and not moved since. We arrived in July 1944, a month after D-Day and stayed just two months. But what a lengthy two months they were!

Release finally arrived with a posting to a real training station, to No. 9 Radio School at Yatesbury, in Wiltshire. So this was it: radar here I come! There were fifty of us, and within hours of our arrival I was craning alongside the others to see which group I was with. Had I learnt nothing? For of course, my name was missing. The present influx meant that the courses were over-subscribed, so until the backlog cleared I was to be assigned to the station orderly room!

It transpired that I was to work under what had to be the one waste-of-space warrant officer who hadn't found a niche at Hartlebury. Instead, he'd entrenched himself here at Yatesbury, just to make my life a trial.

'Roose, can you play the violin?' he demanded, coming up behind me. And having got my reluctant negative – I couldn't believe anyone on earth would still go through that hoary pantomime, but he did! – 'Then get yore 'air cut.' Even he, though, was but a passing thorn, lasting only a fortnight and swiftly forgotten when a new intake arrived and I was allocated to a course.

The month-long radar operator's course was packed with information. We started with learning the basics of wireless and radar, all new stuff to me, although some trainees were radio buffs. The system we were to operate was known as Chain Home, and was designed to detect aircraft at a distance of up to 120 miles, cathode ray tube displays enabling us to count down their range, also to establish both their bearing from us and their altitude. We were warned that this was very much a first-generation radar system, that even so it had proved itself, notably in the Battle of Britain.

We were shown that fan-shaped radio pulses sent out from one aerial array would bounce off a target aircraft and be received as echoes by a second aerial array. The outgoing pulses, we learnt, were sent from a fixed-wire aerial suspended between 360 foot high, open-lattice metal towers. The echoes reflected off the target, it transpired, were received by two aerials mounted on 240 foot high wooden towers, this array being made directional by having the aerials set at right angles to each other.

Our job, as operators, was to manipulate a comparator control – a goniometer – which would bring together the two received signals on our displays to give the most solid return: gonio-bashing to the initiated! An associated scale would show this combined best-return as the bearing of the target, the range being indicated by the distance along the timebase. Another aerial array, low down on the tower, similarly used, enabled the altitude to be determined. Further, we were told that an experienced operator could even estimate the numbers of aircraft involved.

Chain Home aerial towers

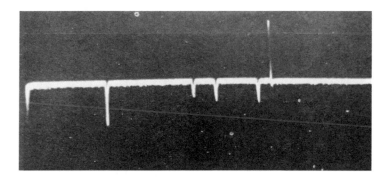

The operator's cathode ray tube timebase

Theory was fair enough, but the skill lay in learning to bring the signals to a peak. In fact, it was all classroom stuff, but signal generators gave us all we needed. The wireless enthusiasts among us tutted, muttering that there were radars now, even in the new heavy bombers, with dish-type aerials that turned around – scanned – and gave map-like displays.

'Chain Home is old now,' the instructor agreed, 'but it works.' And he told us what the system's inventor – a chap called Watson-Watt – had said to the government in the late 1930s, that although he considered the system to be 'third best', it would work, that if they waited for second best it would be too late, while best might never arrive. And so the vital defensive chains were built in the nick of time.

On qualifying as a radar operator I became an aircraftman class two, put up my signals' armflash, and moved onto three shillings and sixpence a day (plus sixpence war pay), although sixpence a day was held back as a 'stoppage' to be sent home. A month later, after another exam, I became an aircraftman class one, a status which brought me in a gratifying four shillings and threepence a day (plus war pay, minus the stoppage).

At course's end we were asked for preference for postings. Although often a formality, consideration to personal choice was given wherever possible. Fred Bater, again, had spoken highly of the Orkney Islands – 'Nobody bothers you way up there' –, so I put that down. And got it. Initially I was required to report to No. 70 (Signals) Group Headquarters at Inverness, only despite having been on a course, there was no mention of leave. Finding, therefore, that the train was routed through Chesterfield I simply got off and treated myself to a few days at home. That done, I resumed my journey, 'arrived' at headquarters, and nobody ever queried where I'd been!

I discovered the Orkneys to be an archipelago of some seventy islands separated from the very northern tip of Scotland by the Pentland Firth. I was to be concerned with the largest island, Mainland, which forms the northern shore of the naval anchorage of Scapa Flow, itself the prime reason for the Chain Home early-warning stations sited on Orkney.

The ferry, the *Earl of Zetland*, ran from Scrabster, near Thurso (to the west of John o' Groats), to Stromness, on the western coast of Mainland. I was to do the Pentland-Firth crossing several times in the next year and a bit and found it varied from the horrendous to the spectacular, depending upon the currents flowing. It could take as little as ninety minutes, most often took two and a half hours, and when conditions turned really rough it could leave you heaving and pitching outside either harbour indefinitely. And even having disembarked at Stromness, it was a case of bouncing about in the back of a lorry to Kirkwall, the main town, then on to my assigned station, Deerness, ten miles beyond, a total of twenty-six jolting miles.

Deerness turned out to be a conglomeration of aerials, wooden huts, and brick-built buildings. What first struck me, though, was that the aerials were not the sort I'd expected, but those of the Chain Home (Low) system.

Back at Yatesbury we'd concentrated on Chain Home, but we'd also covered the supplementary low-level system. This was made necessary because the 'long' 10 metre wavelength pulses of the main system couldn't detect targets below 2,000 feet or so. Shorter wavelengths, however, could sweep to the surface, so Chain Home (Low) used pulses of just 1.5 metres wavelength, enabling it to detect not only low fliers, but ships. Further, as shorter wavelengths and smaller aerials went hand in hand, the aerial arrays could be mounted on a rotating turntable.

No change in the prospective job, though. This still called for an operator to sit in semi-darkness at a cathode ray tube and report to a filter room which would evaluate the readings and pass them to a control centre, in this case to the Combined Gunnery and Sector Operations Room at Kirkwall.

Chain Home (Low) aerial system

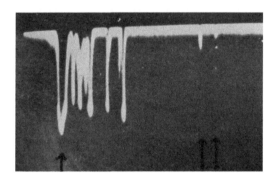

Operator's cathode ray tube display

The Deerness site, I found, had a permanent establishment of about thirty, commanded by a flight lieutenant assisted by a sergeant. Most of the staff were operators, for we ran a three-watch system, with six of us on duty at any one time. Supporting us were cooks, an admin chap, a medical orderly, a driver or so, and a trio of lads who ran the three incredibly noisy diesel engines which supplied electricity to both the radar and the domestic site. The thump, thump, thump grew to permeate our lives, indeed, I can hear it to this day! Of more concern back then though, was that the three acolytes so stank of diesel that by mutual consent they messed together in a hut of their own.

The power supply aside, any technical problems were sorted out by mechanics summoned from the Chain Home station nearer Kirkwall, at Netherbutton. This was staffed in part by WAAF operators, but though operationally linked through the Kirkwall Control Centre, and although we went across for the occasional dance – for our part, read piss-up –, the two stations were administered separately. We did, though, I recall, have the WAAF flight officer move in for a while when our CO was on leave. And lest I forget, we had two NAAFI girls of our own!

This late in the war the entire British coastline, east and west, was covered by the two Chain Home systems, with Scapa Flow having come under their protective blanket early on. Indeed, though the Kentish systems became best known, it was the Firth-of-Forth station, not all that far south of us, that claimed the first ever German raider! True, our Orkneys' sites were not best positioned, but the bare, relatively flat – and singularly treeless – terrain offered few ideal locations, while high winds necessitated our rotating aerial array being able to withstand 120 mph blasts.

As it happened, all our radar equipment was American, which meant that being Brits we needed a password to gain access! The equipment, though, was far more efficient than the first-generation gears we had trained on. Even so there were anomalies, so that on VE Day (8 May 1945, the end of the war in Europe) when we tracked ten surfaced U-Boats making their way into Scapa Flow to surrender, we found that they gave exactly the same echo returns as the two-metre-wingspan gannet, only the speed distinguishing submarine from seabird.

Looking back, time went swiftly, though there was little laid-on entertainment. As I've indicated, when we were invited to dances we spent most of our time at the bar. Solo became the great pastime, with schools running day and night, members of one watch taking over as those of another reluctantly tore themselves away for duty. We did do a few cultural things, however, such as visiting some of the famed archaeological sites. I suppose watchkeeping kept us pretty busy. Just the same I found time to qualify as a heavy-vehicle driver and also as a radar mechanic, so making me a radar operator/mechanic. I was also made up to leading aircraftman (LAC) which saw a two-bladed propeller appear on my arm and swelled my income to five shillings a day (plus war pay, minus the stoppage ...)

Off-duty watches

We got home leave, of course, but only every three months, although then we were allowed travelling time, for it could take, for example, thirty-six hours to get to Derbyshire. The rail journey began on *The Jellicoe Express* – with its snow-plough attachment when needed – and the single-track Far North Line from Thurso to Inverness. Began, that is, trusting that, when going south, at least, the sea wouldn't be too rough to enable us to either board or disembark, or both.

With the war over, the intensity of activity died down and the day came when I had the distinction of closing the last watch at Deerness. The few of us remaining were posted across to Netherbutton, but within a short while I was re-assigned, once more travelling almost the entire length of the country, this time to No. 78 Wing Headquarters, at Maidstone, in Kent.

Only days later, however, I was again uprooted, initially to No. 90 Group headquarters at West Drayton, but then on detachment to Heathrow, though why, nobody was prepared to tell us. Once at the airfield – soon to become London Airport –, the thirty of us so gathered viewed askance the tented accommodation. But it was only after we had been set to the repetitive drill of constructing and erecting aerials, then taking them down again and loading them onto lorries, that it was borne upon us that we had been assembled to form a mobile Chain Home unit. Not too welcome a discovery for we were all in demob group fifty-seven and others in that group were already leaving the Service. We moaned, but there was nothing we could do about it. Indeed, we were even made to read and sign the Official Secrets Act, although why and where we were to operate remained as much a mystery as ever.

Rumour swiftly filled the gaps. There had been reports from Sweden of ghost-rocket sightings, with lurid speculation about them being extra-terrestrial. It was also postulated, however, that our former Russian allies were using the experimental establishment at Peenemunde, in their sector of Germany, to turn captured V-2 Rockets into directable projectiles, so giving them a truly formidable capacity. Our unit, rumour had it, was to be based in Sweden to monitor this activity. Certainly it was enough to get us all buzzing. But eventually it fizzled out.

We suffered a number of frustrating false starts, until suddenly orders came through, and next morning we moved in convoy to Tilbury Docks where, in my turn, I drove my lorry onto a Landing Ship (Tank) which eventually delivered us to Hamburg. No pause there, though, for we were immediately directed onwards for Lübeck, at that time on the very border of the Russian Zone.

Ready to erect our aerials, Lübeck

With snow covering the ground, the days chill, and the nights absolutely freezing, it was not the best of seasons for camping out, nor did we have the cold-weather clothing suited to such conditions. Even so, training paid off, we got our aerials erected, our gears set up, and within a short space of time were fully operational. It was all hush-hush, so even at this remove suffice to say that we were well situated for monitoring Russian rocket sites, also that the screen watching we had formerly done was now carried out by automatic cameras. All went well, and we were given to understand that useful results were being obtained, when the Russians caught on and withdrew their rockets beyond the range of our radars. After which it was into circus mode once more, and back to Tilbury, our demob status now very much in mind.

Having dropped off our heavy equipment we were sent to Group Headquarters, presumably while someone decided what to do with us. Up to now I'd not spent long at West Drayton, but I soon got the impression that while the RAF hadn't quite decided what to do with us, they were determined to get the Service itself back onto a proper – that is, not a wartime – footing. So we found ourselves marching about, reporting to the guardroom before going to town, and checking-in to camp again before a certain time. Of course, we soon found a short cut to get around all that nonsense. But evidently the RAF was serious about re-setting peacetime standards, for on emerging from this short cut one night I found myself face to face with Sergeant Angel – how could one forget his name! – the senior service policeman.

'Breaking out of camp, breaking into camp, and no 'eadgear,' he announced, 'you're on a charge.'

Next morning, accordingly, I found myself not just up before an officer, but before the topmost officer on the station, a group captain!

'A clean record up to now,' he nodded gravely, 'and your corporal due any time. Fourteen days confined to camp.'

Well, that was a shock to the system. But even more so at 0700 hours next morning when I had to present myself for the first of the day's punishment parades. The snag being that I was to be subjected to a kit inspection. Only, with all the time elapsed since recruit training, the lads in the billet had to have a whip around to collect together a full set: I did have a hat though, it was just that the night before I'd lent mine to someone who'd lost his in town but, having booked out through the guardroom, would have been charged on booking in sans headgear.

Fortunately, just an hour or so after that first inspection, an immediate-movement order reached me, so that was the only punishment report I did, for on arriving at my new unit, a Chain Home (Low) station on Flamborough Head, in Yorkshire, I was checked in by a fellow LAC who had been appointed to carry out provost duties.

'It seems you're on fourteen days' jankers, mate,' he said, scrutinizing my papers.

'You can forget that,' I told him. And so he did.

My promotion to acting corporal duly came through (two stripes, and a daily pay rate of six shillings and sixpence – only no war pay now, just the stoppage ...), and with it my final posting, to the Chain Home station at Fairlight Glen, on the south coast. We were transported daily to the site from Rye to carry out a shipping watch. Again I found myself working with American equipment, only this time one which, once shut down, required nearly an hour to set up. Indeed, it was such a palaver that only two of us Brits were shown the procedure. Which was all very well until it came to Easter weekend 1947, when everyone else went off on leave, and I was left to keep the gear running. This meant I had to sleep on site, becoming, in effect, the station commander. I even had the key to the armoury, and indulged myself by taking out a Sten gun and trying – though totally failing – to decimate the local rabbit population!

A little later, however, my demob came through, and having reported to No. 101 Personnel Despatch Centre at RAF Kirkham, near Preston, a pen stroke turned me into a civilian once again.

On balance I had thoroughly enjoyed my service, even though none of it had gone as I had anticipated. Indeed, had Estate work not been so satisfying, I might well have stayed in, for that I'd seen so little of aircraft hadn't in the least diminished my interest in all things aeronautical. Having made the break, however, my concern lay in catching up with my career. And I should say that from the start this went very well, so that when I finally came to retire I'd spent many years in the post of Chief Clerk of the Chatsworth Estate. It had not all been work, by any means, for in my off-duty hours I'd been able to indulge my love of fishing, presiding over the activity on the Estate for years on end.

Since 1947, however, there had been an equally absorbing interest, for back then I learnt that the Royal Observer Corps (ROC), which had been stood down in early 1945, was to be reactivated. My interest whetted, I signed on as an observer, thereby ushering in a forty-year association.

Throughout the war the ROC had played a very necessary role in air-raid reporting, supplementing the Chain Home system as raiders approached, and actually taking over once they had crossed the coast. Now, immersed as we were in the Cold War, the ROC was needed once again. Volunteers wore RAF uniform with the ROC shoulder flash and received a subsistence allowance when on duty.

The duties centred upon weekend exercises during which we'd observe and report air activity from the original brick-built posts sited high on prominent points: our post, for instance, was situated between Baslow and

Hassop. Operationally we liaised with posts at Buxton and Ashover, all three reporting to a control centre at Leeds. Reports were sent, however, by telephone and that, I always felt, was an inherent weakness, with landlines being so vulnerable, yet the Corps was never to adopt the more secure radio comms.

By the beginning of the fifties command and control by radar had made such giant strides that we became fearful for the future of the Corps. Before it could be blighted anew, though, the nuclear threat arose, presenting it with the revised role of reporting the position and magnitude of any explosion, and thereafter monitoring the residual radiation.

With this role change the operation moved underground. At Baslow, for instance, we now had to descend some fifteen feet – eighteen rungs! – to reach our workplace, a fifteen by seven foot monitoring room with a ventilating system, twin bunks, a battery to give lighting, a store of tinned food and water, and a separate chemical-toilet cubbyhole. We also had what was, in truth, some pretty Heath Robinsonish equipment connecting to the surface: a pinhole camera whose paper film would be holed by the flash and so allow the direction and size of the burst to be determined, and a recorder to show the resulting level of radiation. But still no independent radio communications to guarantee getting our reports through!

The plan was that after a nuclear explosion we would remain underground for up to three weeks, however, when the Suez Crisis passed without even the preliminary stand-to order being issued, we took the possibility less seriously, though continuing to exercise and even to carry out night binds underground. On one notable occasion, while detached to the Ashover Rock Post on a weekend exercise, the hilltop above us was overrun by activists from the Campaign for Nuclear Disarmament. However, although they called down the shaft on occasion it was all very amicable.

The ROC bunker, Ashover Rock, The Fabrick, 2012

In the course of time I took on the responsibility of instructing and was appointed to leading officer, but finding that the commitment clashed too much with my Estate duties, I reverted to being a ordinary observer once more, moving in turn to the post at Beauchief, in Sheffield, and finally, to Ashover Rock, on The Fabrick [say Faybrick!], above Ashover.

I had never lost my yen to fly, and membership of the ROC gave me the chance to log flights in Ansons, Beverleys, Valettas, Varsities, and even a Dragon Rapide biplane; the latter sticking in my mind as the pilot held it down on take-off, only to zoom it skywards, just for the joy of it, to the detriment of the equilibriums of those behind him.

ROC membership was great fun, with the added fillip of knowing that we were doing a job of national importance. The end came, though, for the rank and file, in September 1991 although some elements remained until December 1995. I was sad to see it go, of course, but I was proud to have served for forty years and to wear my ROC medal with its two bars, for twelve and twenty-four years service respectively.

Royal Observer Corps Medal, with 12- and 24-year bars

Observer Charles Roose, ROC

I can say much the same of my years of service on the Chatsworth Estate, especially as, on stepping down, I moved into an Estate retirement flat. At one stage I left to spend time with my son-in-law in New Zealand but, on returning, took on the tenancy of another Estate flat, this one adapted, would you credit it, from the very office where I started off my service as a boy clerk! As I sit here in my front room, therefore, I can mark where my great, brass-adorned desk once stood, below what was then a skylight, and before what is now my fireplace. It could be said, then, that Chatsworth is in my very marrow. But my bookshelves and my pictures speak of my other abiding love, that of all things Aviation, with the Lancaster overflying the nearby Derwent Dams, but the Spitfire, of course, still taking pride of place.

Charles Roose, 2014

6. For The Duration Of The Present Emergency

Warrant Officer Eric Reedman, general duties, air movements

Aircraftman Second Class Eric Reedman, 1940

After leaving school I began working for the Co-op in Chilwell, just outside Nottingham. My social life lay in attending dancing classes with another Co-op-ite, Alf Marlow, and going on the prowl together at the hops held in the Long Eaton Peoples' Hall. There was a war on, however, and in 1940, as I turned 18, I applied to become aircrew, only to have the doctors discover that I was colour blind. Though disappointed, I signed on as an Aircrafthand (General Duties), and as the attestation papers had it, 'For the duration of the present emergency'.

A year later, and quite by chance, I was to meet up with Alf again. He had actually been accepted as aircrew and, resplendent with sergeant's stripes, a wireless-operator's badge on his arm, and an air-gunner's brevet on his left breast, had just been posted to a Bomber Command squadron. Lucky old lad!

For my part I'd been sent to No. 2 Recruiting Centre at RAF Cardington for kitting out, and having experienced its effectively unheated wooden huts and mediocre food, had been only too glad to be posted on to Bridlington. Here, the empty boarding houses we were accommodated in, though at first sight an improvement on Cardington's huts, were invariably in a poor state of repair and not infrequently bomb damaged, the only furniture being metal-framed Service beds and straw palliasses. Stoically accepting that, we messed and had lectures in the Spa Ballroom, had PT and drilled – and learnt to salute! – in the streets and on the seafront when the weather permitted, or in the ballroom when it didn't.

RAF departments were dotted all over town, among them the dental section, to which we were marched as a body. Two weeks later, alone and bearing an appointment chit, I once more entered the curving terrace's carbon-copy doorway and climbed stairs that had been plushly carpeted in the interim. I knew the drill: far end of the corridor, no need to knock – and enter. To find myself in a lady's boudoir, complete with lady saying Eek! and Out! in that order. The carpet, of course, had been the clue!

For much of the time we were in the hands of the physical training instructors (PTIs) and drill instructors (DIs). Our especial DI, though, must have had PTI blood in him, for he liked taking us on long route marches. We'd be on our last legs as we re-entered the town. 'Right, Lads!' he'd snap. 'Smarten up. March at attention.' We'd obediently brace up, the action setting the adrenalin flowing. Only instead of dismissing us at the ballroom where our kit was, he would halt us two or three streets away. 'Bastard', we'd moan as he dismissed us, 'he could have marched us all the way. Now we've got to bloody walk.'

With recruit training over, I was posted to the postal section of Headquarters, No. 5 Group, Bomber Command, at Grantham, which suited me fine, being only some thirty miles from home. I had yet to realise that such proximity was two edged, with relatives expecting you to visit whenever a pass came up, whereas on returning to camp it was to find that the most incredibly interesting things had happened in your absence.

These, however, never included the only too regular week-long Ground Defence Training exercises organised by RAF personnel known as Ground Gunners: wearing a wreathed GG sleeve badge, they were the forerunners of the RAF Regiment.

Ground Gunners badge, worn by the forerunners of the RAF Regiment

Aside from playing at warriors, however, we sprog airmen still had much to learn. As when four of us set out on a jaunt to town. We had passed muster by the snowdrop [service policeman] at the gate and were some way down the road when our station commander pulled up in his staff car and offered us a lift. Rather stunned by this, we clambered in, and had just got under way when I noticed I hadn't closed the door properly. I tried to secure it, only to have the air rush practically take it off its hinges. The CO said nothing. But when, still somewhat overawed, we reached Grantham and got out, and having thanked him politely, began to walk off, he discovered a great deal to voice off about. Heinously, we hadn't saluted! And despite all that seafront practice!

I was now an AC2 – aircraftman second class – and part of the RAF's Letter Delivery Service, a facility which used motor-bike despatch riders and also small vans and cars, often swanky models requisitioned from private owners. A complementary service was provided by the Air Despatch Letter Service whose twin-engined de Havilland Dominie – Rapide – biplanes served such remote destinations as the Scottish Islands.

One of my regular duties had me starting at 1800 hours, sorting mail into deliveries throughout the night, then acting as co-driver on the delivery run, heading westwards from Grantham and calling at every RAF establishment as far as Fauld, in Staffordshire. We'd arrive at Fauld at breakfast time, then go to bed until 1600 hours. Then we'd reverse the route, arriving back at Grantham at 2200 hours. I suppose the same routine would still have obtained on 27 November 1944. Little day rest for anyone then, though, with Fauld's deep-mine bomb dump exploding in what is still reckoned as the biggest non-nuclear explosion known.

The Fauld crater

In June 1943 I became an AC1 (aircraftman class one) General Duties, and celebrated by dating a newly-arrived and very attractive WAAF sergeant PT instructor. On our first outing we were walking hand in hand, when, without warning, she swung my arm forwards, then rearwards, and effortlessly tossed me onto my back. 'Just in case you get any ideas,' she told me. Strangely, that wasn't our last date. However, on a planned visit to her family at Doncaster we inadvertently caught the wrong train and finished up at York, lack of further trains that day, and shortage of funds, compelling us to walk back … And that finished me!

At just that time, the RAF began trawling the ranks for aircrew volunteers. Eyesight standards had been reduced for certain categories, and flying goggles with corrective lenses were now available. As no mention was made of colour blindness, I volunteered, and in August was posted to Blackpool on a sixteen-week air-wireless-operator's course.

By an administrative hiccup the fact that I was a serving airman was overlooked, and I had to undergo square-bashing over again. So it was that I spent my twenty-first doing an assault course, and coming face to face with a monster toad in a muddy tunnel. With that encounter bravely borne I had no qualms in facing the Mobile Aircrew Selection Unit when it dropped in, emerging smiling and earmarked – like Alf Marlow before me – for a posting to Bomber Command. The course continued, but a week before we were to move to the signals school for the final phase of training, the Mobile Aircrew Medical Board arrived, re-discovered my colour blindness, and sent me packing, not with an avuncular pat on the shoulder for keenness, but with a flea in my ear for wasting everyone's time. And that was it. A toad in the hole, and a flea in the ear, and my aspirations to fly on operations against the enemy had to be shelved, for good.

As it was, when I finally left the RAF after thirty-five years service I was still colour blind. But alive. Unlike erstwhile Co-op employee Wireless Operator/Air Gunner Alf Marlow, who had been shot down and killed over Germany on 29 September 1944.

Having cleared from Blackpool I was posted to No. 100 (Bomber Support) Group at RAF West Raynham, in Norfolk. Not long before, the station had been heavily bombed but was now back on top line and carrying out long-range intruder operations, particularly against airfields, in support of Bomber Command's main-force raids, its two squadrons – Numbers 141 and 239 – flying the de Havilland Mosquito wooden-wonder fighter-bomber. The whole place was buzzing with activity, the tone being set by the youngest group captain I've ever seen – said to be just 28 – who treated us all to a pep talk. With the station being fully operational once more, he told us, we would now be paving the way for the Second Front.

It was an enterprise they were to undertake without me, however, for I was suddenly posted to RAF Radlett, in Hertfordshire, to the newly-forming Advanced Headquarters of No. 80 Wing, the controlling-authority-to-be over three mobile signals units. In a real departure from the norm we were issued with khaki battledress and detached to Norfolk where instructors from the Scots Guards introduced us to such un-airmanlike pursuits as unarmed combat, jumping off moving lorries, and cliff scaling. It was clear, then, that our future, too, was to be intimately tied up with the invasion!

My Identity Discs: one directing, Do Not Remove

Once back at Radlett we practised what we had learnt, living under canvas, digging latrines, and preparing our own meals. We also took possession of vehicles, as befitted a self-contained unit, but vehicles modified to allow them to be driven off landing craft into up to five feet of water. Speculation on the date of the invasion had been rife for months past, with daubed messages everywhere, urging 'Second Front Now'. When I arrived home on leave, however, a nephew remarked, 'It can't start for two weeks, though, not with Uncle Eric here.'

He was not that far wrong, for within hours of my return, with even compassionate leave banned, we moved to Old Sarum, in Wiltshire, into a guarded perimeter, our holding base, we learnt. The one amenity was a tented bar which we shared with a Royal Canadian Air Force police unit, tasked to marshal traffic on the invasion beach, and various Works' Squadrons kitted out to construct forward landing strips.

Just two days later, on 5 June 1944, we heard armour and heavy vehicles start up and move off, while throughout the night an air armada roared overhead, troop-carrying gliders ghosting among them. The weather, though, had not been as finely judged as my leave, for instead of our unit landing in Normandy on D-Day itself, it was not until the night of the fifteenth that the backlog cleared and we drove our thirteen vehicles onto a Landing Craft (Transport).

After an uncomfortably choppy crossing we landed in the early hours on what was designated 'H' Beach, splashing down into a considerable depth of water, the tension being only slightly broken by the CO's fifteen-hundredweight plunging into a below-surface shell hole and affording us relatively dry-shod others some light relief as the Royal Engineers towed them out to join us on the beach.

We were then directed to Tour en Bessin in the American Sector where we parked along the hedges of an orchard with continuous air activity overhead and incessant gunfire towards Caen. This gave the lads impetus in digging slit trenches while I was set to rig camouflage-netting over our high-standing radio-transmitting vehicle. I was on its roof, bending head down to join two nets when an aircraft dived our way. I glanced up, registered, 'Spitfire', and continued lacing. Until machine-gun bullets began hosing about me. Comprehension dawned. I leapt for the ground, only to have a toecap snag the nets and leave me suspended, head down, as the Spitfire-become-Messerschmitt completed its strafing run.

The tenacity with which the Germans denied Caen to the Allies was to hold us in our orchard for a full two months before the thousand-bomber raid on the city led to the breakout and allowed the British armies to join the Americans in an eastwards flood. Perhaps bizarrely, though, from the earliest days of the stand-off, ENSA (Entertainment National Service Association) had set up stages on lorries and put on variety shows; not only that, but a small theatre reopened in Bayeaux and I actually saw a performance by the Halle Orchestra along with French-born star Alice Delysia, 'the greatest trouper of them all'!

Once released by the breakthrough, and having laboriously negotiated the rubble of Caen, our convoy followed in the wake of the fighting troops, establishing a communications net whenever we were halted. Initially we advanced swiftly, but on approaching Brussels we were forced to wait for two days until the city was cleared of Germans. After that we turned for the coast until we reached Wenduine, seven miles beyond Bruges, where we set up our tents in some tennis courts. As the chilly weather started in, however, we were directed to more sheltered accommodation in what had been a German naval training school. Only to find the front gates securely chained. The back entrance was open, though, so we took possession, parking to the rear.

It was only next morning that the Royal Engineers, wrong-footed by our haste in getting away from our chilly tennis court, arrived to formally clear the place. Having opened the front gates they immediately lost two of their party to a mine, then had to deal with twenty-four more devices along the length of the drive!

We'd already found that some of the toilets would not flush, despite our tugging and banging at them. Now the Royal Engineers discovered that they had, in fact, been booby-trapped. Even so, some of our lads failed to learn, and became casualties on setting off an anti-personnel mine when souvenir hunting.

Another feature of our time here was to have the Royal Marine Commandos use Wenduine to rehearse their role in the assault on Walcheren Island. Indeed, on their triumphant return they made us free of their booty of liberated German rum.

The highlight of my stay, though, was being sent into the woods with the pay-accounts corporal after a report that a German soldier was on the loose. In fact, we came upon two of them! They came quietly, but I was left facing forwards from the tailgate of the truck to cover them. It would have been a fair toss-up as to who was the more nervous, but the corporal, at the wheel behind the partition, remained blissfully oblivious to the fact that, had I actually had to use my rifle, he would have been directly in the line of fire.

The war was drawing to a close when our next uprooting took us back to Brussels to install Headquarters No. 80 Wing in a large chateau at Schepdal. Recommendations for awards, had been submitted, it seemed, resulting in twenty mentions in despatches coming to the Wing. The way of such things, however, has to remain a mystery, so that a recipient who had done no more than clean out the NAAFI was as puzzled by his distinction as the rest of us.

On the subject of meritorious rewards, however, surely nobody would deny the Peacemaker to be truly deserving. And yet … After five weeks of nerve-chewing anxiety the German last-gasp Ardennes breakthrough had been stemmed, although one of our mobile units lost a vehicle in getting clear. Once the signals traffic had finally settled, however, a group of us were whooping it up in the Montgomery Club in Brussels when the civilian manager mounted the stage and, stopping the band, dramatically announced that the war in Europe was over. It was stunning news, and well worth extending the evening for. Having done which we fanned out into the streets, proclaiming the peace to all and sundry. Only to meet with universal disbelief. This could have been attributed to language difficulties, but the same thing happened when we arrived back at Schepdal. In the end it transpired that our peacemaking was a full fortnight too early.

Official peace really did break out on the due day, 8 May 1945, and then we renewed our celebration, only this time with everyone in Brussels joining in.

Two days after VE Day we drove to Ostend and embarked for Harwich on a landing ship (tank). Just as well that we were under no illusions that this was really Peace, however, for we were earmarked, we learnt, not for a prolonged stay in Blighty, but for the Far-Eastern Theatre.

Our preparation base was RAF Swanton Morley, in Norfolk, where personnel were vetted and set to training for the specialist roles they were to fill. I was selected for a code and ciphers course. First, though, I was to become a senior NCO: from Leading Aircraftman I was to jump to sergeant! Again I found myself back at Cardington, this time attending lectures on Air Force Law and conduct in the sergeants' mess; also acting as sergeant in charge of a flight on the parade ground, and indeed, as parade warrant officer. It was all very heady. However …

The however in this case was due to the overloading of the system, so that, on passing out, our course was divided. Half were sent to get started on their specialities while the others, me included, would follow after seven days' leave. Only, during that leave, Japan surrendered. This, of course, was stupendous news. The really stunning blow, though, was the diktat that those who had already begun on their speciality training would continue, and remain sergeants. The rest would remain as they were: me as a leading aircraftman.

I then went through a period of intense disillusionment. From Cardington I was sent to RAF Sudbury, in Suffolk, newly redesignated No. 16 Recruit Centre. It was not to prove a happy sojourn, with virtually everyone misemployed, as highly qualified technicians were detailed to be mess waiters, others set to fatigues. I reluctantly accepted the job as officers' mess barman. That, though, meant I was let off certain station duties, and that, in turn, put me onto the bad side of the station warrant officer (the SWO, or Swo-man), the station disciplinarian, hardly a politic side to be on at any time. In this case, protected as I was by my privileged post, he merely warned me that he had a long memory …

He didn't have to tax that memory overly long, for learning that I'd fallen into the practice of reopening the bar after the CO's departure at night, he reported me. The result was that some junior officers were posted, while I not only lost my position but was put into the care of that self-same Swo-man.

He promptly charged me with having dirty boots, for which I was awarded 14 days confined to camp – CC, or jankers, a minor punishment involving fatigues and disruption of off-duty time. Considering this to be unfair, I applied for a redress of my grievance. Only to have the original sentence doubled. After two days, however, I received a chance amelioration of my sentence. Sudbury had now begun to receive National Service recruits, with jankers being awarded like confetti. As a leading aircraftman, therefore, I was detailed to march the defaulters to wherever they were to carry out their fatigues, a much less demeaning situation.

I wonder, had counsellors been invented back then, if one would have told me that my recent disappointments had to be aired. Certainly, when I was posted to the demobilisation centre at Cardington just days before the Victory Parade, I blatantly kicked over the traces. A group of us had planned to spend the occasion in London. So I tore up my movement orders and went to ground at Sudbury. In fact, while 'underground' I actually came face to face with the SWO twice! each time ducking off before he realised that I should have been long gone.

It all worked swimmingly, we had a fantastic time at the jollifications, and when it was over we went our separate ways. And even on arriving at Cardington there was no problem, I was simply directed to begin issuing NAAFI coupons for cigarettes.

I also kept my eye on the main chance, reserving for my own use the snappiest demob outfit there was, the issued clothes not being to everybody's taste. Even so, spivs would congregate outside the gates offering to exchange them for cash. Though as this got around, the wilier of the new-civilians replaced the issue clothes with cast-offs, resealed the box, did a deal, then swiftly disappeared by train.

Eventually, my own demob group came up: number forty-one. Predictably enough, however, just days before I could take possession of my snazzy outfit, Sudbury closed, and on 19 August 1946 I was demobbed from RAF Kirkham, in Lancashire, vowing, as I left the last five years behind me that I would never again, ever, join as much as a Christmas club.

Though not at all impressed by what I saw in civvy street I eventually settled upon a career in the civil service. More successfully, I also resumed my dancing at the People's Hall in Long Eaton, where my arguably eccentric performance attracted the attention of a police sergeant's daughter named Margaret. And that could not possibly have been more successful.

If we were to marry, though, we needed to earn a crust. And when one of our frugally-based dates took us into a recruiting caravan on an RAF Queen Mary low-loader in Nottingham's Old Market Square I found the display so incredibly compelling that – I signed on the dotted line, and for five years! The Chief Regional Officer was horrified when I proffered my resignation.

'But with diligence and care,' he protested, 'and in the course of time, you'll become an established civil servant.' 'As of today,' I told him, 'the first of December, 1947, I'm an established regular airman.'

Finding myself kitting up at Kirkham, with its ice-cold huts and every toilet frozen, made me wonder whether I'd made the right decision. But all such doubts were dispelled when I arrived at RAF Hospital Ely, in Cambridgeshire, finding it the most attractive place I'd served at yet. Even being assigned to the station warrant officer's staff held no terrors, for what a contrast with the last unregretted specimen of the breed, this one being both a medic and a gentleman.

My job was to take working parades and to compile duty rotas. All very straightforward, though the odd bod might complain about too frequent duties. But I was nonplussed when the senior surgeon himself, an air commodore, arrived in high dudgeon pleading with me to sort out one of his surgeons who was deliberately dodging weekend stints by taking leave!

It was a good posting, and after a year, I became a corporal, Margaret married me, and in June 1950, we moved into our first married quarter. Only, as if our settling was the catalyst, a posting to Singapore arrived, with two weeks' embarkation leave to start at once. Except that after just six days a telegram summoned me for an immediate air passage. Accordingly, shouldering two weighty kitbags and with arms swollen with throbbing jabs and vaccinations, I reported to the Personnel Despatch Centre at Hednesford, on Cannock Chase, in Staffordshire.

A classic case, it turned out, of hurry up – and wait. For the Korean War was being held and the Handley Page Hastings workhorses of Transport Command were overextended, so that after a period of frustratingly kicking our heels, we were sent by sea.

The trooper out left no happy memories. We were incarcerated below decks where there was not enough space for everyone to sling a hammock, many being obliged to spread their bedding rolls on the deck or on table tops. Then again the food was not good, while the air below would have remained foul even if we'd been above the water line and able to open portholes. Nor did conditions change as we wallowed on, with brief calls at Port Said, Suez, Aden, and Colombo. When we finally reached Singapore, however, the sight of lush green hills, many-coloured bushes, and above all the flame trees, made up for practically everything.

Of course, the tranquil scenery belied the political reality, for it was now July 1951 and the Malayan Emergency, declared on 16 June 1948 after the murder of British rubber planters by Communist terrorists, was in full swing. Indeed, four months after I arrived Sir Henry Gurney, the British High Commissioner, was to be assassinated by terrorists on the road to Fraser's Hill.

Most military activities, however, were confined to the mainland, whereas my job was at Changi, on Singapore Island, where the task was to run the technical stores, and most particularly to ensure that parts were available the moment they were needed to keep the theatre's aircraft serviceable. Computers were yet to come, of course, but we made full use of our tried and tested filing and card-indexing systems. Such methods aside, knowing what items existed, and where they were held, became our stock in trade.

It was a busy tour, but a gratifying one, especially after Margaret joined me, when the social element became so much more important. It was not without considerable regret, then, that in December 1953 we sailed for home, our destination, RAF Church Lawton, near Stoke, in Staffordshire.

Perhaps we had been cosseted at Changi, for both of us loathed Church Lawton. From my point of view it was demonstrably a haven for fiddlers. Suffice to say that within days of arriving I had submitted a request for a posting. And a posting anywhere. Just away.

In the event, my prayers were granted, for I was posted to RAF Kidbrooke, in London, to do a six-week senior movements course. At that time movements still focussed on ships, but with much attention paid to the complexities of moving personnel and materiel by rail and road. At best we paid lip service to air movements, this part of the course being covered by the seeming-afterthought provision of a Hastings and a York fuselage and some empty packing cases to be secured with unwieldy 'S'-hook chains. The critical weight-and-balance calculations were a real pain, and a very far cry from the sophisticated trim-sheets of later years. However, with the course over, joy of joys! in July 1955 we were off to Singapore again.

I went first, reporting to the Personnel Despatch Unit, newly located at RAF Innsworth, near Gloucester, where I was appointed NCO troops on a Hastings. Due to unserviceabilities, however, the outbound flight took, not the scheduled three days, but a full three weeks. And three weeks punctuated, I have to say, by a constant whining from the troops – mainly airmen – I had to nursemaid. The route, for the record, was from Lyneham to Istres (Orange, France), then Idris (Tripoli, Libya), Mauripur (Karachi),

Negombo (Ceylon), Kuala Lumpur (Malaya), then Changi. My specific destination, though still on Singapore Island, was the Seletar Maintenance Unit, the main equipment stores for the whole of the Far East Air Force.

The stores job had hardly changed, but in March 1956 I was detached to Colombo, in Ceylon, to supervise sea movements. In September 1956, however, when volunteers were sought for an initiative aimed at regularising the status of movements personnel who flew on duty in RAF transport aircraft, I cited my senior movements qualification, and was accepted. The aircrew category of air quartermaster would not be instituted until 1962, but that was the role I filled, in embryo as it were, with the Far East Air Force Communications Squadron.

It had been a long flog since my attempts to fly had been thwarted by colour blindness, but now I was to fly to my heart's content, for being a one-off, I habitually found myself airborne far more often than the regular crews. And that suited me just fine.

Largely we flew on demand, although we had several routine routes, but 'Specials' lodge best in the memory. Up to Kuala Lumpur, for example, carrying Tungku Abdul Rahman, who would become prime minister when Malaya gained *Merdeka* – its independence – on 31 August 1957. That such dignitaries valued the contribution made by the Commonwealth's armed services to that independence was widely acknowledged at the time. Ironically, it would be some fifty years before that acknowledgement took the form, not of the '*Merdeka*' medal people spoke of then, but the elegant *Pinjat Jasa Malaysia* medal (PJM) of 2006.

Pinjat Jasa Malaysia *Medal, 2006*

Other specials took me to Phnom Penh, in Cambodia, and in various combinations, to Hong Kong, Saigon, Bangkok, and Rangoon. The latter special was particularly poignant, its purpose being to dedicate the memorial to those who had died constructing the Burma railway.

After a spell on the Communications Squadron, I was posted to No. 52 Squadron, one of the three Valetta squadrons operating from Changi. The regular schedules were northwards to Hong Kong and westwards to Negombo, in Ceylon. Hong-Kong bound flights routed via Labuan, in Borneo, then America's Clark Air Force Base, in the Philippines, with the return flights staging through Saigon. The Negombo flights routed there and back via Car Nicobar Island.

No. 52 Squadron also rotated with Nos. 48 and 110 Squadrons to carry out air-supply sorties from Kuala Lumpur: parachuting supplies to jungle patrols. The low flying called for by this task, over mountainous, jungle-covered terrain, with aircraft not that well suited to such operations, inevitably led to losses. These were due, in part, to crews switching from route flying to this highly specialised field and were to fall off markedly once a composite unit was formed to concentrate on jungle supply-dropping, the crews doing just enough route flying to maintain their Transport Command passenger-carrying currency. However, at about the time this Air Supply Force (Malaya) came into being, No. 48 Squadron received the long-range Hastings, and in August 1957 I transferred to them.

The Hastings vastly extended the ranges we could travel without refuelling. We could now route directly to Hong Kong. And there were monthly 'trainers' to Japan and to Australia. The latter commonly took the form of routing to Darwin, then staging through Richmond (Sydney), and Laverton, the major Royal Australian Air Force base, near Melbourne, and so to Adelaide's Edinburgh Field. Again, there were specials, a now-treasured one involving a three-week tour of New Zealand, virtually a flying holiday, the professional high spot for me being to despatch a parachute display team to celebrate the twenty-first anniversary of the Royal New Zealand Air Force.

All too soon, however, our second Far Eastern tour came to an end, and Margaret and I returned home courtesy of Skyways Airlines, whose Hermes took us via Bangkok, Calcutta, Karachi, Teheran, Beirut, Brindisi, and Stanstead, from where we were coached to the Joint Trooping Centre, at RAF Hendon.

By now the air movements world had come into its own and I was posted to supervise one of three passenger-handling shifts at RAF Lyneham, at that time – the start of the Bristol Britannia turbo-prop era – Transport Command's long-range base. Before long, however, I was detached to Nicosia, Cyprus, where the Greek Nationalist EOKA – union with Greece – organisation had mounted a terror campaign. My task was to handle transport operations involving Hastings, Valettas, and Beverleys, but although I managed to get on operational flights, and these included contact work in the Troodos Mountains, scenery always pales from the air and this initial visit to Cyprus left me unimpressed.

In 1960 I was part of a movements team detached to Kenya in response to unrest in the Congo and elsewhere that heralded problems culminating in the East African mutinies four years later. Our team operated first at Nairobi's civil airport, Embakasi, then at neighbouring RAF Eastleigh.

A full two-year unaccompanied posting followed in January 1961, to Aden, and I duly reported to RAF Innsworth, in Gloucestershire, to No. 50 Movements Unit, fully expecting to be flown out by Britannia. Only to learn that I was to travel on the last voyage of the trooper MV *Dunera*. This veteran motor vessel was being used to carry an infantry regiment, with just 50 RAF personnel to take up the available capacity. Yet another trooper voyage! Only made notable in that, during our passage through the Canal, we were frequently buzzed by suddenly-daring Egyptian fighters!

In Aden I worked from the Steamer Point headquarters, handling sea movements, running the baggage depot, and supervising the Military Forwarding Office. After a while, though, I was transferred to the very busy air-movements section at Aden's airfield, Khormaksar, where the norm was to have eight aircraft to handle on every night shift. At least, on becoming tour-ex in December 1962, I was able to personally see to the loading of my own duty-free car!

The posting following on was to Abingdon, in Oxfordshire, but least said about that, the better: Church Lawton not excepted, I hold this to have been the worst period of my service. This unhappy sojourn was relieved in March 1965, when I returned to Cyprus, this time on a three-year accompanied posting during which both of us grew to fully appreciate the island.

Reluctantly returning to the UK in March 1968, I served for just 15 months at Manston, in Kent, before being posted as a flight sergeant to Hendon, the Joint Services Air Trooping Centre, where my sphere embraced all Service aerodromes used for trooping. It also involved liaising between the Ministry of Defence and the various civil airlines chartered for trooping, as well as handling Service movements from all civilian airfields.

The withdrawal from the Gulf was well under way when, in November 1970, I was sent to Bahrain, unaccompanied, and posted 'for eight months, or until the withdrawal from the Gulf is completed'. No trooper this time, not even a Britannia, but a smart VC-10 jetliner from Transport Command's new long-range base at RAF Brize Norton.

Aden had gone, as had the coastal-ring of staging posts and bases at Riyan, Salalah, Masirah, and Sharjah. My role in the final withdrawal, then, was to supervise the Bahrain Air Booking Centre, also its Port Office, in the latter role coordinating the activities of the combined-services staff dealing with merchant ships. Work intensified as stores were shipped to either the UK or the Far East: equipment, vehicles, and lethal ordnance of all sorts. By Christmas 1971, just 30 men remained in Bahrain, mainly army, all employed in selling off the remaining stores to Arab buyers. Finally, there were just two movements staff left, me, and an army major. And with the last voucher signed, we boarded a civil Jumbo, and waved a final farewell to the Gulf. And that it really was final, I, at least, was certain.

From March 1972 postings followed to Wattisham and Waddington, both Strike Command (formerly Bomber Command, effectively), and in August 1974, having received my Warrant, the highest non-commissioned rank, I was posted to Headquarters Strike Command at High Wycombe, to its Priority Provisioning Centre, the task being to visit and liaise with contractors.

Back in 1952, when the RAF had introduced a new trade structure, I had re-engaged until the age of 55. But now, in 1976, after a year at HQ, when applicants were sought to join Airworks Ltd, for service with the Sultan of Oman's Air Force, I was released to take up the appointment. In fact, although it heralded a lengthy period of unaccompanied life, the appointment proved rewarding in all other ways, and it was not until 1985 that I left Oman and really did say farewell to the Gulf.

Two years of driving an ambulance in High Wycombe followed, but in 1989 we moved back up to the East Midlands, to Belper, and I finally retired. From 1940 until 1985, then, forty-five years of service in the RAF and the Sultan of Oman's Air Force: so much for the 'duration of the present emergency'.

Warrant Officer Eric Reedman, 2013

Flight Sergeant Phil Harvey, General Post Office skilled worker, air observer

Aircrew Cadet Phil Harvey, 1943

It was April 1943 when I decided that, life being altogether too full of hazards for a civilian in what had become known as Hellfire Corner, I would volunteer for aircrew as a safer option. I was very nearly eighteen and was training with Post Office Telephones, in Folkestone, Kent, to become an 'Unestablished Skilled Workman'. This was a reserved occupation, but volunteering to fly offered a way around that.

Taking a yet firmer grip on the ladder I was dangling from, I eased my overalled buttocks upwards off the final coil of barbed wire – don't even ask! –, ignored the howls of laughter from the outdoor gang to whom I was 'The Youth', and thought back to that time, just weeks before, when an anti-aircraft officer had complained that a redundant run of telephone wires was obstructing his field of fire.

Obligingly allowing that the wires could be removed, I had promptly found myself perched on a pole, the job nearly complete, ready to cut the last wire. Already, only feet below me, the muzzle of the Bofors quick-firer had swept menacingly by as its elated crew were able to exercise it in full traverse for the first time. Even so, my main concern had been that when I cut that last wire the pole would sway like a palm: indeed, just months later a friend would be killed when his pole actually snapped beneath him at that juncture!

I had cut the last wire, and was duly swaying, when two Focke Wolfe Fw190s had come screaming overhead, lifting my hair, while Bofors' shells instantly erupting past my feet had flattened it again. Ironically, once I joined the RAF I would never come that close to the Luftwaffe again!

For many months before that, however, the German air force had loomed large in all our lives, and particularly since the end of the phoney war. As early as October 1939, as a fourteen-year-old, I had cycled from my home in the Kentish hamlet of Rhodes Minnis to see some unexploded German bombs, and had been disappointed that, being incendiaries, they had been so small. My first real memory of the air war, though, is of a Blenheim passing low over our playground with a great hole torn in its left wing.

The Battle of Britain was fought in the next summer, that of 1940. Consequently throughout our school holidays we became avid spectators. Indeed, supporters, for we kept the score by totalling local crashes. That this did not tell the full story we were well aware, with stricken German aircraft heading out across the Channel, yet ultimately ours proved a far more reliable tally than that given daily on the wireless.

And so, in that summer of largely cloudless skies, we watched the struggle, cheering British successes, sombrely watching our own machines fall. But cheering madly again once we saw a parachute blossom. Though

Germans too, took to their 'chutes, notably *Feldwebel* Karl Bubenhofer, of *Jagdgeschwader* 51 (effectively, Sergeant Bubenhofer of No. 51 Squadron, Luftwaffe) who baled out of his Bf109 on 29 October 1940 and whose descent my bigger brother Benn and I tracked for minutes on end before chasing towards him through a growth of saplings. In fact, what started as a carefree lark suddenly became seminal as Benn shouted, 'Run parallel to me, and that'll put him off his aim.' In that instant, at the age of just fifteen, I suddenly knew the meaning of fear.

In the event, long before the arrival of two builders, some unarmed soldiers, and a revolver-brandishing police sergeant, we'd used our schoolboy French to establish that the pilot – he was hardly older than Benn – was not wounded, and that his weapon, together with one of his flying boots, had gone with his machine, smashing into the ground a mile away. Chagrined, though, to find us there first, the army gave the builders credit for the capture.

We were fully sensible that as our area contained Hawkinge, Lympne, and Manston airfields it must be key to the air defences, and we had long suspected that the tall pylons erected on the coast had significance. As indeed, had the Germans, who fitted Graf Zeppelin Two with detecting equipment and had it deviate from its designated track on a number of occasions to nose past them. However, had the Zeppelin's captain had a hammer dropped from 150 feet to warn him off, as happened to my brother, Arthur, and me! it might have swayed the doubting German scientists into believing that Britain really did have a viable early-warning system. Later, both the radar pylons and the airfields would come under serious attack; which meant that the surrounding countryside too became a target.

Not only that, but eastern Kent had to be overflown both ways by the enemy attacking London. It followed then, that bombers too closely engaged by fighters might choose to jettison their bombs to give themselves greater flexibility. During one such encounter I was out mushrooming when some randomly released bombs whistled down, and with no cover whatsoever, I ran about like a headless chicken before taking shelter – beneath a hedge!

Another time, during harvesting, when I was perched on a loaded wagon, it was the driver who panicked, eventually tumbling the whole concern so that I had to be extracted from beneath the sheaves of corn.

Then again, returning bombers and fighters would gain speed by diving low and opportunely lightening their loads in expending any remaining bombs – and ammunition – on anything that moved. We might even be hazarded by our own side, as when a Spitfire chased a Messerschmitt directly over the heads of a crowd of us congregated by our pillar box. We hadn't seen the Spitfire, so could only fixate on the hole in the 109's spinner where his cannon was; in fact, I see it yet! Fortunately the Spit, flashing overhead instants later, held off firing until the Messerschmitt pulled upwards, when it let fly very purposefully indeed, causing the enemy fighter to belly-slide into the ground.

My eldest brother, Fred, was in the army and my third brother, Arthur, at university on an RAF scholarship. Before joining up, though, Arthur had been among those sixth-formers detailed to supply refreshments to the troops brought into Folkestone from Dunkirk. Strikingly, despite all the chaos, and all the special troop trains laid on, our school train would always be given its due place. As us younger lads waited, therefore, we could wave the soldiers off, but how we ached to become more actively involved! We dreamed, in particular, of our flung stone actually hitting one of the German fighters speeding by.

For me such overflights became personal after I had left school and four Focke Wulfs sprayed our group of cottages with cannon fire. They became more personal yet when, just a little later, one of a pair skipped a bomb past Folkestone telephone exchange where I was working and into the fortuitously-empty Christ Church beyond.

The desire to strike back yet further solidified in me when I was warily cycling along the long, and therefore dangerously exposed, straight of the A20 and came upon the body of another cyclist who had been strafed only minutes before. However, my only chance to actually take action was during a Home-Guard firing session on Shornecliffe range when I rolled over and let fly as a pair of FW190s sped by. This, though, upset our major, who bawled, 'If you'd hit one they'd have come back for us.' All I could offer was, 'But, I thought there was a war on, Sir.' To which he retorted, 'You *stupid* boy!' So pre-empting Captain Mannering by a clear twenty-six years!

My presence in the telephone exchange, and indeed the Home Guard, reflected that as the Battle had run its course, so had schooldays. Too young for the services proper, I had joined the Home Guard, but had also succeeded in gaining a place with the Post Office Telephone Department as a Youth-in-Training; in essence a two-year apprenticeship which would involve me in every aspect of telephony. An early surprise during a fortnight spent as an operator was to find that it was our switchboard that set off the air-raid sirens for the entire Folkestone area: when a purple light came on, we'd throw the appropriate switches. Another surprise was to find that we duty operators didn't then take shelter, but merely carried on! Mind you, we were being paid to do so, in my case a one and sixpence war bonus to supplement my weekly income of a guinea.

Later, during a secondment to Dover, I would come upon 'shell spotting', another refinement of life in Hellfire Corner. The drill was that one member of any team would eye the sea-horizon for the flash denoting a cross-Channel gun firing in occupied France. A countdown would then be started, until at the announcement, 'Twenty seconds to go …' the rest of the group would take cover, and as the count reached zero, and the projectile completed its twenty-mile trajectory, it would detonate.

There were occasions, of course, when no warning was possible. As when I was working in the chambers behind the White Cliffs and went to relieve myself. I was standing at the stall, contemplating the Channel through the cliffside ventilation slits, when a shell exploding on the chalk face below instantly transformed me into a a pier-end minstrel in reverse.

More drastically, there was the occasion when a shell exploded on the window sill of the Dover exchange, killing all three night operators yet leaving two of my counterparts unhurt, if covered in rubble. Despite which, when the exchange became operational again, just twelve days later, the replacement staff stoically resumed the service, though fully aware that they were no better protected than their dead colleagues had been. For, of course, it was the civilians who bore the brunt of what became everyday war, enduring anything, in effect, in order to 'keep 'em flying'.

In fact, in very rare cases, civilian employees received meritorious awards for carrying on in particularly hazardous circumstances. Although when a colleague, 'Bob' Martin, received a British Empire Medal for, as the citation had it, 'remaining up a telegraph pole as German bombers dive-bombed Dover Harbour', his response was, *'Remaining?* What else could I do? I was strapped to the bloody thing.'

Working with the outdoor gangs was intended to complement the more technical aspects of my training. Which it did. Enormously. It swiftly became evident, for instance, that my light weight and slight stature was a great asset. And so, as I have intimated, I was the obvious one to be employed when poles had to be straightened, in situ, over the ubiquitous barbed wire: even multiple coils of the stuff! Or when it came to renewing the telephone wires damaged on land adjacent to an artillery range.

'Why's the field divided by barbed wire?' we asked.

'One side's mined,' the artillery officer told us. Adding doubtfully, 'But we're not sure which side.'

And so I found myself gingerly traversing the field, on foot, with my toolbox and the lightest ladder we had, paying out a coil of cable. All very well. But when they came to clear the field after the war it was discovered that mines had been thickly laid on both sides of the barbed wire!

The RAF had accepted me as suitable PNB, their top category, suitable as pilot, navigator and bomb aimer, however, my decision to leave the Post Office so miffed my immediate supervisors that, until the call came, I was reassigned to the tunnels behind Dover's White Cliffs. Originally built as a barracks in the Napoleonic wars, they had been extensively developed since, and had most recently been used to control the Dunkirk evacuation. For the Post Office the ongoing task was to extend and upgrade the telecommunications network to support new operations rooms in anticipation of the Second Front. In fact, so important had this development become that Churchill decided to make a personal visit. It was essential, though, the brass decided, that civilians were kept out of his way. As the visit progressed, therefore, we were ushered from one connecting tunnel to the next. Until we were inadvertently ushered into the very path of the great man.

'Who are you chaps?' he wanted to know.

'Post Office engineers, Sir,' I replied, 'installing the new communications. But we've been told you mustn't see us.'

'Being civilians,' a colleague put in.

'*Civilians*?' Grunting, Churchill spun on his entourage. 'But I'm a bloody civilian, aren't I? And you're not hiding me!' With which he settled in to chat to us, probing especially for any bureaucratic hold-ups. Finally, adopting full-blown Winnie mode, he told us how vitally important our work was, that the Second Front would be utterly dependent upon the control communications we were installing. Need I say, the encounter bucked us up no end!

Winston Churchill, in his boiler suit

I had been signally unsuccessful in bringing down a German fighter both as a schoolboy and a Home Guard, but in the days before leaving, I did help save a Spitfire. We'd been pursuing a boffin's idea that the current caused to flow down a barrage-balloon cable by an impending thunderstorm could be used to warn of such hazards. We'd just made the connections when the roar of a Merlin heralded a Spitfire. It was only a mile away, so we had precious little time. Waving produced no result, nor did pointing up at the balloon. In desperation I flung myself at the cable and pantomimed climbing it. And that must have got through, for even as we dived for cover so the pilot splitarsed around the cable with literally inches to spare.

As it happened, on my first leave as an aspirant flier I was to make a further visit to the caves' complex. The sentries were probably fazed by the white cap-flash, so I was able to make my way to the sanctum of the Air-Sea Rescue Operations Room where I began mutually catching up. Until the ex-aircrew controller entered the room and instantly recognising my lowly status brusquely ordered, 'Out.' It was, after all, although I couldn't know it then, just weeks before D-Day: before, that is, the Second Front that my workmanship had empowered Winnie to open.

I count my aircrew time from 13 September 1943 when I began the Initial Training Wing course at Torquay where, besides General Service Training, my intake started to study aviation-related subjects. Off duty, the spirit of the times was reflected when an old lady urged, 'You go over Germany every night and risk your life. You really must take heed, before you meet your maker.' Not a word, though, about the evil of dropping bombs. Not back then!

In truth, our reality was not the night ops she erroneously credited us with, but drill. And more drill. Although the drill instructors (DIs) did their best to vary it by feeding us a whole sequence of commands at once, then standing back and letting us get on with it. So, our squad would silently count off, until, with not a command spoken, we would go through this, ever more ambitious, continuity routine. Meanwhile, yards away, other squads would be following suit, the various DIs merely chatting together in a group. Early on, we noticed two American soldiers stopping to watch, then a few more, until within a few days our performances were being clapped by virtually every GI in Torquay.

Our next training stage was grading school, where each candidate was allowed up to fifteen hours' instruction in a Tiger Moth to determine what aircrew category he was best suited for. Throughout our allotted hours, therefore, we did circuits and bumps, general handling – spins and aerobatics –, flew navigation exercises, and went through the motions of dropping bombs on our base, Wolverhampton's municipal airport.

My instructor was a Sergeant Jim Arnold [James William Roy], and in the seven weeks we flew together I grew both to like him and to respect his judgement. And seven weeks to do just twelve hours – the time it took for me to be sent solo –, because the UK's bad weather meant interminable delays! Like all the instructors, he had two pupils. He would give one a lesson from Wolverhampton, then land at the satellite field at Penkridge, where the other, bussed across from Wolverhampton, would take his turn.

Once a week two instructors would get airborne together to brush up their own skills, Jim Arnold's preferred partner for this being Flight Sergeant Evan John Evans – 'Taffy' –, a Welsh pilot so short in stature that he had to put a cushion into the bucket seat of the Tiger before settling onto it with his bottom-slung parachute.

On this particular day – it was 5 March 1944, how could I forget it! – we'd been on a route march and seen various Tigers going through their evolutions, wondering that one, in particular, had pulled out so low that a hill had hidden its recovery. Later, at flights, I was waiting to be picked up for my lesson when another instructor broke the news that both Jim and Taffy had been killed. I walked back to the Nissen hut, took off my flying kit, lay on the bed, and wept. Investigation would show that Flight Sergeant Evans' cushion had slipped, jamming him forwards onto the stick and locking the aircraft into an irrecoverable dive.

Life goes on. Having landed off my next lesson, the instructor climbed out with those wonderful words, 'It's all yours.' It was 15 March 1944, and I was flying solo!

I duly left Wolverhampton securely graded as pilot material. Having arrived at the aircrew holding unit at Heaton Park, in Manchester, however, my intake was devastated to be told that the RAF presently found itself flush with pilots, navigators, and bomb aimers, but was in desperate need of air gunners … As far as we were able, we kicked up, and in the event, just two of our group were assigned to air-gunner training, but only two to pilot training; the rest, including me, being re-assigned to train as observers. Meanwhile it was a question of awaiting a passage to South Africa.

In the interim, however, Winnie's Second Front was launched. But in short order, so were Hitler's V-1 Flying Bombs, or Doodlebugs. Indeed, brother Arthur had the narrowest possible escape from one. Snatching a leave from his Mosquito unit, and helping with the haymaking, he had stalled a tractor en route to the barn. And in the moments it took to get the motor going again, so a Doodlebug arrived, blowing the barn into oblivion.

We sailed to South Africa on the SS *Pasteur*, a Mediterranean cruise liner that made very heavy work of the North Atlantic as we took the circuitous course necessary to avoid U-Boats. Eventually, however, having refuelled in Freetown, we finally, and very gratefully, docked at Cape Town.

It had been a rough voyage, and though most of the lads had been wretchedly sick for a good deal of the time we were cheered by having mystified the iron-stomached, and so, somewhat superior, mariners on one point, at least. We'd been detailed to help man the ship's Bofors and already had enough navigational know-how to work out the angle of a star using the gun-laying graticules. 'So, where's the Line-Crossing ceremony?' we demanded, as we steamed over the equator, 'King Neptune and his lot.' That mere airmen should actually know where the ship was caused not a little sensation. There might even have been a little less disdain …

On disembarking we were given a break of three weeks before being entrained along the Garden Route – surely the most beautiful railway journey on earth! – to begin our training at South African Air Force (SAAF) station Woodbridge, at East London. At that time Woodbridge was the home of No. 48 Elementary Air School and here we studied navigational skills, calculating all manner of courses, keeping both air- and track-and-groundspeed plots, using drift sights, and beginning stellar navigation. But we had been selected as observers, as opposed to navigators, which meant that we also had to master bomb aiming, air gunnery, and effectively, wireless operating. The training was both intense and exacting, but as it was also absorbing, time passed swiftly.

The only fly in the ointment was that the area was a hotbed of the pro-Nazi Afrikaners known as the *Ossewabrandwag*, or OBs. We'd been briefed on the situation, of course, but after their extremist militant wing, the *Stormjaers*, killed one of our lads by driving a car at an off-duty group of cadets we took the threat very seriously. We were in a Commonwealth country, and it came as a great shock to realise that not everybody was on our side.

What does stay with me in that context, is the attitude of some South Africans actually training alongside us. For example, after we'd landed from a maritime exercise the SAAF trainee-nav hurried to his de-briefing officer to report an aircraft down in the sea. 'I felt I should report it to you, Sir, before declaring it to the others.' The others being the RAF crew members! (In fact, his sighting proved to be erroneous).

Having completed what was largely ground school, we moved again, first back to Cape Town, to No. 66 Air School (Navigation and Bombing) at Youngsfield, and then, when that closed down, to No. 44 Air School (Navigation and Bombing) at Grahamstown, a university city in Cape Province. At these venues, flying in Ansons, we began putting into practise the lessons learnt at East London.

There is, of course, a significant difference between navigation done at a desk, and that done in a jolting aeroplane. As confidence grew with experience, however, so things more frequently came together. There were strains, of course, but we found regular relief in low flying, the fliers' historical remedy for tension.

This rule-bending practice, however, had grown so prevalent, and there had been so many accidents, that the second navigator on any training sortie was required to log the aircraft's altitude at frequent intervals. Of course this simply meant that everyone merely added a healthy 500 feet to what was shown on the clock, then settled back to enjoy the countryside flashing by.

Remembering those returning German aircraft similarly hugging the ground in Kent, I might wonder if any had the problem we gave ourselves one day, of explaining away a freshly-washed shirt which draped across our pitot tube and deprived us of our vital airspeed for quite a worrying while before it ripped its evidential self away. Unlike another crew, we didn't have to explain a pitchfork jammed angrily into the bomb doors!

A major source of, at the very least, frustration, was when pilots failed to heed what we were telling them. My hairiest experience in this line came when one of our engines failed midway across the Winterbergs, the lower slopes of the dramatic Drakenberg Mountains. Now Ansons were not at all happy on one engine, and many pilots would have directed the transmission of a full-blown SOS. Ours, however, would not even authorize a lower-priority Urgency message.

Fortunately, this was not my main concern, for I had already directed his attention to an airfield pretty well below us. Only to have him ignore me. Indeed, instead of putting down, he began threading his – *our* – single-engined, inexorably-descending way back through the hilltops. None of my protestations seemed to reach him.

Then, just as we cleared the hills, but now with fog moving in below us, base transmitted an instant weather-recall. And suddenly, our pilot wanted a course for base. Except that he immediately began to spiral downwards, blindly descending into the overcast.

I passed him a snap heading and fortunately, he broke cloud above ground level. A minute later, in what was gratifying confirmation of my directional sense, we found ourselves trailing another Anson whose undercarriage was just coming down. At which, dispensing with my services altogether, our pilot tagged on, then bumped us in for a landing. After which he closed down the good engine, and stamped off.

As a mere pupil, I feared the worst. But I found myself amply backed by the wireless operator and the other trainee nav, and the course progressed.

We concluded that the pilot, who was on an extended rest tour following ops in the Western Desert, must have been more traumatised than anyone had appreciated.

At the end of the course we received our 'O' for Observer brevets – the revered 'flying arsehole' –, and proudly sewed them to our breasts. There was also the matter, though, of our ranks. Successful candidates became sergeants, unless they had been recommended for commissions. Our commanding officer, however, had a personal foible, and where commissions were concerned only considered interviewing university men and ex-policemen. In fact, the 'university' man he selected on our course had merely been sent to an Oxford college during training to get him up to speed. The other, fair enough, was one of the many policeman who had been released from their formerly reserved occupation, as I had, by applying to fly.

What finally soured us on this episode, however, was when we broke into our training records on the homeward voyage: given into our care, we soon realised the wax seal was impressed by nothing more than a South African halfpenny! Shared, these showed that fully nine of us had consistently been assessed as 'officer material'.

I have to say that this experience changed my view of authority figures for good. Since then neither rank nor position have ever, of themselves, drawn my respect, but only personality and ability. Certainly, this stance has enabled me to more ably adjust to any given situation.

All that really mattered back then, however, was that we would very shortly get the chance to fly on operations. Although I must confess to being given some cause to think when news came that Johnny Cairns, a Post Office lad who had taken the shorter, air-gunner's course, had just been shot down and killed.

Just the same, being young, I couldn't wait to get home, and embark on the final training stage. After all, my observer brother, Arthur, now had forty-two Mosquito ops beneath his belt, very nearly two full tours … Except that even as we awaited a sailing date at the Westlake Transit Camp near Cape Town, so the war in Europe ended. Jubilation, of course. But there was still the Japanese war to finish.

I arrived home just in time to support brother Benn – co-capturer of *Feldwebel* Karl Bubenhofer, and now of the Royal Horse Guards – at his wedding. Arthur too had got leave, so after the jollifications he took me back with him to RAF Little Snoring, in Norfolk, where his night-intruder Mosquito squadron was stationed.

After training establishments, it was an eye opener to be shown around an operational station, albeit that its squadrons were disbanding. But the relative chaos was timely, for Arthur was able to get me airborne with his pilot on a fighter-affiliation exercise with a Flying Fortress, briefing me on the difference between navigating at 300 mph and the 120 mph I'd been used to. I knew of the Gee navigational aid, also the Airborne Interception Radar (AI), and the rearward-looking radar they had, but Arthur took time to check me out on all three. Then I was off.

As we approached the exercise area I turned my attention to the Airborne Interception Radar, to become utterly fascinated by discovering that I could both identify the target and guide Arthur's pilot into an attack. Looking up at the last moment, though, I was disconcerted to find the Fortress just where I had expected it to be, but upside down! Indeed, it took a double take for me to realise that it was, in fact, right way up, but that Arthur's pilot had decided to barrel-roll towards it, the slight application of 'g'-force this called for not having registered with me.

Good laugh! But then came the crunch. 'What's the course for base, Phil?' I did a gulp. For I'd been flashing around the featureless North Sea at 300 mph with my head in the radar screen. 'Fly due west,' I said, betting on that directional sense of mine, 'and we'll hit the Wash.' And just as in South Africa it paid off as, within minutes, we entered the Wash, and turned left-hand-down-a-bit for Little Snoring.

Too quickly, time came to part, but as Arthur and I agreed, it had been far too long since we had last foregathered: not a state of affairs, we vowed, to be allowed to happen again. Sadly, it was not to be.

Throughout the RAF, units were girding themselves for reassignment to the Far East. Still not operational, however, my immediate destination was RAF Desford, in Leicester, with its Tiger Moths, to learn how to map read in cluttered England: a far cry from the wide-open spaces of South Africa.

The next acclimatisation stages were carried out at Bishop's Court, in Northern Ireland, and Wigtown in Scotland, a combination telling the initiated that I was destined for Coastal Command. And sure enough, my next stop was No 3 School of General Reconnaissance at Leuchars, near St Andrews.

The end of the Japanese war caught us dallying with marine sextants. Then, though, we progressed to the airmen's bubble variety, a far more sophisticated product which included an averaging mechanism to ensure that during operation any reasonable weaving was cancelled out.

As for the weather, in stark contrast to our months in largely sunny South Africa, our stay at Leuchars was marked by cold, bleak, lowering conditions which only too often turned the runways into ice sheets, with crabbing down them after touchdown an everyday occurrence.

In that bad-weather period, though, the night of 28 January 1946 has to stay in my memory. As a minor introductory, at about 10 pm I sprained my ankle. But at just that time my brother Arthur and his pilot were leaving nearby Montrose to ferry a Mosquito to RAF Hemswell, in Lincolnshire. Being a new delivery, the aircraft was not equipped with radar-navigational aids, nor even basic wireless – unthinkable later, but commonplace then. As they neared the Humber, however, so the whole country went out in fog. They worked through the various lost procedures, but eventually, above unbroken cloud, in the dark, and running short of fuel, they made the politic decision to bale out. The pilot touched down successfully near Spilsby, but Arthur, landing in a tree, suffered a broken neck.

How poignant it is now, to look at a photo of us four brothers, taken not that many years before, in the branches of what I captioned as, the family tree!

Our Family Tree, 1939: from the bottom, Fred, my eldest brother, a soldier; Self; Arthur, Mosquito observer; and Benn, forestry commission, then soldier.

The Service laid on an Anson to get me to Arthur's funeral, but navigating through the tail end of the long-standing poor-weather system proved no easy task. I got the pilot to make the slowest possible descent, then fell to map-reading with a fury once we began to see the ground, ultimately hedge-hopping into a yet fog-wreathed Hemswell. Dicey, of course. But as with the whole sad episode, very much of the times, imbued as they still were with the wartime 'press-on' spirit. Beyond that again was the way all those involved took the tragedy in their stride, and simply carried on.

The war was over, Arthur was gone, and I suppose, to some extent, I saw myself as simply marking time until my release, for despite my best endeavours I never had, after all, managed to get operational during wartime. However, finally fully qualified, I was posted to Coastal Command's No. 224 Squadron, equipped at that time with Liberators and later, Lancasters, and stationed at St Eval, in Cornwall. The job was the nationally-vital one of gathering meteorological data from up to 700 miles into the Atlantic and patrolling the sea lanes, tasks involving days of flying patterns over the trackless, if never entirely empty, ocean, with sorties lasting up to twelve hours.

True, the routine was occasionally broken by periodic mail deliveries to Lagens, in the Azores. Our first of these trips, however, from start to finish, became something of a drama.

Our own skipper, Flight Lieutenant Mac Matheson, had just built up hours enough to permit him to carry passengers, but on this first trip he had to be supervised. The supervising pilot was a flight lieutenant, known to all, we were to discover, as 'Pranger'. He duly accelerated us down the main runway at St Eval, but as it dipped towards the end, where most pilots lifted off, he roared on, only just scraped over the boundary fence, and then, convinced that something was wrong, circled, and thumped back in for a precautionary landing.

Our groundcrew worked their way through the called-for technical checks then, finding nothing untoward, re-cleared the aircraft as fit to fly. Mac and Eddie Hannowin, our flight engineer, carried out an air test, found nothing whatsoever wrong, and duly accepted it in their turn. And so, at our second attempt, we successfully made our way to Lagens. 'Pranger' was still aboard as nominal screen captain, but with our crew having made it quite clear that he was to have nothing to do with the conduct of the flight.

My Crew, from left: Eddy Hannowin, flight engineer; Les, second pilot; Self, navigator; Mac Matheson, skipper; Paddy Kempton, wireless operator/air gunner; Danny Cronin, navigator; Paddy Ryan, wireless operator/air gunner

The actual return did not go entirely to plan either, for due to adverse headwinds, we had to put in at Gibraltar: that, though, only added to the novelty of the trip. What made the exercise truly memorable, however, was that, on getting back to St Eval we found ourselves on the carpet. We'd had a great stay in the Azores, had unashamedly got a little too merry, and had put up a black with the local commander. Our own CO, however, made little of it, although he went through the motions of banning us from further Azores visits. We rank and file overcame this ban by flying piecemeal with other crews. But on the following August Bank Holiday even Mac, our skipper, got a further chance.

He woke me at 0230 hours, long before a dawn which promised a dismal, wet, and cloudy day. It seemed that two American ships had collided some 700 miles off Land's End, that one had been abandoned and may even have sunk.

'We're to get off the moment there's a workable cloud base,' Mac advised, but despite the dismal weather, looked unaccountably cheerful. Once I got into the planning, however, it became clear to me too, that if the search was in the least extended then an Azores diversion was very much on the cards.

Some 300 miles into the outbound flight the weather broke, leaving a cloudless day. I was acting as second navigator, splitting my time between visual searching from the front turret, and providing any assistance called for by my opposite number, Danny Cronin, who was taking the first-nav's slot. In fact, a half an hour or so before reaching the search area, and more for a lark than anything else, I took advantage of the clear-sky conditions and obtained a very excessive four sun shots. At the same time I nudged Paddy Ryan, at the wireless, to furnish me with a similar number of Consol (long-range navigational aid) bearings. Then, straight-faced, I plonked the results on Danny's desk. I was mildly surprised that he didn't simply curse me, and dump them. Instead, although he moaned a bit, he got down to it, and plotted all eight of them on the chart. And not many minutes later, we saw the first collision victim.

This was the SS *William J Riddle*, which we found proceeding under its own steam, learning, as Aldis-light signals passed, that it had everyone from both vessels aboard. Having transmitted back that information to Coastal Command and Admiralty, we then set off to search for traces of the other vessel, the SS *American Farmer*. In fact, we soon came upon her, listing markedly, yet very obviously afloat. Again, we shot off her position and all the requisite signals.

The SS **American Farmer,** *still afloat, but abandoned*

The *American Farmer's* captain would later claim that, having got all his charges aboard the *William J Riddle* for safety, he had intended to re-board, only to be frustrated when fog came down. Essentially, though, after we had told the world where the crippled vessel was, the British SS *Elizabete* had arrived and taken her in tow. Only to have the SS *American Ranger*, from the *American Farmer's* company – and under the eye of the Yankee destroyer, *USS Perry* –, dispossess the British salvage crew, and subsequently contest the *Elizabete's* claim to salvage rights.

Long before this, with our job done, we had transmitted a final update, found that fuel considerations did indeed make it necessary to divert to the Azores, and enjoyed an extremely pleasant weekend off. On the Monday, however, we saw something more of the drama when we were ordered to dwell over the collision area, before leaving the squabbling little fleet to their own devices and heading back for St Eval.

Just as I count the months spent on Hellfire Corner as the highlight of my youth, so I count the *American Farmer* episode as the acme of my flying days, for with hostilities over, my release date pressed, and I had both a life and a career to carve out, the latter, it transpired, as a Plessey design engineer, a fascinating occupation which would take me all over the world.

As for the collision, the press turned it into a cause célèbre. The High Court of the Admiralty, seeking to rule on salvage rights, found for the SS *Elizabete*, noting in so doing that it was the RAF who had supplied the position of the derelict. The USS *Perry*, however, supporting the SS *American Ranger*, objected, arguing that the RAF – we! – had supplied a position at least fifty miles out, its captain advancing confidently, 'Our shipboard calculations were based upon a midday sun shot, taken only the previous day.' Which is where my prankish overkill paid off. For Mac, as aircraft captain, produced the nav log showing that we had depended upon an unassailable eight-position-line fix taken just 30 minutes before the sighting. With which the claims of the SS *Elizabete* were granted, and Mac received the King's Commendation for Valuable Service in the Air.

My last real contact with the RAF – long-term involvement with the Aircrew Association aside – was in connection with this event. After reflecting for a while I contacted Air Ministry, inquiring, not entirely tongue in cheek, what the navigator's share of the prize money might be. There was what I felt was a shocked pause. But then, following not too long a delay, I received a cheque for eighty pounds, sixteen shillings, and twopence. Also a brace of accompanying comments, both brusque. 'This is salvage money, not prize money.' And finally, 'There is to be no further communication on this matter.'

No communication. And yet, from my earliest involvement in the war effort, communication had played such an important part. My aircrew service was one great pleasure, in the main … But it was as a Post Office communicator that I feel I truly served, and so propose all those unsung civilian colleagues who, by their understated professionalism, really did help keep 'em flying.

Phil Harvey, with bubble sextant, 2014

8. Frozen Tears

**Leading Aircraftwoman Zosia Kowalczyk, Later, Kowalska,
naturalized as Martin, Women's Auxiliary Air Force,
Polish Forces under British Control, cook**

Aircraftwoman Zosia Kowalczyk, 1943

At twenty-one my life had already taken many unexpected turns. As I joined the crowd around the wireless in Tanganyika's Kidugala camp I was not to know that it was about to change as dramatically again. General Sikorski, our exiled leader in England, was already talking, urging Polish women to help with war work. As he finished his appeal Jasia Grzywa grabbed my arm.

'Well, Zosia, The *Kresy*, Siberia, Uzbekistan, Iran, India, Africa. Now what do you say to England? The WAAFs, the air force?'

I hesitated.

'Well,' Jasia pressed, 'what do you think?'

In truth, I did not know what to think. I knew little of England. And what I did know was not good. Back in September 1939 my father, Blazej, had said that the English and the French had promised to come to Poland's aid if Germany attacked her. But they did nothing. And when two weeks later the Russians attacked too, they did even less. Yet …

'I'll see what Anna thinks,' I told her.

In fact, it seemed a great opportunity. I suppose we'd all been waiting for something to happen. We, being scores upon scores of young women, blossoming back to full health after our privations in Siberia and Uzbekistan, with the men of our own age far away in the army. Undoubtedly tensions had been running high. Just days since, a couple of girls had actually brawled over a particular man, only to have him tell them, 'I've two grown sons with the Anders' army and you're younger than both of them.' Then, when another girl fell pregnant but discovered that her officer lover had a wife back in Poland, she killed herself. At least General Sikorski's broadcast from London helped clear the air.

When my sister, Anna, came off kitchen duty, she listened intently as I told her of the appeal. Then she shook her head.

'Why should we go to this war?'

'It's Poland's war too,' I reasoned.

After that the discussion went on well into the night. As did Anna's objections: she was not educated enough: at thirty she was too old: her eyesight was too poor: she was simply too tired …

I knew early on, of course, that she would not be coming: I knew the power of her will. And who knew better what the last two years had cost her?

'You go, Zosia,' she urged finally. 'It's a fresh start for you.'

It was never going to be an easy parting. At the very least I owed Anna my life. We all did. Me, and our three brothers. But I had to admit that, from the start, I felt an enthusiasm for this English venture such as I had never known.

In our camp, Kidugala, the girls flocked to sign on. And once our train got under way, virtually circling Tanganyika to pick up at the other camps, at

Ifunda, Koya, Kondoa, and Tengeru, we found that the girls in each of them had responded with the same eagerness. Indeed, by the time we arrived at Tengeru, in the shadow of Mount Kilimanjaro, five hundred of us had answered General Sikorski's call.

They held us at Tengeru for some time, and rather than let us get bored, started us in at drill. But those natural tensions were still uppermost in some, like Janka Valntanowitcz, who would disappear every night. 'I've found this Italian prisoner of war,' she told us, 'and he smuggles me into his camp.'

Eventually, though, we were entrained to Mombasa where the troopship SS *Amsterdam* awaited us, and my tears flowed freely once again, for bright as the future might seem, I was leaving dear Anna behind. Understandably enough, in my sorrow, my mind turned back.

My mother and father had married in Chicago where each had gone to build up a nest egg, but then my mother, Maria – but always Mary, to my father –, had returned to Poland with baby Anna to run the holding they'd bought. Father had rejoined her in 1920 and in 1927, when I was five, learning that good land was being offered cheaply to settlers, he had moved us to the *Kresy Wshodnie* – the South-Eastern Border.

This really was frontier land, having only recently been won from the Ukrainians, and as they resented our presence life could be tense. Anna, of course, being eleven years older than me, had lived through all six of our nation's recent conflicts – against Lithuania, Hungary, Austria, both Germany and Russia, and the Ukraine. So even before the September Campaign she must have had her fill of war.

Before Germany attacked on 1 September 1939, many of the recently dispossessed nationals had become militant, their murderous activities putting Polish refugees onto the roads, among them, my cousin Zofia, from Rabka. Having stayed with us for two weeks, and thinking the situation had stabilized, she set off to return home. Never to be seen again.

Refugee cousin Zofia, never seen again

Just a fortnight after the German invasion from the west, of course, the Russians treacherously swept in from the east. And by early October it was all over.

Although the Russians passed authority to the local Ukrainians, the Soviets were now the real controllers of the *Kresy*, a state of affairs my father viewed with unease.

'Eventually, it's going to be Siberia for us, Mary, my dear', he said heavily. For he was a doubly marked man, being both a landowner and tainted – as the Communist's saw it – by having spent time in America. Certainly, that very evening he had us make up packs of essentials. Us, being Anna, me, and the boys, Juzek (sixteen), Janek (fourteen), and Staszek (ten). I remember being upset at how little I was allowed to pack. But Anna put her foot down when father tried to stop her including her national-dress blouse and black skirt; arguably the first display of the indomitable will that was to serve us so well!

For our family the uneasiness lasted until 10 February 1940. Then, at five in the morning, two Ukrainians, neighbours still, but now officials as well, came banging on our door. We were being 're-settled', father was told, and had twenty minutes to leave the house. We were limited to five kilos of clothing and goods, we were to take no jewellery, other than wedding rings, and no more than twenty zlotys in cash – at that time just less than a English pound! An official paper was flourished showing our names on a list. But the porchlight caught both the starred caps and the bared bayonets of two silent Russian soldiers.

I burst into tears, as did Staszek, while Janek bit his lip, but Juzek, always hot-headed, moved purposefully forwards, until a command from father halted him.

'Juzek! These men are acting legally. Help Anna and your mother pack.'

And minutes later we joined a disconsolate column trudging towards the village school. All that remains with me from our arrival there, though, is the bawling of the untended stock, for I remember choking back tears to wail, 'Listen, Mother, even the cows are crying.'

There was to be a lot more crying. Early that evening we were herded to the railway station where a train awaited. But a train of shuttered cattle wagons! Wagons whose doors were slid shut the moment we were packed on board, then locked! In the gloom we picked out bunks, and straw-strewn boards. Then, the train jolted into life, and voices swelled in renewed protest, until brother Staszek's piping tones shocked everyone into silence. 'They're taking us to Siberia.'

At that, I put my head in my hands. I was eighteen, and my world had been torn apart.

In fact, they took us to Kotlas, near Archangelsk, at the junction of the Severnaya and the Vychegda Rivers and on the edge of the Arctic Circle. Kindly time blots out much, but never can it blot out the horrors of the four weeks they made the journey take. Certainly, best not spoken of now. And though journey's end was what the English call Archangel, in Russia, so deeply is Siberia ingrained in the Polish psyche that Siberia it remains.

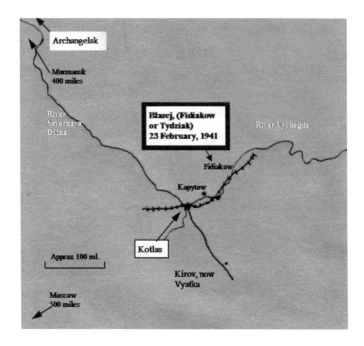

Map of the Archangelsk (Archangel) 'Special Settlements' mentioned

On leaving the train a major shock awaited us as we saw Russian soldiers making a selection of the young and obviously fit, both men and girls. To our consternation, Anna was singled out. Concerned, my father asked a guard what this meant.

'They go to Zadoweje,' the man grunted. And then, 'A lumber camp. A good place. They work. They eat.'

And minutes later Anna's column disappeared into the forests.

The rest of us were taken to the Kopytow 'Special' or 'Forced-Exile' Settlement. As we were halted at the gates one of our number began to weep, at which a woman passer-by, whom we had taken for Russian, paused, to chide in long-unused Polish, 'You'll never be allowed to leave Russia, so learn to live here, or die here. There're no miracles.'

No miracles! It was far from the last time we were to be told this.

There were some 3,000 Poles in Kopytow, and along with the majority of adults, I was set to logging. Mother was drafted into the kitchens, while all three boys were sent to school. Father, though, was sent to a nearby camp, Fidiakow, to make charcoal.

Some months later we were allowed to join him, after which Anna was able to visit. Her appearances were doubly valued, for being both bright and able she invariably exceeded the work requirement, or 'norm', and was paid bonuses in goods, but most importantly, in food. For the normal ration was just 300 grammes of bread a day – a few bites, and it was gone – whereas those, like father and Anna, who exceeded the norm got 700 grammes. Even then, not that very much at all.

In fact, starvation was never far off and invariably underlay the deaths among us. These had started on the train among the old and infirm, but now younger people began to fail. For months though, thanks to our two bonus earners, and to mother procuring kitchen scraps, our family did rather better than merely survive. Just after Christmas 1940, however, catastrophe struck.

Making charcoal called for the open-air furnace to be tended throughout the process, and while doing this father was overcome by the bitter cold. He lingered until 23 February 1941, then passed away. When his condition became critical I was working at a distant camp, and though I was given leave, deep snow, driven by high winds, meant that I arrived too late.

Mother was weeping, but Anna, who had arrived in time to receive father's blessing, turned as I entered and seeing my desolation, gathered me into her arms. 'Zosia, darling, you're exhausted,' she said softly. Then, touching my cheek, she added wonderingly, 'Why! your tears are frozen.'

For months after that, getting food, and surviving, took all our efforts. What we couldn't know was that events in the outside world were once more re-shaping our lives. Later we would learn that when the Germans invaded Russia in June 1941 the Soviet armies, weakened by Stalin's purges, reeled back. Desperate, the Russians suddenly realised that they had an additional, ready-made army in their Polish prisoners of war. In July 1941, therefore, diplomatic relations with Poland were hastily restored, an 'amnesty'! was announced to all Polish citizens in Russia, and an agreement was reached by which captured Polish soldiers would fight Hitler.

And then came the utterly unlooked-for development, in truth, the Miracle! For as the 'amnesty' – the effrontery of using that word! – applied to all Poles in Russia, so civilians too were to be released.

When the news reached us we were highly elated. It meant, no less, that life was back on track!

Initially our group was to return by river steamer to the rail junction at Kotlas, but as the vessel nosed towards us it appeared to be crowded to capacity. Mother and Anna, though, pushed me up the gangplank, so that only at the last minute did I look up at those packing the rails.

We had heard of Russia's criminal political prisoners but these beggared belief. Sunken eyed and shaven headed, their unhealthy grey skin showed through layers of stinking rags that made my stomach heave. The crowd surged, cannoning me into the nearest man – and spilling writhing *somethings* from his rags onto my blouse.

'Lice, filthy lice!' I shrieked, horrified: the creature was smothered with the things! As I jerked back, so he too pulled away the hand he had instinctively extended to steady me. Only as he did so, he said clearly, or clearly until his voice broke halfway through, '*Przepraszam, Pani*': 'I'm sorry, madam.' In perfect Polish!

God! I was appalled! He – they – all these gaunt and shuffling beings from some alien world were Polish! And more than that, Poles only a year or so older than I was! Soldier-lads who had been captured during the September Campaign and then pressed into forced-labour ever since.

Later we would find that many really had been incarcerated in Siberia; that it was commonplace for a group of twenty to have been reduced to four; that, with the amnesty, weeks before, they had been unceremoniously turned out of their camps with neither rations nor transport supplied for the journey. Need I say that from that moment on there was nothing we wouldn't do for them?

The two groups parted company at Kotlas, the army lads carrying on to the Southern Urals where the new army was to form, and us packing into the railhead camp, more than content that we were going home.

High hopes! For what we had yet to learn was that, hard upon making the agreement to use the Polish soldiers, the Russians had realised that they lacked the means to equip them. Because of this a new agreement had been worked out by which the new army was to sent to Iran, where the Western Allies would equip it [See Glossary, Ander's army]. We, of course, knew nothing of this, so fully expected to be sent home to Poland.

I have skipped over much of the trauma of those days. Let me do so again and simply say that to realise that we were not bound for Poland, but for unheard-of Iran, desolated us. We would eventually learn, of course, that when the Germans had invaded Russia they had swept across the whole of Poland; that now we had no home to go to. Meanwhile we were once again loaded into cattle wagons, and this time taken south.

It was an uncomfortable journey, but at least the doors were no longer locked. And we were able to pick up supplies, for now we stopped in settlements, not remote from them. The route, though, has to remain vague, for nobody told us where we were. Late on we saw great mountain ranges, and word went around that we were in the land of the Golden Horde which had once sacked Cracow. But for much of the way we wondered at the vast areas under cultivation, noting, half-disdainful, half-sorrowing, that much of this abundance was being left to rot.

'Yet at Kopytow School,' Staszek puzzled, 'they taught us that Soviet collective farms were the most productive in the world.'

The journey was interminable, but we finally pulled into somewhere whose name, at least, we recognised: Tashkent! We even got off the train there, but only for an hour or so, though long enough to be impressed by the tree-shaded streets, the soaring minarets and the sparkling irrigation ditches. The briefness of the stop did not bother us, for by now we knew we were definitely to leave Russia, if only for Iran. Except that once again wider events were to bear upon us.

With nominally-released Poles already streaming south, the Russians found themselves facing unanticipated problems, among them, whether Jewish and Ukrainian deportees from the *Kresy* should be freed too. Then again, by this time their own armies had stemmed the German advance. Perhaps they needed time to evaluate where this left them. Wherever it was, instead of taking us straight to the border, they sidetracked us, dispersing us among villages in Soviet Uzbekistan, presumably while they had a rethink.

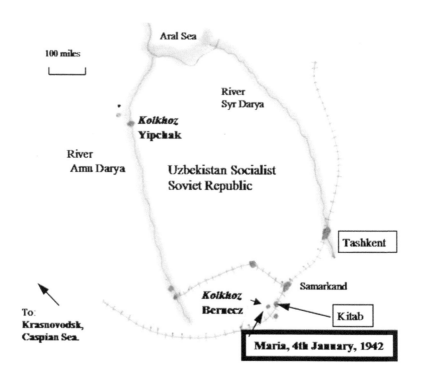

Map of the **Kolkhoz** *collective farms in Soviet Uzbekistan mentioned*

We were taken for six days up the River Amu Darya, initially to Kolkhoz Chipchak, that is, the collective village of Chipchak. This had to be the poorest place you can imagine, but the Uzbek people were kind to us, making room in their circle as we arrived, then passing around the one spoon they owned. Within days, though, we took up more permanent residence at Kolkhoz Bernecz.

To say that there were times that winter when we resorted to eating grasses may stretch credibility, but this was the case, for in the Uzbek collectives everyone lived on the brink of starvation. Certainly, I remember breaking down one day and vowing before heaven that after all this was over I would never go hungry again! Years later I would see the film *Gone with the Wind* and be reduced to tears when Scarlett O'Hara made the self-same vow!

Mother had never fully recovered from father's death, and now she failed rapidly. For her, the end came on 4 January 1942 at a time when Staszek and I were in the throes of typhus and the other boys were sickly too. Nor were any of our male neighbours well enough to labour, so Anna had to bury mother on her own.

Traumatic as that was for her, her main priority was us: she got me back to health by constant care, and saved Staszek's life by keeping him from what passed for a hospital. What undoubtedly saved all of us, though, was a recruiting officer from the newly-formed Polish Army, now at Tashkent, waiting for the Russians to clear us onwards into Iran. When he called in, neither of us wanted the boys to go. Only we knew it was for the best, that the army would feed them …

Juzek was itching to join up, while Janek's only reservation was that he really wanted to join the air force. The problem was Staszek, who was not only too young but small for his age. Anna, though, proved equal to the task, arguing that the lad had been seriously ill, but was rapidly catching up. I could tell the officer wasn't in the least bit taken in, but after a while he nodded.

'He'll make a fine cadet,' he smiled, and signed Staszek on too. It was, of course, a bittersweet parting.

Despite having less food to find there was no real improvement in conditions, but with the boys in safe hands Anna and I were easier in our minds. Then came the day when we made our routine call to collect our meagre grain issue. On this occasion the Uzbek miller laughed off our complaint about the high grit content.

'Why worry, ladies? Tomorrow you go.'

We were utterly taken aback. But he was right, for the Russians had finally agreed to honour the agreement! And a day or so later the army escorted us to the railway junction at Kitab.

Even then there must have been another political hitch for we were held at Kitab for some days, in the open, although the April weather had turned bitter. And sadly many more people succumbed.

At length, though, we got under way again, ending up this time at Krasnovodsk, on the eastern shore of the Caspian Sea where a ship awaited. It seemed hopeful, and yet we were still in Soviet territory! It was in great trepidation, therefore, that we lined the rails as we closed on the Iranian port of Pahlavi.

Except that, as we neared the quay, we saw that it was alive with Polish flags! With women dressed in the gaily flowered blouses of our national dress! And with a Polish military band to instantly reduce the assembled mass to tears! For to us, on board, it meant that, if we were not in Poland, we were, at least, in a Polish enclave in a friendly land. And finally, out of Soviet Russia.

And a timely emergence, our contingent being the last of those permitted to leave Russia under the amnesty. For now that the Germans were being pushed back, the Soviets decided that all Poles still in Russia would be regarded as Soviet citizens. Finally, when the Soviet atrocity at Katyn was revealed by the Germans – 22,000 captured Polish officers and intelligentsia shot dead! – diplomatic relations were instantly severed and the frontier slammed shut.

Although we were free, and despite all the care lavished by the aid services, the deaths were to continue, for with our general resistance so low the slightest infection could prove fatal. Among measures to reverse the decline, our heads were shorn, our bodies disinfected, and all clothing incinerated; only Anna's national-costume blouse and treasured black skirt escaping the flames, Anna, the indomitable, absolutely refusing to let them go!

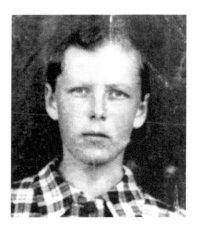

Zosia, with head shorn, Pahlavi, 1942

Having found our feet, our first task was to discover what had happened to the boys. Juzek, we found, was to fight alongside the British in Italy, Janek was to be shipped to England to train as a boy airman, and Staszek was to finish his education in British-controlled Palestine. All, we told ourselves, were in good hands.

Our next move was to cross the Elburz Mountains to Tehran by lorry convoy, the memory of precipitous gorges giving me shivers to this day. We then stayed for varying periods at a succession of recuperation camps, after which we descended by train to Ahvas, at the head of the Persian Gulf. And from here a ship took us to Karachi, in what was, it seemed, British India. Though why British, puzzled us. British Palestine, now British India …

Some Poles were to remain in India, but a week later we left for a protracted two-thousand mile voyage, to Africa. Strangely, though an ocean voyage, it was not a universally healthy one, our feeling being that the sea air quickened recovery too swiftly for many weakened constitutions.

Even Anna, my tower of strength, faltered, the strain of caring for the rest of us for so long finally catching up with her. Back in the forests she, like many others, had suffered from snow blindness. For most, this had passed. Anna's eyes, however, had continued to give trouble, and now reacted particularly badly to the sunlight off the sea.

The ship's doctor did his best, but all he could offer was drops, though a specialist said later that these had prevented Anna from going totally blind. As it was, ever afterwards she needed a strong magnifying glass to read with.

It was September 1942 when we came ashore in what is now Tanzania, at Dar-Es-Salaam – in Arabic, the Haven of Peace. Peaceful, perhaps, despite which sickness and death were to be our close companions for many a month to come. I do believe, however, that Anna truly held it to be a haven. So why indeed, would she want anything more to do with the war?

Kidugala refugee camp, some seventy miles inland from Dar-Es-Salaam, was centred upon a hospital. Across the river was a school and a church, and the accommodation site, where we were housed in fours in native-style huts; round, thatched, and very light and airy. There was an air of permanence about it and yet when the Poles finally moved out the British bulldozed it to stop Africans moving in! So much for British Africa, then …

Certainly, they were not an easy people to understand, the British, or English. For example when we began feeding the African children they told us to stop, or they'd cut off our rations.

As mother had done in Siberia, Anna worked as a cook, while I was made responsible for organizing the supplies for a group of forty women.

Anna, centre, with two colleagues, at Kidugala

We'd been there, gently recovering, but undoubtedly falling into a routine, for just over a year when we heard the Sikorski broadcast, and came to the parting of the ways. And sad though that parting was, I have to admit that as we boarded the SS *Amsterdam* at Mombasa I was bubbling over with anticipation. Clearly my life was about to take an entirely new turn.

We sailed in convoy, putting ashore at Durban where we were sung into port by a lady dressed in white: a soprano called Perla Sirdle Gibson, we later found out, who had lost her son in the war. One song she sang was '*Land of Hope and Glory*', and I was surprised to see it reduce the so-stoical Britishers to tears. For apart from us 500 WAAFs-to-be, there were 1,500 Dominion troops, re-positioning to Britain after the Desert War.

Mixing was strictly forbidden, even so there were scores of shipboard romances. In fact, I attracted the attention of a very handsome Australian sergeant, although I was so shy that I took to hiding if he was likely to be around. What we did do though, was start picking up English words and phrases.

During our week's stay in Durban we were issued with South-African-pattern khaki-drill blouses and short skirts, and were plied with trays of lemon tea and cakes by elegant colonial ladies in wide-brimmed hats and flowery dresses. So different from anything we had known before!

Durban was our last port of call, for on clearing Africa the convoy headed out into the Atlantic to avoid submarines, making it a long voyage. Even so we found ways to occupy ourselves, my friend Rózia deciding to find out what the Scottish sentry wore under his kilt. She dropped some coins, betting he'd bend down to pick them up, which he did, only she was laughing so much she never did see.

Eventually we were set ashore at Glasgow, but whereas I'd expected beautiful white mansions like those we'd known in South Africa, all I saw was a cobbled, rain-slicked quay and sad, black tenements. We then travelled all through the night, arriving at Redcar, on the east coast. And having eaten we were allocated billets in requisitioned holiday villas.

Next day they gave us a medical, two doctors examining us in pairs, unbelievably, giving us an internal examination! something I'd never dreamt of. And although we'd learnt quite a bit of English I was still mystified when my doctor called across to his colleague, 'This one's a virgin.'

Unlike Janka Valntanowitcz who, as a result of her nightly visits to the prisoner-war-camp, came back and announced, 'I'm pregnant.' She was sent up to Scotland, where she had twins! Another girl too, left us for Scotland, a tall, willowy blonde with a beautiful face and a figure that drew all the men, but she went to a TB sanatorium.

In contrast, Caroline Bodnar had a husband fighting in Italy, three sons dead in Siberia, and had never been well in Africa, yet though barely scraping through the medical the English climate must have suited her, for she got better and better.

At this stage some girls were assigned to other war work, most of us, though, were sworn into the Women's Auxiliary Air Force. So I became P.2792488 (the 'P' denoting Polish) Aircraftwoman Second Class Zosia Kowalczyk.

On the first real working day we overslept, to be awoken by a Scottish woman sergeant bawling, 'On the double, clothing parade, let's be having you.' We all rushed out, but Rózia was in such a hurry that she forgot her skirt. To the noisy delight of a crowd of workmen!

We were issued with blue-grey RAF uniforms which had 'Poland' shoulder flashes. We were also given English lessons, although the first education officer began by telling us that he accepted that many Poles were barely literate in Polish. At which one of the girls gave him facts and figures to show Poland to be more literate overall than Britain had ever been. After which we never saw that silly man again.

We also had lectures to bring us up to date on the war, so that we learnt how well Polish airmen had done in the Battle of Britain, and how our bomber squadrons were now flying over Germany every night. However, in early June we could only watch as the invasion fleets passed overhead. But two days later, on 8 June 1944, we were sent to RAF Station Wilmslow, near Stockport, to No 31 Women's Reception Centre, where we did a lot more marching but even more scrubbing. What they also had us do, though, was give our preference for trades. No choice for me, there, for without hesitation I opted to become a cook: cooks don't go hungry! And I had never forgotten my vow! On 13 July 1944, therefore, I reported to the cookery school at RAF Newton, near Nottingham, to begin my trade training.

Newton was primarily No 16 Polish Service Flying Training School, and responsible for training Polish pilots in both basic and advanced flying. Because it worked relatively settled hours, however, it was able to accommodate the cookery school too: the Polish bomber stations further up the Fosse Way, at Syerston and Swinderby, couldn't have done so.

The key figure in my life became Corporal Mihalski, the chef. He had a big moustache which would bristle when things went wrong, as they did, of course, virtually every mealtime, at which, he'd rave, cursing everyone in sight, regardless of rank. When he was pleased with one of us, on the other hand, he'd take us into the storeroom and let us have our fill of cream. Without boasting, I have to say that I grew nicely rounded.

Not that cooking was natural to me, for back at home I'd always been chided for spending more time at my looking glass than at household chores. Effectively, therefore, I had to start from scratch.

Some things, however, were not as bad as I'd imagined, with machines for peeling potatoes and for the bulk mixing of porridge, custard, and stews. And though hard work, it always gave me a good feeling to see people leaving the dining hall satisfied.

For our week's end-of-course leave a few of us decided to visit the Paderewski Polish military hospital in Edinburgh. But oh! the sights. Wards and wards of young Poles. Without jaws, eyes, limbs, hands, and lacking control of bodily functions. Many had been wounded at Monte Cassino. In truth, it was all so upsetting that I was really glad when our leave was up and I was able to get away, especially on reflecting that my brother, Juzek, still fighting in Italy, might any day become such a patient.

I had a far happier encounter, however, just before leaving Newton, fleeting as it necessarily was. I was walking from the cookhouse when one of a group of airmen boarding a lorry called my name. I had to look twice, and even then I could scarcely believe that this tall, uniformed lad was my brother, Janek. He was on a visit from RAF Halton, in Buckinghamshire, where he was on a two-year training course as an RAF apprentice. As you might gather it was a joyous reunion, yet another bittersweet one in that it meant an immediate parting, and weeks on end of settling down again.

Brother Janek, an RAF aircraft apprentice at Halton, wearing the RAF's boy-service 'wheel' armbadge

The final part of my training began on 5 December 1944 at the Polish School of Technical Training at RAF Locking, near Weston-Super-Mare, in Somerset. Corporal Mihalski's basic training clearly paid off, for when Wing Commander Rudnicki, our station commander, sampled the meal I'd submitted as my trade test he boomed out, 'Well, LAC Kowalczyk, judging by this, Corporal Kowalski is going to be a very lucky man. Meanwhile, we'd better keep you here.'

Of course, I was covered in blushes. For a start, it was a compliment for a trainee to be retained on the station, but it was also clear that even the station commander knew of my developing involvement with Corporal Stefan Kowalski.

Stefan Kowalski, 1944

Brought up near Poznan, Stefan had come to England in a very different way from me, though it had been one followed by most Poles arriving in Britain. In 1939 he had been a policeman serving in General Debinski's Penal Expedition against Ukrainian Nationalists. When the September Campaign ended, however, he had retreated under orders into Hungary where he remained for some months before being shipped to Marseilles. He was then sent to Coëtquidan, in North-Western France, where he had been enlisted into the Polish Army under French Command. Just days later, though, France surrendered. Ignoring this technicality – ignoring too the protests of many Frenchmen encountered along the way who argued that the war was over – he was among the thousands of Poles and other troops who made their way westwards to the coast, to St-Jean-de-Luz, to be brought to England by the Royal Navy [Operation Aerial].

Arriving in August 1940 Stefan had been enlisted into the Polish Air Force under British Command as a photographer. In mid 1943, however, while stationed at Northolt on No. 315 (Hurricane) Squadron, a problem with his leg confined him to Hillingdon's Cogarley Hospital for three months. It was November 1943 before he was fit for duty again but then he was allowed to remuster to the police – his civilian job – and posted to Locking.

He clearly feared more trouble from his leg though, and as our relationship deepened, he warned me that if we married I'd be taking on a cripple. Some cripple, for after we married, on 17 February 1945, he was very active for another sixty years, and still annually driving himself to Poland at eighty-four!

Back in 1945 the daughters of the local mayor rallied around to furnish me with a wedding dress while the press made much of us as the first Polish couple to marry in Weston-Super-Mare; even if one paper renamed me Mary and had us coming from Holland! Once married we found a cottage in Locking village. Then in May 1945, the war ended.

In the July we were posted onto the staff of the Polish Demobilisation Centre at RAF Cammeringham, a few miles from Lincoln. I was put in charge of the cookhouse while Stefan policed the station. Although on one occasion he played the shining prince on behalf of us girls. This was when we found that the officer taking station parades would quite unconsciously – but very obviously! – fiddle with himself as he faced us. Until Stefan had a quiet word with him.

A notable who had no such faults was the Hapsburg aristocrat, Acting Group Captain Prince Karol Hieronim Celestyn Maria Konstanty Stanisław Radziwill (later to be related to the American Kennedys). I suppose he too was simply awaiting demob.

With the war ended our big worry was whether we could safely return to a Poland that was now Communist controlled, for we knew from *Kresy* days that people who had been to the west were viewed as suspect by the Communists. But there was another aspect. For we learnt too, that those who had survived the occupation, and in many cases the additional atrocities carried out by nationalist groups, looked down on all returnees, notwithstanding that so many of us had been taken out of Poland by force. Having weighed all this, we eventually decided that we would be unwise to return.

During the next two years Poles by the thousand passed through Cammeringham, handed in their kit, and left the Service, the great majority enlisting with the Polish Resettlement Corps to learn a trade. This might well have been the course we chose, except that when I found I was to have a baby I applied for release and was duly discharged as a leading aircraftwoman on 3 September 1946. Who knows, an extra few months and I might have become a corporal like Stefan!

By the time our daughter, Wiesława [say, vee-ess-swarver], was born on 29 January 1947, Stefan had decided to exercise his right to stay in Britain but not to bother with the Resettlement Corps. Instead, having been discharged on 27 April 1947, and having changed our surname to Martin, he set up as a photographer in Matlock Bath, although his long-term employment was to be with the Qualcast engineering firm in Derby.

During our time in Matlock my far-flung family came together once more. Staszek, his schooling done in Palestine, arrived, but after a while moved to America, settling in Chicago, where his grandparents had worked.

Staszek, in Palestine, 1945

Janek, discharged from the RAF, stayed a while then emigrated to Australia. He wrote just once, advising that I should never come there, that it was too hot, that he had suffered sunstroke in the sugar-cane fields. After which I never heard from him again.

Juzek too, had come to England after a particularly traumatic war with the Second Polish Corps in Italy. In all, he had fought in ten major campaigns, including the Battle of Monte Cassino where he had won the Cross for Valour. It was clear, however, that stress had not sat easily on him, and after he too, left for Australia, we heard nothing more of him.

Juzek, Derby, 1945

There was just my dear Anna to come. As the African camps closed, she settled upon joining me in England. Possibly her protracted stay had purged the stress of Siberia and Uzbekistan. Certainly, not long after she arrived in England she met Michal Ulijaszek, a former Polish soldier and prisoner of war of the Germans, who had retrained as a coalminer, and they too enjoyed a happy and long-lasting marriage.

Our family odyssey was that of so many Poles, but I have always been grateful to the WAAFs for giving a meaningful direction to my life after the terrible years of disruption. In the course of that life I have, of course, had cause to weep on occasion over the years, but never again have my tears frozen. Nor have I ever again gone hungry.

Zosia Martin, 2014

Polish Air Force Medal, War Medal 1939–45: applied for fifty years after the event …

Leading Aircraftman Pat Thorpe, ground wireless operator

Pat Thorpe 1942

I might well have stayed on at Sleaford's Carre's Grammar School, in Lincolnshire, except that early in 1933, when I was fourteen, family circumstances forced me to leave and earn a living.

Having a natural affinity for horses I was taken on initially by Miss Kelly Dickens at her showjumping establishment near Newport Pagnell, but some time later I secured an appointment with Air Vice-Marshal Sir John Baldwin, the Air Officer Commanding the RAF College, Cranwell. My duties included 'stick and balling' his polo ponies – accustoming them to the sport – and attending him at the leading polo venues, at Roehampton,

Hurlingham, and Ranelagh, in London, and Cowdray, near Midhurst. My bread and butter task, however, was to supervise College equitation.

At that time Cranwell College cadets – until October 1933 still accommodated in the old naval huts across the road from the new building –, were expected to learn to ride like gentlemen as well as learn to fly, so while tutoring them I messed at the College, considerably easing my everyday expenses. After a while, however, I moved on, following Captain Smiley of the Rifle Brigade in the now familiar round of polo venues.

For anyone with a passion for horses it was a perfect existence, constantly engaged in jumping, hunting, and polo, and always with prime stock. Even so, intent on broadening my horizons, I then secured a place at top veterinary surgeon Eric Goodhall's establishment at Midhurst. I was employed to look after his pony and his hunters, but once Eric began entrusting me to carry out certain procedures, I determined to become a vet myself. By that time, however, the war had got under way, and when I felt obliged to hand in my notice I was gratified to have Eric ask me to come back when things returned to normal.

I still ask myself why I threw all this up when I could have stayed on for another year or two at least. And at this lengthy remove I have to admit that the word stupidity suggests itself. Mind you, I could also protest that I was approaching eighteen, and that there was indeed a war on. Anyway, I decided to join the Raff. And not only that, but to apply for aircrew. Yet why I opted for wireless operator/air gunner, again, I cannot say.

I went to the recruiting office in Lincoln, did some interviews, and was given a medical, but no aptitude tests that I can remember. Then I was sent home to await the results. On the morning before my eighteenth birthday a travel warrant arrived for the next day. Only to be countermanded an hour later by a telegram advising me that I was too young to join, and that I should continue to wait: even that early on, then, Air Ministry seemed somewhat confused in their plans for me.

Just five days later, however, on 24 Sep 1940, instructions came for me to report to RAF Padgate, near Warrington, for attestation and kitting up.

This routine procedure completed I became an aircraftman second class (U/T) – under training, or as we had it, 'useless' – and was sent on to RAF West Kirkby, near Liverpool, to No. 5 Recruits Centre for square-bashing. The real work, though, was to follow when my group was posted up to Scotland to a wireless training school being run from a college building just off George Square, in Glasgow. Times have changed, of course, but back then we had to salute every time we passed the war memorial!

The three-months' course was run at high intensity, so that, aspiring to operate the air-communications equipment of the day, we lived with morse code morning, noon, and night. For the most part we were immersed in sending plain language, but we were also introduced to a brevity system known as the X Code: so that, for example, X259 in morse, would tell the other operator, 'Receiving you loud and clear'.

The main technicalities were to wait until we reached the next training phase, which took me back to Cranwell, to one of the College's lodger units, No. 1 Radio School. And here I fell on my feet, because with my parents still being in Sleaford I was granted a sleeping-out pass.

This was another three months' phase in which both prospective ground and air operators studied all aspects of wireless theory, with additional airborne exercises for aircrew aspirants. For us, half the day would be spent on the ground, delving deeper into the technological aspects of air-wireless operating, the other half in the air where the bulk of the work was done in Blenheims. These were still worthy, and still being used on operations, though outmoded. By just how much, however, we could not have said, and yet there were portents. So when the buzz went about that something special was happening on Cranwell's North Airfield, we all packed over there.

Parked tail-on to one of the hangars, its shrieking engine hosing out a flaming exhaust that bade fair to buckle the metal panels, we found the weirdest aeroplane ever. For where was the propeller?

We would discover, of course, that this was the world's first jet-propelled aeroplane, the Gloster Whittle E28/39. It was 15 May 1941, and this was to be its first flight. The engine noise rose and rose as the machine made its way to the take-off point. Then, as the shriek hit ever higher levels it began to roll, very slowly at the start, then more quickly, and ever more quickly, until it lifted its nose and with unbelievable swiftness wailed upwards, dwindling to become but a black cross in the sky.

Our piston-engined Blenheims, of course, remained a different kettle of fish, but they served us well as the staff directed us through increasingly more demanding air exercises.

Wryly now, I have to recall how well it was all going. Receiving morse never proved the problem for me that it did for so many others, while I was perfectly comfortable with wireless theory. In fact, having completed the Radio School phase I had put up my lightning-dart Signals' armbadge and was confident that within weeks – after a gunnery course – I would be stitching up my 'AG' brevet; the armbadge and half-wing brevet together denoting the qualified wireless operator/air gunner. Indeed, sergeants' stripes too were in the offing, though this measure was taking time to be implemented.

Then, out of the blue, all trainees were called upon to re-sit medicals. At which stage I was discovered to have a colour blindness which utterly precluded me from any category of aircrew!

It was hard to take in. But there was nothing to be done. Everyone was sympathetic, and as a sop, having agreed to remuster to ground wireless, I was given my choice of posting, opting for Tangmere, because it was near Midhurst, and Eric's stables. In the interim I returned to the classroom, to become familiar with Codex, a device which automatically encrypted messages sent in 'plain-language' morse, and to delve into aerial arrays and the switchery of ground transmitters and receivers. Training completed, I duly left Cranwell in early June 1941, qualified as a wireless operator (ground) and in the established rank of aircraftman class two. In due course I would become an aircraftman class one, and on demonstrating that I could transmit morse – and more importantly, receive it – at twenty-five words a minute, a leading aircraftman (LAC). The rank of sergeant had retreated well beyond the horizon!

Then again, any hopes I'd harboured of riding while exercising my Service duties at Tangmere were dashed when I was warned for an overseas posting. No unit was specified but after a period of embarkation leave I found myself Glasgow-bound once again and on 31 July 1941 departed from Gourack aboard the SS *Orcades* bound for an undisclosed destination.

There was little to cherish about wartime trooping, my overriding memory being of stuffiness and bad smells. For someone used to the open it was particularly hard, especially as we were accommodated well below the water line, where there wasn't the slightest chance of getting fresh air.

We called in at Freetown, but Durban was the highlight of the trip out, for they gave us three weeks off there. And what a time we had! After the dourness of wartime Britain everything was so colourful, Durban being rightly renowned as South Africa's seaside playground in the sun. There was the combination of the warm ocean and tropical vegetation, with not far inland, the natural wonders of the Valley of a Thousand Hills. Then again there was the amphitheatre where outdoor dances were held every evening. But all too soon we were filing back aboard, this time, the SS *Mauretania*. And still without anyone having told me where I was bound.

That Air Ministry actually had a plan for me began to seem more likely when, having steamed up the Red Sea, we disembarked at Port Suez. The Canal, though was effectively closed, so we were trucked over the long, dusty drag north to Kasfareet, on the Great Bitter Lake. After just a short stay here they moved us on to Aboukir, near Alexandria, on the Mediterranean, where we arrived in late November 1941 and where, while I was still awaiting orders, the news broke that Pearl Harbour had been attacked by the Japanese, and that the Americans had entered the war on our side.

It seemed clear now that my lot was to be bound up with the desert army, at that time poised off to the west and awaiting what would be the second of Rommel's offensives. Except that at that juncture a definite posting arrived. To No. 258 AMES, which meant nothing whatsoever to me.

The acronym, it transpired, stood for Air Ministry Experimental Station, a cover name for a radar station (radar: radio direction finding and ranging), the openly-bandied term being RDF, or radio-direction-finding. The function of an AMES was to help secure air control, as had been so ably demonstrated during the Battle of Britain and, I now discovered, in Malta. Fixed installations, however, had a finite range. Wherever a need arose beyond that range, therefore, a mobile AMES would move into the field. And No. 258 AMES was just that, a self-sufficient mobile unit.

The way it was to work was that, having positioned, and set up shop, the radar – sorry, RDF! – types would interpret what their blips told them, after which we wireless chappies would relay the results to a central air-defence-control centre. To fulfil this task the AMES would have some fifty personnel under the command of a flight lieutenant, together with transport to carry all the equipment: we had a pick-up and four heavy Scammels and Bedfords.

The personnel included control-operators for the RDF, wireless operators (like me) for the communications net, technicians, drivers, RAF-policemen-guards, cooks, a medic, and certainly not least, GD erks, or General Duties airmen. The latter we rather unkindly likened to the army's Pioneer Corps, chaps not qualified in any specific trade, but able to turn a hand wherever needed.

Unlike a structured squadron a mobile AMES did not gell by design but rather evolved, with the trade divisions blurring, so that a brawny cook might find a shadow role as an aerial erector, a keen-eyed driver as an aircraft lookout. In No. 258, certainly, the pivotal man was the commanding officer, Flight Lieutenant George A. Chapman, a heady admixture of professional RAF and pirate. Equally key, though, was the adjutant, Flying Officer the Right Honourable Leslie E. Bainbridge Hawker, both a gent and a born fixer. It was no small thanks to the two of them that 'Chapman's Circus' coalesced as quickly as it did.

A circus setting up is, of course, the very model of co-operation, but in the early weeks at Aboukir our efforts fell far short of that. Indeed, shambolic springs to mind. The first task was to erect the aerials. Our W/T aerials were straightforward enough but those for the RDF required two eighty-foot masts, each bearing an aerial array, one for transmitting, the other for receiving. The masts were a two-piece wooden construct, the sections being fitted together while flat on the ground then swung into the vertical using a cantilever arrangement with sundry blocks and tackles. Equally essential, though, were willing backs, together with many grunts, groans, and split thumbs. Frequent cursing seemed to help, too.

We were not utterly without experience, for we had an initiate who had served with a mobile AMES at Tobruk and had now come back to spread his expertise. Swiftly then, our operation became more polished, each of us coming to know where and when a hand could best be given, and where each of the thousands of items of equipment could be located, produced at need, and then re-stowed for the next time.

My own expertise was limited to transmitting and receiving messages and to fumbling through the frequency changes called for as distances and conditions changed, each variation meaning inserting new crystals at best, and laborious and esoteric back-tuning of one coil to another at worst, particularly as no circuit seemed capable of holding its own integrity from one moment to the next.

As for the operational functioning of the unit, the radar-control element was highly specialised and I saw little enough of it, for when the radar watch I supported was on duty, so was I. But in both the radar field, and what I considered to be the more straightforward one of communications, constant drills helped to perfect techniques, and both Chapman and Bainbridge Hawker kept us busy at it.

AMES wireless station

It was not all slavery, however, and we did get time off. And with Cairo, like Durban, being very horsey, that suited my book fine. Indeed, it was on one of my forays that, to our mutual delight, I met up once more with a man I had last worked with years before in Britain, the imposing Chief Syce – loosely groom – Abdul Rahman Mahmood, of the world-famed El Gezira polo team of Cairo: and this amid the swarming millions of the Egyptian capital!

Head Syce Abdul Rahman Mahmood, with small sahib

Unfortunately, we were only to have that single encounter, for within days orders came for us to up sticks, and prepare to move. Only not westwards, into the desert, as we had assumed, but back the way we had come, down the long and dusty road to Port Suez.

We embarked on the SS *Neuralia*, the vessel, I realised, that had taken my career-soldier brother, Russell, out to India in 1936. Back down the Red Sea we went, although not without a disconcerting slew towards the coast at Massawa, in Eritrea – Italian Somaliland –, making us fear that cruel Authority might intend this as our destination. In the event, we sheered off, and headed instead for Aden where the ship bunkered, covering everything and everyone in coal dust.

The venerable garrison port, framed with sharp dun-hued ridges did not look too prepossessing and I doubt if anyone was that disappointed at not being permitted a run ashore. What we did get was our first sighting – if a relatively distant one –, of a fixed-site AMES, No. 240, I believe it was. Aden is basically the shell of a volcano, and the station's aerials were situated on the very highest point, on *Jebel Shamsan*. Though how they got their aerials up there I really didn't want to know.

Having left Aden we skirted the Arabian Peninsular and struck eastwards across the Indian Ocean, until, in late December 1941, we disembarked at Bombay, where indeed, we spent the Christmas holiday.

Early in the new year of 1942, though, we left India again, this time aboard the SS *Indrapoera*. And now where? As a medic friend was to write to me years afterwards, 'To-ing and fro-ing across the ocean one felt like a maritime gypsy looking for somewhere to settle. Any tendency to boredom was countered by endless rubbers of bridge, and solo whist. And I recall you, Thorpie, beating me at darts ...'

In fact, we steamed northwards, then turned left to the very far end of the Persian Gulf, passing close to the oil refinery at Abadan, then disembarking at Basra, in Iraq where, with surprisingly little chaos, thanks to all our practices, we got ourselves together and made our way to RAF Shaibah, a dozen miles to the south-west.

So this, then, was where our war was to be fought, the oil-rich Gulf! Even so, in lieu of further orders, we did not offload our trucks, Chapman deciding – perhaps with insider knowledge – that the moment we did so, we would be shifted elsewhere. And so we waited. For three interminable weeks.

Shaibah had been an established RAF station since 1920, but although there were several permanent buildings it was still pretty basic. Certainly my main memory of the place is mounting guard on a totally unrepentant hussar – I see his bright-red beret still! – who had got so brassed off with Shaibah that he had shot the cook – a true outflowering of what a popular Service ballad perpetuates as the Shaibah blues! I recall too its being so cold there that we set aside our KD (khaki drill), delved deep into our kitbags, and resurrected our Home Dress blue-grey.

But the Gulf was not be our battleground, it transpired, for after the three weeks we boarded the SS *Johan Van Oldenbarmeveldt*, a Dutch vessel, with such magnificent food that our curiosity about the destination waned somewhat. In fact, we reversed tracks, back to renew acquaintance with India, this time, though, at Bombay's Colaban Camp. Where life took yet another upturn. The unit was still accommodated under canvas but the tents were what was known as EPIP (English Pattern, Indian Produce), held just eight men, and even had electric light. Not only that, but with the Raj still very much alive, our every need was catered to. Though mere erks, all we did was drop our dirty kit on the floor and lo! next morning it appeared clean and parade-ground crisp.

There were servants for every task, all paid at an infinitesimal rate, just a few annas – pence – a day. So the *pani* (all same like Gunga Din!) carried water in his leather *bhishti* bag, the *dhobi* washed, the *mater* swept – as did the *matrani*, his female counterpart –, the *nappi* cut our hair (and might well have shaved us while we slept, as my brother had always maintained happened during his service on the North-West Frontier); the *bobagee* did our cooking, and the *dhurzi* could fashion anything in the way of tailoring we might call for. Being enlightened Raff chaps, we studiously avoided falling into the old-soldier solecism of adding wallah – as in dhobi-wallah – to the titles of these dedicated functionaries.

Off camp I spent wonderful times at the racecourse where the privileged many viewed the proceedings from sumptuous enclosures while the populace packed the areas before the rails. Daily, too, we were able to enjoy the Breach Candy swimming pool; we even formed an AMES soccer team. It really was a pleasant, and utterly eye-opening, if somewhat lotus-eating, interlude.

Where the conflict was concerned we still retained the belief that Air Ministry had a purpose for us, after all, our desert veteran, in regaling us with the successes of his AMES at Tobruk, had insisted that there was always a Plan.

Even so, time did seem to be dragging on. A month or so later, however, we received orders at last. We did a final drill, then packed for real, loading everything aboard a special train at Bombay's Victoria Terminus before being shunted eastwards across the breadth of India, to Madras. In fact, to Avadi Camp, an acronym standing for 'Armoured Vehicles and Ammunition Depot of India', part of a vast cantonment situated about twelve miles north-west of the city.

No settling in here, though, not for Chapman's Circus, for with only the briefest of delays we boarded the already steamed up SS *Neuralia* once again. And this time it did seem as if I might indeed be about to use my morse key in earnest, the sustained easterly heading showing that we were bound for Burma, where things were seriously hotting up. For unbelievable as it seemed at the time, impregnable Singapore had fallen. And before it, Malaya, and the Straits Territories. Now the triumphant Japanese had India in their sights.

Having reached the coast, we turned up the River Irrawaddy, taking a full day to reach the capital, Rangoon. I dare say it came as a surprise to others besides me to discover that it was on this selfsame river that the 'old flotilla' of Kipling's poem, *Mandalay*, operated, and not on some ocean bay across which a thunderous sun habitually came up out of China.

Only even now it was not to be circus time, for when we finally docked it was to find Rangoon in turmoil. The Japanese, we learnt, were only fifty miles away, at Pegu, and nearing fast. Accordingly we were turned about, to reboard the SS *Neuralia*, and make our way back down the Irrawaddy to the open sea, passing now black-billowing pyres as oil stocks were fired to deny them to the enemy. After which it was Madras again, though this time we were given time to settle and to enjoy the sun and, between drills, to luxuriate in such venues as the Stanley Club.

We were not left alone too long, however, for having re-loaded our vehicles we entrained northwards up the east coast, passing en route, Amarda Road, soon to become a base for B-29 Superfortresses. The wartime routing made this an epic journey of just under a thousand miles, one punctuated by halts during which we would troop to the engine to get boiling water to shave and brew up. Eventually, though, we entered Bengal, and reached Calcutta.

Our initial base here was Kharagpur Railway Settlement, a major maintenance depot. And what an eye opener to Indian society! We vaguely knew of the caste system, but this was a specialised, industrial form of it. The whole settlement was divided by avenues, the sweepers living in First Avenue, the executives in Sixth Avenue, house numbers within those avenues reflecting the resident's exact position in the pecking order.

Leaving Kharagpur we moved to Calcutta where we were accommodated on Dum Dum airfield, most notable for its mosquitoes. As one of our service policemen found having turned in without his mosquito net, to awake as an absolute mess of bites. Certainly, back then, nets were essential, indeed although things were changing, there were times when orders obliged us to wear the traditional, and virtually useless, sola topis, for protection against sun stroke.

Once again we seemed to be at a loose end. We kept up our skills, of course, for while setting up site took practice, so did taking morse at speed. Off duty, though, we had Calcutta at our doorstep.

For my part I was able to ride in the Maidan, the vast central park, but all of us were frequent visitors to Chowringhee, the main street, although as British other ranks we were barred from such officers-only establishments as the Grand Hotel and the nearby Great Eastern Hotel – Mark Twain's 'Best hotel East of the Suez'. Just the same, when it came to organising a foundation dinner for No. 258 AMES – 'First in India!' – our adjutant, Bainbridge Hawker, the great fixer, had the world-famous, green-shuttered

Firpo's Restaurant do the catering, then loaded the repast into hot boxes and drove it back to camp. Real style: notwithstanding that both other ranks and officers then partook using issue mug and irons.

Even so, perhaps such near exposure to the upper-echelon world went to the heads of two friends of mine, Jack Tweddle, a cook, and Joe Furness, a driver, from Derbyshire's Tideswell – the 'Tideswell Nightingale' we called him, by virtue of his singing voice! Whatever their motivation, a little later they wangled their way to Egra to bag a tiger. Having found one, Joe let fly with his 0.303 Lee Enfield, only to have the wounded tiger leap on his back and claw him from shoulder to buttocks. Fortunately Jack kept his nerve and managed to dispatch the poor beast with his own rifle before it could totally do for Joe – what scars though! Certainly they impressed my sons when, in later years, I took them to the pub Joe had, in Tideswell.

Self on left, with tiger hunters Joe Furness and Jack Tweddle

Back then, however, the Japanese threat to India had become very real. It was not all that long, therefore, before No. 258 AMES was sent some forty miles south, to Mathurapur, to finally set up shop. At last this was no practice, so we raised our aerial towers as if born to the task, every available hand heaving to get them vertical. Then, having established contact, I was able to give free rein to my morse key.

Once up and working our station became a critical part of Bengal's air defences, indeed, we had already plotted Jap recce flights overhead. Accordingly, work was set in hand to disguise the Circus as a Bengali village, scuds of labourers being drafted in to scoop out an acre-sized pool, then to erect native-style *busti* huts around it, the spoof dwellings lacking concrete bases but displaying mud-plastered bamboo walls and thatched roofs to any airborne spy.

As it happened, our camouflage was never to be tested. Or not by air attacks. For it was a natural force that struck, and in the form of a cyclone which battered the area for a full twenty-four hours and really was the most frightening experience. We were accommodated in firmly-built structures, even so these shook with squalls so strong that it was impossible to venture outdoors.

The aftermath was even more terrible, for besides the human toll and the material damage done, the crops were devastated and some ninety per cent of the cattle killed. The situation got even more desperate when drought set in to exacerbate the resulting famine. Even so one of the most distressing sights for us was to see flocks of vultures fighting with packs of pi – pariah – dogs over the carcases, and the cadavers! that lay about in their hundreds.

Despite our assiduous practice in becoming a slick here-today-and-gone-tomorrow concern, having finally become operational we were to remain on site for a full eighteen months! But busy days, at last! If interspersed, in my case, with two bouts of malaria, one of dysentery, and an attack of jaundice which saw me hospitalised at the Gopalpur Military Hospital at Orissa. Such trivialities aside, we ran a three-shift system, and aimed to send reports to the control centre every fifteen minutes. True, there were occasions when the ionospheric level which radio signals bounced off – the Heaviside Layer, fifty to ninety miles up – changed height, and we lost contact for a while. For the most part, though, we maintained the watch.

Our main task was monitoring the skies to the south-east of Calcutta, where we had most RDF range, though the screens were able to give adequate cover in other quadrants. Further, the overall coverage was vastly extended by wireless reports of enemy air movements sent from units in the field.

Where communications were concerned, constant activity quickly honed our skills, so that we could not only recognise the 'fist' of the distant operator but often dispense with more long-winded formal procedures, so that a bib-bip from one station, and a bib-bib-bib response from the other, would say all there was to be said. Indeed, we soon found that we could abbreviate virtually anything, whether plain or encoded language: yet today's devotees think texting breaks new ground!

As the months went by, however, and the fighting intensified, and especially as the Japs were first halted, and then pushed back, so the demands on the various AMES units changed; and I say 'various', for while we had been the first ostensibly-mobile AMES in India, we'd been followed by scores more. The need now was for forward reporting units, and many of them, spread across the fighting fronts. These were known as Wireless Observation Units, or WOUs – Woos, in the parlance –, some being staffed by three men, others by up to twenty. Personnel would include wireless operators, cooks, and general-duties men, all armed, but without vehicles, the equipment being carried by mules or ponies, or backpacked.

The WOUs took up position in the field – some moving north to the Imphal and Kohima areas where the Japanese were fighting savagely –, strung up an aerial, then eyed the skies, maintaining the fifteen-minute check-in schedule with air-defence control, but instantly transmitting back any actual aerial activity. Their base AMES', meanwhile, carried on the radar-location task.

My especial province became long-trek WOUs into areas where there were no roads, my facility with riding proving invaluable, albeit that the mules and even India's light, fairy-footed ponies – though kindred – were a far cry from the polo and hunting mounts of a few, now-so-distant, years before.

A WOU (Wireless Observation Unit) at Kultali Forest Station,
self on right

Once the Japs had been held at Kohima, however, and even before the push-back began, wireless-operator volunteers were sought for a WOU to be attached to No. 5 Royal Marine Commando, the unit tasked to spearhead the force committed to oust the Japs from the Arakan, the western coast of the southern extremity of Burma. Having been accepted, I became a member of No. 879 AMES and underwent a composite of infantry, jungle-warfare, and seaborne-assault training at a commando camp near Cox's Bazaar, some way south of Chittagong, making the first of what would be seven opposed beach landings at Akyab, further south still.

The drill for such assaults was that our flat-bottomed landing craft would run in under close air support, the ramps would go down, and everyone would storm ashore, splashing through the shallows, up the beach, then through the jungle fringe. We WOUs being burdened by paraphernalia, the marines would scamper ahead. By the time we caught up, therefore, they'd normally have quelled any opposition, and have taped a safe enough passage through any mines.

'Don't step over the effin tape,' their rearguard'd grunted as we puffed by on the first landing, 'or you'll effin lose your effin legs.' Accordingly we took great care where we put our feet in searching out a suitable reporting site. We'd then string our aerial up a tree, tune in, and get down to business of keeping our support aircraft, and control, aware of the situation.

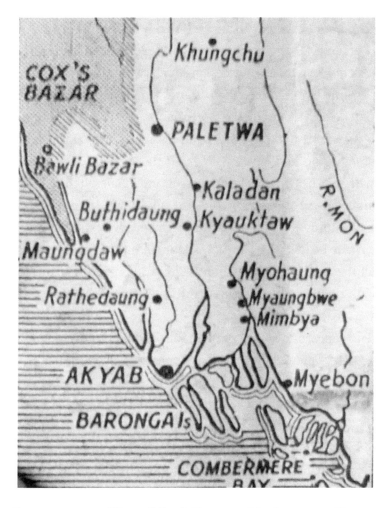

Contemporary Map of Cox's Bazaar–Myebon area, Burma

Ironically, it was RAF information which came closest to doing for me. And that on my sixth landing, and what was arguably the most significant of all such operations, the assault on Myebon, in Hunter's Bay, thirty miles south-east of Akyab. On running in we'd been amply supported with P-47 Thunderbolts softening up the beach defences. Only the planners – it transpired – had misinterpreted an RAF reconnaissance photo and timed things for the wrong tide state. When my own landing craft grounded, therefore, it did so on a sandbank which spilled off, not into inches of water, but into some five to six feet of the wretched stuff. Far too late, of course, for our beachmaster to remedy the matter, so down went the ramp.

Fair enough for the commandos, stripped to the buff for battle. We, though, were like Christmas trees, particularly us wireless operators with our back-slung Type-22 sets, the batteries alone weighing twenty tons – I swear! Not being a strapping six-footer (among our bearers I'd been known as *chota* – small – *sahib!*) the water closed up way above my head. Luckily, hands grabbed me, and I eventually made the shore. But it was hard going to cross, first the beach, and then the scrub and jungle, all the while choking and spluttering, shedding sea water and half drowned.

Such ventures, though, were always fraught, even without mishaps, for we'd normally be held there for a week or so until the sector was secured, aware all the time that Jap infantry were close by. In the nature of jungle operations, though, the only live enemy I saw were those being taken off to a prisoner-of-war compound.

'Weird thing,' one of the commando escorts commented, 'we 'ands 'em over and they're packed in, yet the compound never gets full.'

A mystery. But just conceivably to do with the fact that the compound guards were Ghurkhas who were never that partial to Japs.

Our own concerns, understandably enough, I suppose, had to be with creature comforts. For months now we'd subsisted on a mix of army and navy rations air-dropped by low-flying aircraft – Dakotas, Austers, and Lysanders – the aircraft driving in from the sea, then sensibly breaking away before overflying the Jap-haunted jungle. By the time we took Myebon, however, the Americans were round and about and in great strength. And how we welcomed them, with their 'K' rations: the Hersey bars, their high-quality toilet paper, and their coffee tablets, complete with milk powder and sugar!

Strange people, though, they'd rush to exchange their luxuries for the tins of bully beef we loathed! Sybaritic people too: I'll swear that even before a beach was cleared their engineers'd have rigged up a pipeline and fashioned a shower! And so generous! During our stay at Myebon they made over one of their jeeps to me so that I could rush up and down the beach during ration drops. Not quite as good for unwinding as charging through the shallows on a good steed, but with the added zest of knowing that the seat was packed with explosives so that the vehicle could be destroyed should a Jap counterattack succeed.

My seventh, and what turned out to be my final, opposed landing was that at Ramree. And this time everything went fine. Or rather, far, far better than just fine. For having crossed the beach, strung my aerial, and tuned in, I immediately copied a signal from headquarters telling me that my tour was up, and that the moment I produced myself back at main base, at Calcutta, I would be returning to the UK!

By this time Chapman's Circus, with all its splinter acts, had been fully employed for a year and nine months. There had been hard times, especially in the last phase, with the Royal Marine Commandos. Now, though, it was a question of getting myself up to Calcutta. My travel orders were to proceed by any means, so having collected my three rupees and eight annas 'hot meal and ice allowance entitlement', I thumbed a lift in a Dakota to Dum Dum and duly presented myself at main base.

And in the fullness of time, and having hitched westwards across the width of India to Bombay, there was the good old SS *Johan Van Oldenbarmeveldt* awaiting me for my eighth, and last ever, troopship voyage. No time-consuming passage around the Cape on this occasion, for by now the Med was open (VE Day had been celebrated a month back in Europe) and we used the Suez Canal. I had left the UK on 31 July 1941, and we docked in Glasgow on 31 July 1945. Gratifyingly, King George the Sixth had kept his bargain: married men, he had assured us before sending us off, were to serve three years overseas, single men, four. And he had ensured that I did so. To the very day.

I arrived back quite late, in a sense. But then I'd come a long way. In my absence my soldier brother Russell had transferred into the Airborne, been captured at Arnhem and spent nine months as a prisoner of war, yet was already home. On a particularly warm day in early August 1945 we sat together, waiting for the pub to open.

'Well, Babs,' he said reflectively, 'I finished my war. How long do you think it'll take to finish yours?' – *Bab's*? Family stuff …

I thought about it. I'd seen what fanatical fighters the Japanese were on the Arakan. And I thought back to an open-air film-news the Americans had shown about their taking of Iwo Jima (it was re-screened on TV only recently, nearly seventy years on!). The defenders had died, virtually to a man, the commentator stating drily, '22,000 Jap dead really gives Uncle Sam some sanitary problem.'

With that in mind, 'Fifteen years,' I said.

Some forecast! Two days later, and the Japanese war was over. Yet what moral controversy the use of atomic weapons ushered in! But consider the 'sanitary problems' for everyone concerned had the Japanese had been forced to fight for their homeland, having so tenaciously clung to scores of essentially worthless – to them – foreign beaches in the Pacific Islands and at least seven in Burma!

With disembarkation leave over, I reported in quick succession to Padgate, and then to West Kirby. After which I was posted to await my demob at Shepherds Grove, near Bury St Edmonds. And when it came through, I reported to Cardington, drew my demob suit and my trilby, but not my raglan overcoat – there wasn't one to fit, so that had to be sent on. I pocketed 110 clothing coupons, sixty pounds in cash, and hurried away to a further, and final, six weeks' paid leave.

On 15 May 1946, then, my six years of Service was done. Had I been wise, or foolish, to rush in when I had? What I fully appreciated was that had I not been colour-blind – a condition of no concern whatsoever in ordinary life – I would have become a wireless operator/air gunner, and almost certainly died on operations.

As for my new life, rather than take up the offer I'd been given of returning to Eric Goodhall's Midhurst practice, I applied to become a student at the Royal Veterinary College at Camden Town, was accepted, and awarded a grant. Only to find that returning servicemen had swelled the waiting list to five years. While pondering this, I took on a pub in Lincolnshire. But time passed, stirrings returned, and seeing a *Horse and Hound* advertisement for a job, involving horses, over in Sudbury, Derbyshire, I successfully applied. And one day, in the way of things, I had cause to enter the village shop, where I met the owner's daughter … After which my many-facetted life really took off.

Pat Thorpe, 2013

10. An Easy War

Flight Lieutenant Alex Peace, pilot

Sergeant Alex Peace, Elementary Flying Training School, Cambridge, 1940

I was brought up in Sheffield, and did well at school, but on leaving, and despite a keen interest in aviation – making models, reading books, and even having a flight with Sir Alan Cobham in an Avro 504 in 1933 –, I was unable to get taken on by any of the major aircraft firms. However, in September 1937, when I was eighteen, family 'pull' got me into Rolls-Royce in Derby – it were always thus, and still is at Rolls! –, where I began my studies in the Experimental Shop.

By the second year of my apprenticeship it had become clear that war was on the way, so in May 1939 I joined the RAF Volunteer Reserve as a trainee pilot. There was a stiff medical, but no aptitude tests, though I recall the shorter candidates being sat against a wall with their legs stretched out to determine if they would be able to reach the rudder pedals. On acceptance as aircrew cadets we became sergeants, began drilling, started learning the morse code, and spent our weekends at Burnaston airfield where I had an air-experience flight in a Magister but received no formal flying instruction.

On 3 September 1939 we listened to Neville Chamberlain – 'My long struggle to reach Peace has failed' – telling us that we were at war. Two days later I had been called up and sent to the Initial Training Wing at Hastings where we were accommodated in sea-front flats and began our basic training in earnest, and in particular the automaton-creating square-bashing, one of our drill instructors being tough film-star Victor Mclaglen's even tougher brother. And automaton-creating? Coming face to face with a bus conductor in a peaked cap, I instantly threw up a salute. We also refreshed our arithmetic and morse, and it was probably here that, as a result of general interviews, they decided whether they thought we would be suitable material for commissioning.

Even tougher than Victor Mclaglen ...

The next stage took me to Marshall's at Cambridge, at that time, No. 22 Elementary Flying Training School, where I soloed after some seven hours on Tiger Moths. What I especially recall, however, was drooling over a Gloster Gladiator, for me, at that time, the very epitome of aircraft design, standing on equal terms, it could be, with the other apple of my eye, the phenomenally successful racing Bugatti Type 35. In fact, I came very close to becoming the owner of a Type 35, a glorious example, too. I traced down its owner in India and offered the asking price of £150, only to learn that it had been sold just a week before. Nor did I get any closer to the Gladiator.

I thoroughly enjoyed flying training and having been used to motorbikes, cars and horses, took to it like the proverbial duck to water, certainly where seat-of-the-pants and light hands were concerned. I suppose this showed through, as I was recommended for fighters.

A fair bit of the time on Tiger Moths seemed to be spent in practising forced-landings, perhaps more than normal, indeed, as my instructor had a propensity for chopping the throttle over the pub at Caxton Gibbet, on Ermine Street. I'd put down in the field alongside, then he'd climb out, settle himself with a pint, and watch me carry on with the exercise.

As well as flying there were technical lectures, our bible being the two-volume *AP129*, an Air Ministry Publication which included virtually everything known about aircraft and their operation but was as dry as dust and never seemed to cover the point we wanted to know about. We also had educational talks, one in particular delivered to us by the 'Father of the Royal Air Force' Lord Trenchard. I'm sure his words were golden, but all I recall was his urging us to pee on incendiary bombs if they came our way.

Lord Trenchard, Father of the Royal Air Force

My next move was to No. 5 Flying Training School at Sealand, in Cheshire, an established RAF Station where every meal met the standard of what I imagined a Masonic banquet to be. Here, we flew the Miles Master, a performance step-up designed to bridge the gap between the slow Tiger Moth and first-line fighters. The Master was easy to fly, but had problems with its Kestrel engine which had a tendency to overheat on take-off and blow up. The Mark Two, with the radial engine, was much better and was said to compare well with the Hurricane in both performance and handling.

There was, I recall, an introduction to instrument flying, but very little of it, and although by the time we sewed on our wings we'd soloed at night, the flying we'd logged was mainly daytime, eyes-on-the-horizon stuff.

Now, with wings secured, I was among those appointed to a commission. There was no special knife-fork-and-spoon course, we simply moved into the officers' mess, and that was that, although in the course of time I received my commissioning scroll, stamped top-right with, 'Tenable for the duration of hostilities'. More immediately I fell into the hands of the reps from both Burberrys and Gieves, each intent on persuading me that I needed every conceivable thing on his firm's extensive – and very expensive – list, not forgetting a folding-tripod canvas washbasin!

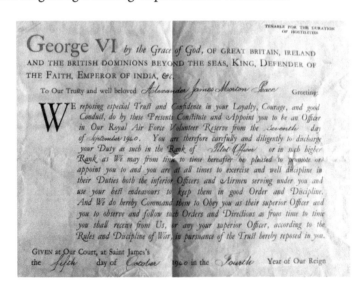

'Duration of Hostilities' commissioning scroll, 1940

In September 1940 I was posted to nearby RAF Hawarden, which was then No. 7 Operational Training Unit, to convert onto the Spitfire. The conversion consisted of boning up on *Pilot's Notes*, sitting in the cockpit as an instructor pointed out the various switches and dials, then getting airborne on your own. It may sound daunting, but from the start the Spitfire proved a delight to fly. You might say it was so sweet a machine that it flew itself, a quality of prime importance operationally, of course, for it allowed the pilot to concentrate on the job in hand rather than worry about the nuts-and-bolts of handling. Certainly, with my twentieth birthday looming, it left me speechless with admiration.

Admittedly the undercarriage on the early marks was a problem, for it had to be pumped up and down. Accordingly it was easy to tell a novice by the way his Spitfire bucked about until the wheels were retracted, after which things smoothed out again. It was undeniable too that with the Spitfire's undercarriage being so narrow, directional control on the ground could be debatable, though as we invariably landed into wind this was no problem.

Then again the airscrew on the Mark One was a two-pitch type and required some getting used to: set to coarse for high speed, then turned to fine for landing, it smacked of changing gear from top directly into bottom in a car. There was also the marked urge to swing on take-off due to the rotational effects of high power, but judicious use of stick and rudder readily counteracted this. Besides, these were mere niggles, and nobody could have failed to enjoy this phase of training.

It was now mid-September 1940, and as we were well aware, fighter casualties had soared: at that time, of course, the term 'Battle of Britain' had yet to be coined. With such losses in mind we were rushed through training, the powers that be envisaging that the high wastage of fighter pilots would continue. So it was that, unprepared as I felt, I found myself reporting to No. 74 (Tiger) Squadron, presently at RAF Coltishall, in Norfolk, and under the command of the celebrated 'Sailor' Malan. When I joined, his was already a name to conjure with, and to this day he remains one of the not-that-very-many people I take my hat off to. (Sailor? He was christened Adolph Gysbert Malan, gained the 'sailor' from his time in the mercantile marine, and his wife called him John.)

'Sailor' Malan

As a very new lad I began to settle in, discovering that the squadron had just been rotated to Norfolk from the south for a rest. I flew a few sorties, including a formation exercise during which, as we changed to line astern, the aircraft ahead of me took the tail off our leader. The leader's machine plummeted straight into the ground, but the number two, despite his mangled prop, managed to make a safe landing. As witness, however, I found myself being interviewed by the awesome 'Sailor' and the flight commanders, possibly as daunting an experience as seeing the tragedy unfold.

The investigation found that when the leader's tailplane had been cut off, the control wires had pulled tight, trapping the pilot's feet on the rudder bar. This happened because the Spitfire had two rudder pedals on each side, the lower set for ordinary flying, and an upper 'combat' set for use when tight manoeuvring was envisaged, the raised feet minimising blood-loss to the brain. With his feet trapped between upper and lower pedals, the leader had been quite unable to bale out.

My own most notable flight was when my undercarriage refused to lower. The squadron's Spitfires no longer had a manually operated system, using pneumatics to do the job, but though I tried and tried again over the course of a circuit or two I still couldn't get the wheels down. Then, just as I was about to declare to the world that I must belly land, I remembered the emergency air bottle, operated it, and got an instant undercarriage! My main feeling was of embarrassment for having even momentarily forgotten the emergency system, leading me to apologise to everyone remotely concerned, as if the original malfunction had been my fault.

Just under a fortnight after I joined them No. 74 was recalled to operations, to Biggin Hill, still the centre of much aerial activity. This faced me, of course, with the immediate prospect of battle. Yet still I'd never once fired my guns, not at a drogue, not even at a ground target, and there'd been no instruction whatsoever in air combat. Possibly had things been less hectic overall it would have been different, but that was how it was for me.

With the ease of long practice, the squadron gathered itself for the move. Until then, as a new boy, I had been rather out on a limb, the others knowing each other so well and having the shared bond of operational experience. All they'd gleaned of me was that I had a great interest in cars, and that I was Rolls-Royce trained. To them, that meant that I must be an expert on Rolls-Royce cars, and therefore in chauffeuring them: no use protesting that all I'd ever driven was a girlfriend's Austin Seven! So it was that the flight commander asked me to take his prized Talbot Saloon down to Biggin.

The others all took off and winged their way south, while I had a great time boring at high speed in their wake, propelled by aviation fuel the said flight commander had drained from an aircraft. I finally arrived at Biggin and returned the car to its owner, but was always a little miffed by his frequently repeated insistence that it 'had never been the same since'.

This flight commander, John Freeborn, was a personality in his own right. In the early days of the war he had been among those scrambled when two British formations had inadvertently been set upon one another. In the resulting melee he had shot down a Hurricane, killing its pilot. A court martial had exonerated him from all blame, however, and he was presently distinguishing himself, frequently being given operational control of the squadron by Malan.

Back at Coltishall, another of the personalities resting there had been Douglas Bader, the legless fighter pilot. At that time he was an acting squadron leader and commanding No. 242 (Canadian) Squadron which he had revitalised at Duxford. He was still busy developing the Big Wing strategy he and Air Vice-Marshal Leigh-Mallory were so keen on, and our squadron had flown along on some of the practices. The only time I actually encountered him, however, was during a doubles tennis match. Overreaching for a wide ball he overbalanced and fell. His partner reached to assist him, only to be brusquely waved off. Bader clearly wanted no assistance, and was not overly prissy-mouthed in saying so.

Douglas Bader

At Biggin the squadron moved back into action without delay. By this late stage of the conflict, though, casualty rates had fallen so much that it was no longer necessary to hurl new chums like me into combat, sink or swim, now we could be nurtured, then eased in. So it was that I saw out the last stages of what we were beginning to know as the Battle of Britain from a deck chair, watching contrails being etched in the sky, and counting home the operational pilots.

What I did do was manage to make several evening visits to London's West End, seeing the tube stations crowded with families seeking shelter from the bombing, hearing the bombs exploding myself, but discovering that the night clubs were still heavily frequented.

Families sleeping in the Underground

Eventually someone must have realised that I was, effectively, surplus to requirements with No. 74 Squadron, and I was posted up to RAF Kirton in Lindsey, north of Lincoln, to join No. 616 Squadron, the City of Doncaster (Auxiliary) Squadron. The tasks here were to patrol over convoys, and to attempt to intercept enemy intruders in the Hull area, the latter meaning, in practice, constantly being scrambled to intercept bombers we never saw.

There was a Boston flight too, trying out Leigh searchlights in order to identify enemy aircraft by night. At the same time attempts were made to make the Spitfire better suited to the night-fighter's role, the basic problem being that the flaring discharge from the exhaust stubs dazzled the pilot. A metal shield was rigged up to mask the flames but the experiment never seemed to amount to anything.

Also sharing the station was No. 121 Squadron, the second Eagle Squadron, Eagle being the generic name given to the units made up of American pilots who elected to join the fray before the United States entered the war. One character who stays in my mind is Vernon 'Shorty' Keough, who had been a pre-war parachutist and then a key member of the first Eagle Squadron. At just four foot ten inches tall, he was the smallest pilot in the RAF and required two seat cushions in his Spitfire. He went missing off Flamborough Head on 15 February 1941.

Another acquaintance I formed during this period resulted from my enthusiasm for guns: my first gun, at about fifteen, having been a French army Lebel, the 1886 pattern, 8 mm, ten-shot rifle – with bayonet – which cost me 7/6d [37.5p]. I remember my old-soldier dad observing, 'I don't mind you getting the rifle into good order but don't let me catch you sharpening the bayonet.'

Since then I'd tried out a fair number of guns – if not those on my Spitfire. But recently I'd paid ten pounds for a mail-order 0.38 Smith and Wesson nickel-plated revolver. There was another pilot on the unit, another Midlander, who had a similar interest. His name was Johnson, and although at the time he had already flown operationally, been decorated, and was four years older than me and a graduate civil engineer, we became quite pally. He had a 7.62 Luger automatic which I immediately coveted. So we did a swap. After which I pretty well lost track of him. Left to his own devices, however, J.E. 'Johnnie' Johnson became the highest-scoring Allied pilot (with thirty-eight confirmed kills), remained in the RAF, and retired as an air vice-marshal.

Johnny Johnson

At least I finally got to try out my Spitfire's guns at Kirton, if not in anger. And flying alongside such illustrious company who knows what might have happened? Except that, in boarding my aircraft on a scramble, I slipped off the trailing edge, crashed to the ground, and hurt my right wrist. Examining it at station sick quarters, the Eagle Squadron's doctor, doing duty man, gravely decided that, being badly sprained, it needed strapping up. It was, in fact, broken in two places! Hardly surprising then, that even with the recommended strapping, I found myself unable to handle the stick. As a result, after various consultations, and as the wrist didn't appear to improve, I was posted as a Link-Trainer instructor to RAF Heston, where a Spitfire Operational Training Unit (OTU) was forming.

Left: Self, at RAF Kirton in Lindsey, 1941, with yet undiagnosed doubly-broken right wrist. Right: Link Trainer

It was here, five months after my fall, that the double break was finally discovered, when Heston's medical officer, failing to detect any improvement, sent me to the RAF hospital at Halton. There, they mulled over giving me a bone graft but eventually decided that comparing X-rays showed that a slow healing was, in fact, under way. And so I was sent back to Heston with my arm in plaster, to carry on in the Link Trainer, first swotting up, and then instructing on blind flying and – at an essentially fine-weather Spitfire training unit! – beam-approach landing techniques!

In due course the now fully-formed No. 53 (Spitfire) OTU, moved to RAF Llandow, near Cardiff, where the station commander was the well decorated Group Captain Ira Jones, celebrated as a scout-cum-fighter pilot with my old squadron, No. 74, in the First World War. He had remained in the Service until 1936, then retired, but had been called back to the active list in 1939. He was a larger-than-life character, a Welshman with a pronounced stutter, who loved a drink, and would have given anything to have been allowed to have a go at increasing his score of First World War kills, a total variously given as either 37 or 40.

Ira Jones

He was very taken to find that I had recently been flying with his old unit, but my abiding memory of him was when he got a bee in his bonnet about pilots leaving their undercarriages down too long after take-off. This, he pointed out, lost them valuable seconds when scrambling for action, for the earlier the wheels came up the sooner the Spitfire became its sleek, speedy self. Accordingly he announced that he would do a demonstration. With every eye on him Ira roared off down the runway. At not-quite take-off speed, however, he hit the notorious Llandow bump, was thrown into the air, selected his undercarriage up nonetheless, and promptly settled back onto his belly. When we reached the wreck and began to release him he was muttering, 'I m-must have hit an air p-pocket.'

But then he was no stranger to crashes, writing in 1938 that as a pupil pilot he had learnt to avoid injury by taking his feet off the rudder bars just before impact and tucking them under the seat, a technique he had proved in twenty-eight crashes. Which made the show he'd laid on for us his twenty-ninth.

Seeing the CO put up such a black might have been of some comfort to a pupil who took off from Llandow, got lost, and eventually put down at St Athan. Unfortunately, he got confused with the position of his undercarriage – most likely forgot to lift it after getting airborne from Llandow – so that on his approach he made the selection blindly, put his wheels up instead of down, and bellied in, damaging the aircraft but walking away unscathed himself: just as Ira had. It just might have been some comfort, but then he was a pupil, and Ira was the CO. And a hard man, to boot.

Even so, poor Ira, I might say. Deep in one of the hangers was a relic from older days, an Avro 504K, which Ira would drool over. The time came, however, when, paying yet another nostalgic visit, he found an airman, not only sitting in the cockpit but waggling the controls.

'What the hell do you think you're doing?' Ira demanded wrathfully.

Recognising his CO, the airman immediately scrambled out, and stood to attention.

'Well, Sir,' he offered respectfully, 'it *is* my aeroplane.'

The aerodrome was partly on requisitioned land, and he was the son of the landowner.

One of my own trips might have had a similar outcome to those Ira specialised in, when I got airborne and found that I had no reading on my airspeed indicator. At that period – with scrambling being the order of the day – the norm was that the groundcrew prepared the aircraft for flight, after which the pilot would sit by the dispersal hut waiting to be called. When the call came it was a matter of sprinting to the aircraft, clambering onto the trailing edge – preferably without tipping arse over elbow –, being helped to strap in, and then getting airborne with the least possible delay. On this occasion the pitot-head cover had been left on. Most embarrassing. But no real problem, for the Spitfire was such a wonderful machine that one could sense when it was happy with the airspeed, and with just a little more concentration on the 'feel' than normal, I was able to land without mishap.

Another strand of my job at Llandow was to command the Air-Sea Rescue flight, flying a Lysander over the Bristol channel whenever summoned. My learning to fly the machine was a question of a circuit hanging over the back of the pilot I was to replace and watching the way he did things. After which he left on posting, and I became the expert. But in the context of soloing in unfamiliar machines I remember being so impressed as a Spitfire did an impeccable touchdown, and even more impressed as a diminutive, and shapely, young woman emerged, forcing me to reflect that Air Transport Auxiliary pilots like this lass moved from type to type with even less instruction than I had.

Even before my wrist healed properly it had become disturbingly evident to me that once the training world got its teeth into a pilot it regarded him as its own property. In endeavouring to get free of its clutches I had time and again sought out my various flight commanders to plead with them to get me back to where I might finally fly on operations. They were all sympathetic, but nothing came of my pressing. Indeed, I soon found myself posted yet again, only this time even further from an operational unit. In fact, back to Derby, to the Rolls-Royce Aero Engine school where RAF maintenance personnel were taught about the firm's various engines.

My role was to run a supplementary section of the school designed to teach engine handling to aircrew: to pilots, and a trickle of that new breed, flight engineers. The requirement for this, I discovered, was driven by a change of strategy. Hitherto fighters, especially, had been required to get airborne with minimum delay, meet the incoming bombers, fight, and return to base. In the limited time this took the engine would, effectively, be run at full bore, often at combat boost. Now, with the fight being carried across to the Continent by both fighters and bombers, lengthy, far-ranging, sorties were called for, so that 'miles per gallon' became the aim, the mantra being 'High boost, Low RPM': a technique that could halve the fuel consumption.

The five-day handling course was taught by RAF pilots with Rolls-Royce experts in support. As for our students, they came from all the user nations, did the handling at Derby, then visited Hucknall to liaise with Rolls' test pilots.

The value of the training was clear enough, but being full of youthful vigour I regarded it as a soft posting, resenting it for continuing to prevent me from engaging in operations. This was especially the case once the course was running smoothly and I could use the company's communication-flight Spitfire to make visits and talk engines with operational pilots. Only I had nobody to moan to. Indeed, from this time on – and arguably without precedence in the Service – I was never again to find myself in a role where I was directly responsible to a senior officer.

In desperation, determined to force my way to the very top and argue my case to get onto ops, I presented myself at Fighter Command Headquarters at Bentley Priory. I fancy, though, I was finally fielded off by a leading aircraftman clerk or the like, and the trip accomplished nothing whatsoever.

Quite likely, the reverse, for shortly afterwards I was contacted by Rolls' chief test pilot, Squadron Leader Ronnie Harker. An inspection tour of the Middle East had convinced him that an engine-handling school out there would pay dividends. If I was interested in setting up such a unit, he told me, he would make the necessary recommendations to Air Ministry. Despairing of ever getting onto ops in Europe, a switch of theatre seemed to offer at least some chance. And within weeks I found myself at sea, en-route to RAF Station Heliopolis.

The vessel I sailed in was the RMS (Royal Mailship) *Highland Brigade*, operating for that voyage as an RAF transport. The division of responsibilities on board was clear cut, the ship's crew ran the vessel but left all passenger concerns to the Officer Commanding Troops – the OC Troops. In this instance the 'troops' were predominantly airmen who travelled in rather cramped conditions in the holds, sleeping in hammocks, and battened down for the most part, the hatches being lifted periodically to relieve a little of the fug. There was a small detachment of Seaforth Highlanders, a few ATS and army officers, and a scattering of RAF engineering and administrative types, some relatively senior. Finally there was a number of naval prisoners being sent on some form of a punishment posting.

The accommodations proved first-class for officers and men alike and for my part I settled back to enjoy a luxury voyage to foreign climes. But, the best laid plans! For shortly after departure the OC Troops, a wing commander, fell ill, died, and had to be buried at sea. And my days of ease were at an end. The RAF warrant officer for the draft flung me up a quivering salute and advised me that, although not the highest-ranking RAF officer on board, I was the only representative of the senior branch of the Service – the General Duties (Flying) Branch –, that I was, therefore, Officer Commanding Troops.

Fortunately this stalwart knew all the ropes and was able to take most of the weight off my untrained shoulders. Or at least, until the day when the imprisoned sailors, breaking free, disarmed the hapless RAF tradesmen on sentry-go, and raided the liquor store. After which I was suddenly OC Troops of a ship full of drunken sailors running riot.

I found myself confronting one who presented himself at the door of the officers' lounge where the ATS ladies were sheltering. He was wielding a whisky bottle in one hand and an open, cut-throat razor in the other. My instinct was to seize a bottle from the bar and bring it down on his wrist, but on seeing the disapproving headshakes from some army officers sitting well back from the action – but now, at least, looking up from their newspapers and chessboards –, I resorted to shouting at him instead, at which he ran off.

Eventually, aided by the one or two airmen I could find willing to interest themselves in the matter, it became a case of chasing the sailors into the very bowels of the vessel, though as they seemed to know all the crannies I soon saw this to be hopeless. In despair I approached the Seaforth's officer for assistance. Without hesitation, he deployed his men, and the mutineers were rapidly rounded up. In the aftermath I was haranguing a group of recaptured prisoners at the foot of a companionway when one began to get shirty. The Seaforth officer gave a rather bored nod, at which the nearest jock brought his rifle down on the bolshy's head, abruptly ending all resistance.

So we returned the sailors to their detention, lodging two in a padded cell we found below – a padded cell, ready fitted, on a luxury liner! –, and unloading the lot at Durban, the first port of call.

I took advantage of the free time we had in Durban to visit an aunt of mine, duly finding my way to her bungalow only to have a neighbour tell me that I'd just missed her, that she'd gone to another property up-country and wouldn't be home before my sailing time. And even that turned out to be a moveable feast, for when I arrived back alongside I was told that I was to transfer immediately to a vessel even then preparing to get under way. I promptly gathered up my kit, said farewell to the warrant officer, and hurried aboard. To find myself Bombay bound!

No flying, then, let alone operational flying, but things were looking up; first Africa, and now India! A lot less luxurious this new vessel, but I found the facilities fair enough, and after all, India beckoned. As did another shipping-company official, though, once we docked at Bombay. I was just in time, I was told, to transfer to a vessel even now getting up steam. For Aden.

So much for India. But now, Arabia! Only there was to be no getting ashore there, not for any length of time, for the ship did its business at Aden, and steamed on, to finally drop me at Port Suez, at the far end of the Canal from Heliopolis. However, Canal or not, no more ships for the world traveller, only, for all my youthful stamina I must have been jaded by then, for the rail journey up to Heliopolis via Cairo left no impression at all.

Heliopolis, the RAF Headquarters, I discovered, was a sizeable and long-established cantonment, the station housing, among other units, a large maintenance unit (MU) where aircraft were rotated for major servicing. I have to say at once, that, no doubt hearing of my imminent arrival – and my desire to see some operational flying –, the Axis forces had given up the fight in the North-African desert: Monty from the east and Operation Torch from the west had proved too much for them. So it was that whenever I found time to get into Cairo it was even more of an eye-opener than it might have been, lit up in pre-war style and with all manner of goods on offer.

When I reported in nobody seemed to know anything about my mission, but eventually a works-and-bricks man (Air Ministry Works

Department) joined me for a planning session during which I sketched out my requirements: classrooms, a bay for two engines – the in-line Merlin, and a radial type –, storerooms, and offices for the staff. He soon found an empty building which could be converted to my requirements and work got under way. In the course of time more pilot-instructors were sent out from the UK while locally I was given the services of three very enthusiastic chaps, a corporal and two airmen, who were only too glad to get away from their more routine tasks.

Had I known it, my last chance of getting back to an operational unit had gone, for now I was not only in a training environment but overseas too. Not that I had that much time to brood, for we could hardly have been busier, with so many units in the theatre feeding us pupils, notable among them Spitfire pilots from the Egyptian Air Force.

In any spare time I still kept my hand in at flying, particularly after a ferry pilot dropped a Harvard off at the MU. I'd asked, a little tentatively, if I might fly it, to be told straightly that it wasn't his, and that I could do what I liked with it. After which I was able to get airborne regularly, including taking the occasional jaunt to Jerusalem. However, we'd been given free access to the prestigious Heliopolis Sporting Club, and I spent most off-duty time at their swimming pool.

Where the job was concerned, it remained the case that I never did have anyone to report to, and perhaps this rubbed off, for I clearly upset one seriously senior officer. He'd expected his aircraft – a Fairchild Argus which he used as a runabout – to have been refuelled and ready exactly when he wanted it. When he discovered he would have to wait another ten minutes, he became extremely angry. 'Really, Peace,' he flung at me, before departing skywards once again, 'you should realise that I am, in fact, a very important person.'

I suppose I might have become quite an important person myself, for just days later I was rung up by a staff officer who was rationalising establishments in the theatre. 'What about that post of yours,' he opened, 'that rates a squadron leader, surely? We'd better promote you.' But as the school seemed to be ticking along nicely under a mere flight lieutenant I assured him that there wasn't work enough in it for a senior officer. And so stultified what might have been a heady rise to power.

The war ended, and in the course of time my sailing orders arrived. I travelled by sea as far as Marseilles, then entrained – in a British rolling-stock coach! – to the Channel, and so back home.

After various leaves and clearing procedures, I returned to the engine school at Rolls-Royce, to find it short-handed, the Service personnel having been demobbed. I became a manager, met and married Dorothy, my wife – with whom I enjoyed fifty-nine happy years – and gave little enough thought to flying and to the RAF. Many years later a young man did turn up asking to take down my story for an oral-history bank. Having got his recording he was quiet for a moment, then he said reflectively, 'So you had an easy war then.'

An easy war? Certainly, it was once suggested that I was kin to the doorman of the Dorchester, having done nothing myself, but having met so many of those who had. And yet, but for slipping off that trailing edge! Perhaps, had that not happened, I would not on occasion even now feel anywhere near so keenly the guilt of being a survivor.

Alex Peace, 2013

11. We Too Kept 'Em Flying: A Vignette

Stella Read, civilian fabric worker, Vickers-Armstrongs (Aircraft) Ltd, Weybridge

Stella Read, 1941

I was 16 when war broke out and already working for Vickers, in Weybridge, as a fabric worker, cycling there from Staines for every shift. Or at least, until I became engaged and my husband-to-be, Len Crofts, from Egham, began taking me on his motor-bike.

Throughout my time at Vickers we were building the Wellington, to my mind, the most significant bomber of the Second World War. After all, it was to serve the RAF from 1938 right through until 1953. That other one – with four engines – yes, the Lancaster –, you always hear about that. But I've always said that the Wellington was never given half the credit it deserved; it should have been praised much more, bearing the brunt, as it did, for so long. For a start nobody at Weybridge ever called it anything but the 'Wellington', never the 'Wimpy'. It was respect. There was something about it that drew the affection of everyone who came into contact with it, whether factory worker, groundcrew, flier, or public at large.

Vickers' workers assembling geodetic frames

One thing that made it special was the geodetic framework. The fuselage, the tail, the wings, they were all geodetic. Bar the wing tips, which were ordinary metal. Our job as fabric workers was to cover the geodetic. In some areas we'd use wooden strips, pre-drilled with screw-holes, and press them into receiving recesses in the geodetics. Then we'd lay the fabric – the skinning – over the geodetic and use pump-action screwdrivers to secure it to the wood, finally taping over the screw heads. In other places we'd spread the fabric over the geodetic then lay wire along the framework, securing it using hooked needles and waxed string. We'd bring the needle up, over the wire, and down again, all along. All very neatly, of course; our version of the Victorian sampler, we'd say. And finally the whole skin would be doped. We were so proud of the finished job!

After some time on the shop floor I joined Amy, a cousin of mine, in a gang sent on detachment around the various operational airfields in order to patch up the more seriously damaged machines. It was painful to see the way some of them limped home, with an engine stopped, perhaps, and at times with simply enormous amounts of fabric missing, not to say rear turrets; fortunately, in such cases the underlying, and virtually indestructible, geodetic frames had seen them through.

Simply enormous amounts of fabric missing ... not to say rear turrets ...

The Indestructible Wellington

What was particularly poignant was when the RAF chaps would keep us girls back from the damaged Wellingtons until they'd hosed down the interiors, the need for such preparation speaking for itself.

Not every part of these detachments was heavy, however, and certainly not when we were at Mildenhall working alongside No. 149 Squadron during the filming of *Target for Tonight*. A sectioned Wellington was set up in a hangar and I was able to help with re-attaching the fabric, and generally showing the film people how things went: strangely I'd find myself doing the same thing for the staff at the Brooklands Museum at Weybridge during a visit over sixty years later!

What made the 1941 film stand out was that they didn't use actors but genuine RAF aircrew. Dicky Bird was the rear gunner, the observer was Alex Moon, and the second pilot, Gordon Woollatt; a very friendly, unassuming bunch. The one nobody could forget, of course, was Percy Pickard, the pilot, who went on to make such a name for himself, carrying out some very daring raids, particularly his final one when he led a force of Mosquitoes in bombing the ground-level parts of a prison to free prisoners held in its upper storeys. He was killed during the raid and it was said that the French wanted him to be awarded the Victoria Cross, though whether they gave him anything themselves, I don't know.

Another of those I met on the film unit was the WAAF officer, Constance Babington Smith, who later discovered where the Germans were developing their V-2 Rockets.

Constance Babington Smith

The filming aside, we'd always be made much of when we were with the RAF, which was wonderful for us, being so young, though Len wasn't that keen on my going. The objection he actually raised was that being on operational stations was too dangerous. Fortunately, none of the airfields was ever attacked when I was on detachment, but in truth it was what he saw as my flirtatiousness that worried Len. And in fact I have to admit to brazenly accosting a soldier I came face to face with in Lincoln, right up in the midlands.

'Hello!' I beamed. Only to have him stalk by head high. 'You *are* allowed to talk to me, Paddy,' I called after him, 'I am your sister-in-law.' It was my sister, Flo's, husband!

To give Len credit, though, both he and I had been on shift on 4 September 1940 when, during our lunch break, and while the afternoon shift were clocking in, the Germans had bombed the Weybridge factory, killing eighty-three workers and injuring 419. Lucy Fuzzins, who was to marry my brother, Eddie, survived unhurt, though emerging puzzled, complaining, 'I couldn't think why this man suddenly threw himself on top of me. I'd never set eyes on him before.'

As I have said, we were all so very proud of the Wellington. And how proud we were too, to have served, even temporarily, alongside all the lads, and the many Service lasses, who kept our creation fit to do its job. Working in the factory was satisfying enough, but being out there on the airfields, seeing the Wellingtons go off, then hours later, seeing them come home, is what comes to mind whenever I reflect that, even as unseen factory workers, we were among the many who could boast, yes, indeed! we kept 'em flying.

Stella Crofts, Weybridge 2010

12. The Eavesdroppers

Leading Aircraftwoman Barbara Hutton (née Wood), ground wireless operator

Leading Aircraftwoman Barbara Hutton, Isle of Man, 1944

I was born in 1922, in Rochdale, and on leaving school took a job working for a firm that made footwear; quite inexpensive footwear, you might say cheap and cheerful, though I liked the slippers in particular. It was basically a family firm with just a couple of young men working alongside me, but after 1939 both were called up for War Service, one going into the army, the other into the RAF.

Although men were conscripted at eighteen, that early on there was no call-up for women. By the time I was twenty, however, the government were conscripting women aged twenty to thirty, offering a choice of either the armed forces or munitions work. A year later men would get an additional choice, lucky lads! they could become Bevin Boys, and work down the mines. Munitions didn't appeal to me: I'd had a cousin taken to work in that line and the chemicals turned her yellow! When my time came to register, therefore, I had no hesitation, and opted for the armed forces, and specifically for the Women's Auxiliary Air Force (WAAF): I wasn't that keen on khaki.

I knew nothing about the women's branch of the air force, but during recruit training lecturers told us that before the war its work had been done by what were known as the 'Royal Air Force Companies' of the Auxiliary Territorial Service, the ATS. Had the WAAF not been formed, therefore, I would have served in khaki after all.

Even before that, it had been made clear to us that while the WAAF was to help the RAF, it was to remain quite separate from it. Even at the recruiting stage we were assured, 'There is no question of W.A.A.F. personnel flying'. Neither was there a question of us bearing arms, notwithstanding which, a year or so later I'd suffer a sore shoulder after firing off a 0.303 rifle! Even so, despite such indulgences as not having to fly, and not being required to riddle people with machine guns, we'd be getting paid at quite two-thirds the rate of men in equivalent trades.

As for those trades, initially, we learnt, the WAAF had preferred women who were already qualified before joining. But that had been when it offered just five trades. When I joined, though, there were some twenty-six to be filled. Before we could declare a preference, however, we had to prove ourselves suited to Service life.

On 4 February 1943, having presented myself at the recruiting office on the date prescribed by my call-up papers, I was given a medical, filled in various forms, was interviewed, swore to be faithful to the King, at least for the duration of the present conflict, and received a railway warrant authorising Aircraftwoman Class Two Woods to travel (third class) to somewhere called RAF Innsworth, way down south near Gloucester. I did have time for a quick visit home, however, before reporting, calling in too, at my former workplace. The latter visit, in its own way, was rather sad, for the semi-retired family who owned the firm were unable – or unwilling – to switch to more lucrative fields, for example, to the production of uniforms. Even so, it survived the war.

RAF Innsworth was a large, permanent station which, among other units, housed No. 2 WAAF Depot. Here we were to spend six weeks doing recruit training, getting to know the Service, and getting to know each other. Although there several brick barrack blocks, our intake was accommodated in large wooden huts each holding some thirty girls. Oh! and equally important, it being February, a centrally located coal-burning stove which had to be both kept alight and black-leaded: 'bull' being the key at recruit training.

For a lot of the girls it was the first time away from home, so the first week or so saw many a sob scene. It was my first time too, but I seemed to thrive on it. Strange as it may seem, and despite the aim of our stay there being to have us conform to authority, it could well have been my first taste of real independence.

Early mornings and late evenings were spent in domestic chores like sweeping floors, aligning beds down the hut, making up bedding into blocks, arranging kit-layouts for the daily barrack-room inspections, washing and ironing of kit – on scrubbed-white deal tables – and polishing shoes. The days themselves saw us busy with lectures, on everything from pay to personal cleanliness, and moral living. We learnt a smattering of Service history and customs, rather more of Service law, certainly enough to know that once we were given walking-out passes we could be shot for not being back before lights out. We had, of course, joined a fighting service.

When we were not in the classrooms we were on the barrack square, a vast expanse we got to know intimately. Most of us found square-bashing enjoyable enough, although both the RAF and the WAAF drill instructors were adept at the most colourful set-downs.

'Aircraftwoman Wood, you about-turn like a –'

Well, like something unprintable. But I have to say that their ribald observations were invariably funny and certainly lightened the atmosphere.

Then again, the WAAF sergeant in charge of our intake was like a mother to us. And we were young, of course, indeed, I celebrated my twenty-first while I was training.

Drill became part of our lives, for wherever we went, we marched: to the cookhouse – with the steaming, malodorous, scum-surfaced zinc trough provided to rinse off our 'mug and irons' after eating; to the lectures, to physical training, to pay parade: as recruits we got one and four a day (5.5p), plus fourpence (1.67p) war pay; to stores to be issued with our uniforms, after which we were marched back to the billets laden with everything from 'Undergarments WAAFs for the use of', through sidepacks, and a white kitbag, to coarse grey-blue battledresses, and greatcoats: a one-pound ten shillings (£1.50p) fine for losing the latter – or for not having it to hand in on the far-off day of your release. Subsequently we would be marched back again for various fittings, until, after ten days or so, we were all fully kitted out.

What we said about certain items of the equipment, should perhaps, be left unmentioned. It would be impossible, of course, to universally please any collection of women when it came to clothing, especially with uniform being specifically designed to minimise individuality. Some girls found expression by wearing the lisle stockings inside out, so that the seams showed; then again, seams could be ironed into garments where none had been looked for, though most us were satisfied with folding the skirts – they had six gores – and putting them under the bedding, after which, being wool, they took on perfect creases. In a similar way hats could be variously coaxed into a more desirable shape – they could never find one small enough for me so I had to pack mine out with paper. All in all, though, I think most of us felt that the uniforms were smart, if falling somewhat short of actually being fetching. Undeniably, trying them out in the billet furthered the process of us getting pally – surely one of the aims in crowding us together! – so our comments, whether for or against, were uninhibited to say the least.

Indeed, the barrack room was like a melting pot of society, for there were girls from all backgrounds. Certainly, reactions to the periodic FFI inspections – freedom from infection: an extremely intimate, yet communally-mounted, health check – were markedly varied. The majority, of course, were ordinary lasses, but there were others who seemed to me a cut above. Some of these would later be taken off to become officers, but I seemed to get on with all of them, whatever their – well, class, as we used to say. Then again, with such a jumble of different types, and with little enough to do in the long, winter evenings but write letters home, make down our beds, and listen to the wireless, the barrack room might have been viewed as a little university. Undoubtedly, despite the daily regimentation, and now the uniform dress, you really did see personalities develop.

This was particularly the case when we were confronted by the various trades the Service needed to be filled. All the medical branches were out, of course; you had to be qualified. Except that you could be trained as an orderly: though they seemed to specialise in bedpans ... And I had not the slightest interest in mechanical things, which ruled out driver, or any sort of mechanic, popular though such things were to many of the girls. Then they wanted clerks, but that smacked of office work, and I had avoided that – and serving in shops– on leaving school. There were openings for waitresses, and for batwomen, but although some girls went for it, I decided that I didn't join up to become a skivvy. I felt almost the same when it came to becoming a cook. Of course, this had its attractive side, one always had to prepare food. And there was so much to learn. But the thought of slaving three or four times a day over great greasy cauldrons full of soup, or stew, or worse still, cabbage, turned the stomach. It was beastly enough when we had to scour utensils during stints in the 'tin room' on cookhouse fatigues.

The list of trades seemed exhaustive. And as they worked through it and course members expressed their preferences, I narrowed down those that might interest me. One of these was, in fact, clerk, but clerk (special duties). Then there was radio operator: although before being accepted there was a selection board, which I didn't fancy. And there was wireless operator, which required good arithmetic, spelling and English; all of which seemed fine. There was also teleprinter operator, but preference was given to girls who could already type. I suppose, in the end, the pay rate might have had something to do with swinging the balance between the four.

The trades were divided into groups from Two to Five, with Group Two being highest paid. Teleprinter operator, clerk (special duties), and radio operator were all Group Four, but wireless operator was Group Two and, at 2/4d (12p) a day (plus war pay) brought in 2d (0.84p) more than the other three. In the event, whatever I based my decision on, wireless operator was the one I plumped for.

Recruit training carried on, with girls periodically being called away from the drill square or lecture room for interviews. Not all were accepted for the trades they wished to enter, but I was fortunate, and although they recommended that I train as a flight mechanic, they agreed to my choice of trainee wireless operator. When the course ended, therefore, I was posted to do my trade training at No. 3 Radio School at Compton Bassett, in Wiltshire.

RAF Compton Bassett, a mainly-hutted camp ...

RAF Compton Bassett, I discovered, was a very large, mainly-hutted camp set pretty well below the Cherwill White Horse, and not that far from Calne: home of Harris's sausages. Throughout the war virtually all the RAF's communications personnel were trained either at Compton Bassett or at nearby Yatesbury, so there were thousands of trainees, undergoing scores of courses. Male trainees predominated, so although at Compton we marched between venues to the unceasing blare of tannoyed martial music, the fact that we were doing so under the critical, and far from silent, notice of crowds of chaps, helped spruce us up as neither drill corporal nor brass band ever could.

And there really were courses of all sorts going on, from the mundane to the slit-your-throat top-secret, though the group that sticks in my mind was that from the RAF Regiment – they guarded airfields – whose U/T (under training) signallers could be seen from the classrooms, out in all weathers, using Aldis lamps to flash messages in morse to fellow stalwarts on the far side of the camp. The majority of those being trained were destined to become ground personnel, but some aircrew – wireless operator/air gunners – also trained there.

Once settled, we faced six months of wireless-associated activities. Taking precedence over all of these, however, was the morse code: not Morse code: through high usage, we learnt, the RAF had dropped the eponymous big 'M', of Samuel Morse. And high usage because at that time most communication with aeroplanes was done through old Sam's code. Voice contact was possible using radio-telephony (R/T – speech), but only at very short ranges. For longer ranges it had to be wireless-telegraphy (W/T – morse), with messages being tapped out with a key, in the way that telegrams were transmitted. The first task set us, therefore, was learning to send and receive morse.

I stress, 'and receive', for although, having learnt the symbols – alphabet, punctuation-marks, and numbers –, it was easy enough to rattle away on a morse key, it was far more difficult to assimilate the same symbols coming through a headset. To qualify as basic wireless operators, and so become Aircraftwomen Class One, we would be tested in sending and receiving twenty words a minute in both plain language and five-symbol 'psycho' groups containing letters and numbers: a 'word', in this context, comprising five letters. The process was essentially one of repetition, but it was effective, so that to this day my ears prick up whenever dots and dashes skitter out from TV wartime films …

The morse-instruction rooms were equipped with a wireless receiver, headphones, and morse keys. An instructor would sit at his own key, and tap out messages to us which we'd hear either through headsets or from the wireless loudspeaker. We'd copy down what we heard, and when he'd done, pass him our results for checking. What we increasingly found as the working rate quickened, was that to try to guess what was coming next was fatal. If you'd written down C-A- and thought he was going to send Cat, when, instead, he sent Can, it so threw the mental process that you could well miss the rest of the message. What was required, therefore, was to turn yourself into an automaton, jotting down the individual symbols without the slightest idea what they were building up to. At our stage, only when the transmission stopped could you take in the whole, and see what it was you'd written down.

This learning process dominated our lives, with some girls resorting to reading out roadside notices in morse as we marched to that so-stirring tannoy. Even so, as the speed increased above twelve words a minute, some couldn't cope, while others found the strain of the periodical tests too much for them. So, as the speed increased, the class dwindled, with girls departing to remuster into other trades.

Morse, though, was a long-winded way of passing information, so frequently-used messages were themselves encoded. The code we used most was the three-letter 'Q' Code, so that instead of tapping out, 'Please send more slowly' (twenty symbols) you sent 'QRS' (just three). There was an also an 'X' Code, which was highly secret, and a military 'Z' Code, which we never used where I was to work. We also had to familiarise ourselves with 'Procedures', particularly the way RAF air/ground messages were structured. This helped, because although 'reading ahead' was disastrous, a knowledge of the form communications took made life easier. So that, for instance, if we heard 'QTH' – My position is – we'd know the format of the position report to follow: heading and airspeed, altitude, type of aircraft, nature of any problem, and pilot's intentions …

I was among the fortunate ones who were able to take the increasing morse speeds without too much trouble. I was equally fortunate, however, in that they didn't want us to know too much about wireless theory, though the RAF seemed to believe that the more you knew of the background to anything, the better you'd be at your own bit of the job. All that stuff they wanted us to know about signals bouncing off layers in the atmosphere, 'schematic diagrams' of wireless circuits, and valves! They were inconsistent, however, for although every message had to be timed, they never required us to describe the innards of a clock!

I duly reached the required standard of morse, twenty words a minute – this meant, I was told, that I'd a calm mind, and a good sense of both rhythm and touch. I also did sufficiently well in the final exams to be asked if I would like to go on an advanced course as a 'W/T-slip' operator. I'd already got a vague idea what this was, for as the course had advanced the morse instructor had taken to employing a paper tape to play morse to us. This had been welcomed because, as tests grew critical, the tape would send impeccable morse whereas when hand-keying, the instructor might just fluff a symbol, and so disrupt a candidate's flow.

I was now shown the bigger picture. Wireless operators could aspire to handling morse at, possibly, twenty-five words a minute. There were machines, however, that could handle it far faster. Essentially, an operator would spell out the message into a special typewriter that punched – perforated – holes in a half-inch wide paper tape. This tape, or slip, could be fed into a transmitting machine and be received, again in paper-tape form, at the destination. The receiving operator would gather the emerging slip in one hand, then read off the wavy line that represented the dots and dashes. Having done so, she would transpose it into 'plain' language (it might itself be coded), and type the message into an ordinary typewriter. In this way an operator, given fair conditions, could produce messages at eighty, and even a hundred, words a minute. The basic trade test for a W/T slip operator was to demonstrate eighteen words a minute at ordinary morse – I was already ahead of that – fifty-five words a minute at perforating, and forty-five at slip reading.

Bound up as I was in the Signals world, it was very impressive. But I was, above all, pragmatic. The special course would mean another unspecified number of months in classrooms, and I'd already had my fill of that. More marching too, being bawled at on the square – they had one here, as well! –, and kit inspections. Then again, despite the extra labour involved – learning the special form of morse, and to touch-type –, slip operators and wireless operators were in the same pay group, so no advantage there. Far more importantly, the extra training would delay my doing something useful for the war effort. So while I recognised the invitation as a compliment, I had no hesitation in turning it down. I was posted, therefore as a wireless operator, and to Ramsey, in the Isle of Man.

Just to round off the tale of my progression in morse, after a month or so in the job at Ramsey, I successfully tested at twenty-two words a minute, and was promoted to Leading Aircraftwoman (LACW), which entitled me to wear a two-bladed propeller badge on my sleeve. It also meant an improved pay rate of – I rather think it was 3/3d (19p) a day, plus, of course, that 4d (1.67p) war pay. I remember that a corporal, the next stage up in those days, but with loads of responsibility, got 4/4d (22p) a day – the in-between step, of senior aircraftwoman, with a three-bladed propeller, only came in after the war.

Before reporting to my new posting, I had a term of leave. On this occasion I was burdened with all my paraphernalia, the kitbag alone weighing a ton. But I couldn't leave Calne for the last time without picking up the pound of Harris' pork sausages my leave pass entitled me to buy off-coupon: dad had loved them every time I'd managed to scrounge a weekend pass during training: hitching lifts up-country had no terrors for us then ... Home leave though, as always, went far too quickly, and soon I was walking up the gangplank of the Isle of Man Ferry, kitbag dragging at my heels.

I don't recall what I expected when I arrived on the Isle of Man, probably an RAF station buzzing with aeroplanes and preferably without the acres of huts I'd become tired of after months at both Innsworth and Compton Bassett. I certainly hadn't expected to be deposited in a relatively isolated building that, until war broke out, had been Ramsey Grammar School. That was the case, though, for the whole establishment had been requisitioned by the RAF, so not only did we work in the former classrooms but my group – my shift – actually slept on the stage! Indeed, I rather think our main operations room had been the main hall, or something of the sort.

There were aircraft buzzing around, all right but, as one of the girls pointed out, 'They're local, from Andreas and Jurby, so we don't touch them.' As it turned out, at this stage of the war both these nearby – and neighbouring – airfields were engaged in training aircrews in bombing and gunnery, doing quick flips to the ranges off the northern tip of the Island. Strictly speaking, my colleague was correct, for with them operating overhead, as it were, we had no responsibility for them. In time, however, I would make up my own mind about what, from Andreas, at least, I did and didn't touch!

First though, I was to be briefed in how my wireless-operating function fitted into the overall pattern of things. To which end, besides having the set-up explained to me, I was employed as a runner – a message carrier – for the first day or so, which enabled me to see at first hand how the system worked.

In essence, Ramsey had control responsibility for an extensive, and extremely busy air-training area bounded by Glasgow, Liverpool, and Belfast, an area serving ten local airfields but regularly utilised too by aircraft from further flung bases. In 1939, when the RAF had taken over the new wing of the grammar school, the centre had controlled the fighter squadrons at Jurby and Andreas, but in early 1943, as these airfields turned to training, it had taken on the role of a Training-Flying Control Centre (TFCC) with the responsibility for co-ordinating all the training carried out over the Irish

Sea. Some 200 crashes having shown the necessity for improved control, it was exercised by having all aircraft monitored and controlled by the TFCC during their stay in the area. To do this, of course, the Centre needed to maintain contact with them as they carried out their training – whether navigational, air-firing, or bombing – and to ensure that they were clear of the area once they had completed their training exercise.

Three radar stations helped in this task, but the main controlling was done by W/T messages sent to and from the participating aircraft. When aircraft entered the area, they would send a position report. The Centre controller would then advise them if they were still clear to carry out their planned activity, or whether it would have to be modified because other aircraft had not yet vacated the area. During their stay in the area, the aircraft would send other position reports at both specified locations and at specified times. And having left, they would give the Centre confirmation that they had done so.

The wireless room where my twelve-girl shift worked, had a set and headphones for each of us, our job, as wireless operators, being to monitor the reports, and any other messages sent by the exercising aircraft, and record them. That is to say, we had no direct contact with the aircraft, that being the function of operators at other stations, and a job I might have done had I not been posted to Ramsey. So although we could not participate, we chuckled at the very occasional pieces of badinage that livened the strictly formatted reports. Innocuous intrusions like, 'What's for tea, Ma?' parroting Our Ernie, in the *Knockout* comic; and at times, far pithier indisciplines. You could say we were there to eavesdrop, and then tell teacher what we'd overheard!

The way it worked was that when a given aircraft entered the zone from, say, RAF Cark – Grange-over-Sands –, one of our regular user-airfields, it might fly a route dog-legging over the Irish Sea, bomb on a range, then fly another dog-legging route to clear the area. The WAAF next in line to handle an aircraft would receive its initial report, pencil it into her log, but also onto a celluloid card. This she'd pass to staff in the 'filter room'. The girls there would take her information, add to it information from the radar stations and the like, and display the collated information on a part-metal plotting counter to show such details as callsign, type, height, bearing, and – if a formation was involved – the number of aircraft. The counter would then be passed into the operations room.

WAAF plotters

The floor of the ops room was dominated by a huge table map of the TFCC. One of several WAAF plotters, each armed with an adjustable-length plotting rod with a magnetized tip, would pick up the counter – or plot – and place it on the map at the position presently occupied by the aircraft it represented. The squadron-leader controller and his assistant were positioned on a balcony overlooking the map, a vantage point which enabled him to assimilate the changing picture, and to redirect aircraft as and when necessary. To do this he had a two-way R/T link enabling him to communicate directly with nearby aircraft, and telephones through which he could have messages sent to more distant ones by W/T operators working at our transmitting station.

By the time I arrived there, in early 1944, the system, the brainchild of a single officer, was a very slick operation. Certainly, I was terribly impressed, and while I was not in a position to appreciate it at the time, I was not that surprised to be told, many years later, that the Ramsey TFCC was the forerunner of Britain's modern air traffic control system.

We worked in shifts of five hours, in a pattern I can remember to this day, the cycle starting at 0600 hours. Whether the airspace was busy, as we preferred, or slack, as when bad weather caused most flights to be scrubbed, we still had to strain all-shift-long at our headsets: routine advisory position reports were one thing, but we were responsible for an emergency watch as well – I recall ringing the panic bell for my sergeant on two occasions on hearing an SOS, but although he rushed to the headset, both incidents eventually resolved themselves. Altogether a demanding schedule, with the five-hour duty invariably draining us of energy.

Probably just as well that we did get so tired, for although the Isle of Man offers visitors so much, travelling about the place was far from easy back then. For a start, transport facilities were not that good from the Ramsey area, and there were several restricted zones, some around prisoner of war camps, one very close, near Jurby, and holding over 700 prisoners, and another, rather smaller, nearer Douglas. Then there were 'secure areas' where civilian detainees were held, people of German and Italian origin, who had been uprooted from their homes as enemy aliens: not that many didn't welcome the relative peace of the island.

As for entertainment on the unit itself, there were never more than a couple of hundred of us all told, and many of them were billeted in Ramsey which, in wartime, at least, hadn't that much to offer beyond a few pubs and a cinema or two. This all changed for me, however, in mid August 1944 when, having found myself with time on my hands after exhausting Ramsey's delights, I entered one of the ventures set up by local ladies, this one in a school, where they served tea and cakes. Our favourite venue was the Mission for Seaman, on the quay, but that day I fancied a change. It was hardly thronged, the two dogs who seemed to live there couldn't be bothered, and the two women behind the counter, having served me, had little to say. And then the door opened, and a tall young Lochinvar pushed inside: he was, of course, silhouetted against a bright summer sun … Even so, I have his photo to proffer as evidence.

George Hutton, 1944

I should, of course, be able to remember the words we exchanged that led us to share the table. But perhaps I can be excused by the overlay of some seventy years of being together. Suffice to say that his name was George Hutton, that he was a flight-sergeant air gunner, resting between operational tours, and that only hours before he had arrived at RAF Andreas, just beyond Ramsey, to serve as an instructor on No. 11 Air Gunnery School: that is, he was to be one of those local fliers we didn't touch. Or didn't touch professionally, that is …

We kept company from that afternoon on, whenever each of us could get away from our duties. It was evident to me from the start that George had endured trauma, for all that he played it down. There was piquancy too, in that within a short space he would be recalled to operations. But we were young; and we were in love … Indeed, it was a halcyon summer. And happily, although we couldn't know it then, not by any means the last we'd know together. In prosaic terms, though, we were to have four clear months together before, on 31 December 1944, he was posted back to ops.

He went to a holding unit in Norfolk where a pool of crews waited until one of its Group's squadrons had casualties and needed replacements. He converted onto a light-bomber type that made it inevitable that he would sent across to the continent. But at least we'd had Christmas together, and those four idyllic months before it.

For us eavesdroppers, work intensified, for the RAF build-up of the last few years now bore fruit in abundance, sending a flood of trainee crews into the system. Ironically, the BBC and the newpapers were becoming increasingly optimistic, all the signs suggesting that, in the end, the Service would be unable to use more than a fraction of the crews coming through. I know that, despite our being parted, George was relieved that he'd been recalled before newcomers swamped all the squadron places. For my part I would have had him swathed in cotton wool and held relatively safe at Andreas, but he wanted to stick his neck out, so having him cosseted was not to be …

Early in the new year – 1945 – my father became very ill and I obtained compassionate leave to visit him in Rochdale. I contacted George – he was still in Norfolk – and asked if he could join me. For support, really, there was nothing long-term to be done for dad who had never truly recovered from wounds he had received in the Great War. Despite the inevitability of things, it was a heartrending time, but one made easier by George's presence.

And undoubtedly Fate had a hand. For when I phoned him, George had been airborne with his commanding officer. Once they'd landed, however, the CO, overhearing my request being passed on, had immediately packed George off to Rochdale, with a leave pass and a travel warrant, but without other formalities. The day before George returned to camp, however – it was 25 February 1945 – the CO, and his crew, were killed in a crash, when the lack of proper admin led to the bizarre situation of other crew members assuming that George too had died.

For my part, the major tragedy had been avoided. But bitterly-sweet, George's replacement on that fatal flight had been Warrant Officer Frank Russell, a mutually dear friend from Andreas …

I soldiered on at Ramsey as George was sent to a squadron in Belgium and resumed flying ops into Germany. Again, ironically, as things heated up for him, so they slackened off for me, with the RAF sending unused, yet already surplus trainee aircrew to holding camps while deciding what to do with them. As for us, we got fed up seeing the same film shows, so we were delighted to be allowed to go potato lifting near Jurby, alongside the POWs! except that before we got fairly started a period of excessive rain set in and the enterprise was washed out.

But then, thank the Lord! it was all over, although George and I missed being together for the VE Day jollifications. No matter, we now had a future to look forward to! Indeed, George was able to pay several fleeting visits home, during one of which, on 30 August 1945, we were married.

Babs and George, married,
30 August 1945

No extended honeymoon, of course, for George had to return to duty. In a matter of months, however, the squadron was recalled to UK. Before that, however, George had been totally bowled over when another air gunner had taken him into a tent where the most magnificent display of glassware, lit from overhead, had been spread out on a table. George, as pragmatic as they come, had looked at the others gathering around and, as he told me, scoffed, 'What idiot's gathered this lot? It'll be virtually impossible to get it home unbroken.'

The others had roared with laughter. 'Your problem, George.'

He then learnt that, weeks since, they had sent back to Brussels to buy it as a wedding present for us! There were eighty pieces, one for each of the senior NCOs on the squadron. And far from it getting broken in transit, much survives to this day! But how I'd like to have seen George's face, when realisation struck him.

Being married, the moment it suited us, I was able to request an immediate release. This was accepted and I was sent to No. 105 Dispersal Centre, at RAF Wythall, near Birmingham – where I saw a jet-propelled aeroplane for the first time! –, and was demobbed on 20 September 1945. On 4 November 1946, after George's demob number had come up, he too left the Service.

Settling into civilian life had its problems, but we were more fortunate than many, as we grew to appreciate when we booked into a hotel in Ramsey for our first post-war holiday. There was another visitor, very stylish, but somewhat distant, and most definitely posh. She had a child, and also a nanny, even so everything flustered her. But she had infinite faith in her husband's ability to put things right, once he returned from some, unspecified, business.

'The wing commander will see to it,' was her counter to everything she saw as adversity. 'The wing commander will know what to do.'

I suppose I could equally well have tripped about saying, 'The warrant officer will see to it ...' However, when the wing commander eventually arrived back – on the day we were leaving, as it happened –, he turned out to be the most placid of young men. As for milady's airs and graces, 'She's trying to live in the past,' the nanny told us, shaking her head. 'She doesn't need a nanny. It's all for show.'

In contrast, neither George nor I spent time reflecting on our Service years. The RAF had done us proud, and left us with many happy memories. But we had to move on. George got a job with de Havillands at Chester. And although the money was not that good at first, it was secure employment. Certainly, when he was offered far better remuneration to train air gunners for the Argentinean Air Force, I drew the line: with forty ops in his logbook he'd stuck out his neck enough. And so he made a career in engineering design, remaining in post when de Havillands became Hawker Siddeley, and continuing until he reached retirement age.

When the Falkland's War blew up and we were at loggerheads with Argentina, it was as well for my peace of mind that I had, in fact, drawn that line so many years before. I've always felt, though, that something besides the further risk to George determined the stance I took at that time. It could even be that, having so recently been an eavesdropper, sitting there and listening, but saying nowt, had given me the gift of seeing how the wind lay.

Barbara Hutton, 2014

Glossary

A2 (Qualified Flying Instructor: QFI): RAF QFI categories, and responsibilities:

B2. Copes with three or four students, runs the coffee swindle and two or three inventories. Is really an A1 having a run of awfully bad luck.

B1. Copes with four students, runs the flight, gives all the briefings, answers all the questions, and flies in all weathers.

A2. Copes with one or two students, answers some of the questions, only flies when the weather is bad.

A1. Avoids all students, evades all questions. Only flies when the weather is good. Is really a B2 having a run of awfully good luck.

Ab initio: from the beginning. This referred to aspirant fliers who had passed aptitude selection and were now being tested for suitability in the air.

Afrika Korps: the German expeditionary force serving in Libya and Tunisia. Surrendered in May 1943.

Aircrew: on 19 January 1939 airmen aircrew (observers and gunners) were effectively afforded the status of sergeants, although the measure was not regularised until early 1940 when heavy bombers appeared. World War Two aircrew categories comprised: pilot; navigator [observer, pre 1942]; wireless operator/air gunner; air gunner; flight engineer [post 1941]; bomb aimer [post 1942]; air signaller [post 1943]. There was also the observer radio (radar) of 1941, the navigator/wireless operator category, and similar combinations involving navigators.

Air Observer: a 1915 Royal Flying Corps flying category denoted by an 'O' brevet. In April 1942 its responsibilities were split between the navigator ('N' brevet) and the air bomber ('B' brevet) categories.

Airscrew (propeller): there was a contemporary pedanticism against the use of propeller, or prop. But airscrew and aircrew were so easily mixed up.

Air Quartermaster: an aircrew category (with brevet 'AQ') introduced in 1962 to formalize the role of personnel who had been flying with Transport Command to supervise loading, air-dropping, and the in-flight handling of passengers. In 1970 the category became air loadmaster (brevet 'LM'). Since 2003 loadmasters share the 'WSO' ('Wizzo': weapons, systems, operations) brevet of all non-pilot aircrew.

Aldis: Aldis lamp, a signal lamp for transmitting morse, named after inventor Arthur C.W. Aldis.

Ardennes Offensive: from 16 December 1944 to 25 January 1945 the Germans launched a surprise offensive through the Ardennes Forests aiming to split the Allied armies, capture Antwerp, and ultimately force a peace settlement. It was defeated when the Americans were reinforced, and improved weather permitted air support.

Alvar Lidell: Tord Alvar Quan Lidell, OBE (1908–1981), a celebrated BBC radio newsreader and commentator. He introduced Chamberlain's 'this country is at war' speech on 3 September 1939.

Ander's army: Władysław Anders (1892–1970) was the prisoner-of-war general in Russia chosen by the exiled Polish leader General Sikorski to organise the 75,000 strong army of freed Poles. (In essence) Britain supplied uniforms but when the Russians could not ration the new army, Stalin agreed with a British proposal that all the Poles be moved to Iran where the British held a mandate. Many thousands, however, died of typhus.

Ashover Post: this Royal Observer Corps (nuclear) post is at SK 35836 63662 (928 ft), near Ashover Rock. Though the upper works are visible the underground chamber is sealed.

ATS (Auxiliary Territorial Service): the women's army; from 1949 the Women's Royal Army Corps (WRAC).

Arriving, Arrival chit: when reporting to a station on posting, 'arriving' personnel would check in, on signature, at every section relevant to them (clothing stores, accounts) so that they were known to be on strength for issues and services. Similarly, personnel would 'clear' with their 'clearance chits' on being posted away.

Axis Powers: the name, formally adopted in 1940, for the banding (essentially) of Germany, Italy, and Japan against France and Britain. The term evolved from 1936 when, grateful for Germany's backing against the League of Nations, Italy became reconciled to Nazi policies.

Bader, Douglas: Group Captain Sir Douglas Robert Steuart Bader, CBE, DSO and Bar, DFC and Bar, FRAeS (1910–1982). Lost both legs in a pre-war flying accident, but returned to fly operationally.

Baslow Post: this Royal Observer Corps (nuclear) post was just 100 yards north of the Baslow–Hassop Road (Wheatlands Lane) at map reference SK 24009 72261 (574 ft). It was cleared in 1968, leaving only residual traces.

Beau Geste **(1924), P.C. Wren**: Percival Christopher Wren (1875–1941), British author of several stories set in the French Foreign Legion. Almost certainly never served in the Legion.

BEF: the British Expeditionary Force, set up in 1938. Arrived in France in September 1939. In May 1940, evacuated from Dunkirk.

'Begin the Beguine': a 1935 song by Cole Porter, popular during the forties, the beguine being a combination of ballroom and Latin dance.

Bevin Boy: a conscript sent down the mines rather than into the fighting services. Named after Ernest Bevin the wartime Minister of Labour and National Service ('this is where you boys come in …').

Black (putting up a): gaining a discrediting mark, normally for a minor infringement.

Black-pencil: when personal letters of subordinates were censored, any possible security lapses were scored out with black pencil.

Blériot: Louis Charles Joseph Blériot (1872–1936). French pioneer aviator who made the first powered-flight crossing of the English Channel on 25 July 1909 (For the record, his friend Alfred Leblanc both called him and forced him to eat breakfast).

Blighty: Britain, from Hindustani.

Bod: a body, hence, person.

Bofors: a quick-firing, 40 mm calibre anti-aircraft gun of Swedish design, it fired 120 rounds a minute, was most effective up to 12,000 feet, but could reach 24,000 feet. The public commonly referred to them as 'pom-poms', harking back to an earlier generation of quick-firers turned to the anti-aircraft role.

Burma Railway: a 258 mile (415 km) railway running between Bangkok and Rangoon in support of Japan's campaign in Burma, built 1942–1943, using forced labour. Of the 180,000 Asian labourers and 60,000 Allied prisoners of war (POWs) employed, some 90,000 labourers and 16,000 POWs died during construction.

Buzz-bomb: V-1 Flying Bomb, see Doodlebug.

Canal Zone, British presence: Britain had protected the Suez Canal since 1888, a legitimate presence Britain insisted on maintaining under the Anglo-Egyptian Treaty of 1936. In 1951, however, Egypt repudiated the treaty. Britain finally withdrew in July 1956.

Captain Mannering: the Home-Guard commander (actor Arthur Lowe) in the BBC sitcom, *Dad's Army,* first shown in 1968. Mannering's frustrated rejoinder to the often hapless Private Frank Pike (Ian Lavender) was, 'You *stupid* boy!'

Chain Home: the 1939 early-warning radar system, with aerials mounted on 300 foot towers, set along the east coast. Aircraft flying above 2,000 feet could be detected at 120 miles. The complementary Chain Home Low system detected intruders flying below that. Between May and August 1939 Graf Zeppelin Two, LZ130, would deviate off course to carry out wireless-probing tests on the towers. In fact, these were so inconclusive that the Germans doubted that Britain had serious early-detection cover.

Chamberlain: Arthur Neville Chamberlain FRS (1869–1940). Prime Minister from May 1937 to May 1940 and effective author, therefore, of the RAF's vital expansion.

Char: tea, slang derived from several languages, dating back to the 1500s.

Charge (252, or fizzer): a report, made out on RAF Form 252, that a service offence has been committed. An officer responsible for the airman concerned then decides whether punishment is called for by the *Manual of Air Force Law*.

Circuit(s): a 'circuit' involves taking off into wind, climbing to 1,000 or so feet, turning parallel to the runway, flying downwind past the airfield, then turning back, descending, and touching down. The exercise encompasses all aspects of a normal flight.

Consol: a long-range navigation aid, of German origin. Interpreted using a wireless receiver, it did not give away the aircraft's position.

Cushy: easy, probably from Hindi, *Kjush*, or pleasant.

Despatch (dispatch): contemporary usage was the 'e' form, as in Air Despatch.

Dicey: dangerous.

Doodlebug (Buzz-bomb): the V-1 (*Vergeltungswaffe*: Reprisal Weapon) unmanned Fiesler 103 pulse-jet Flying Bomb. It carried a ton of amatol high-explosive and 7,000 are said to have landed on mainland Britain,

3,876 on London. It might be politic to reiterate that while the V-2 was a rocket, the V-1 [these days, too-often termed 'V-1 rocket'] was a pilotless pulse-jet aircraft.

DUKW ('Duck'): a six-wheeled amphibious vehicle made by General Motors. 'D' denoted 1942; 'U', Utility; 'K', front-wheel drive; 'W', two powered rear axles.

Erk: aircraftman class two (AC2), the lowest RAF rank (hence AC Plonk). 'Aircraftman' replaced the Royal Flying Corps rank of air mechanic. Erk seems to derive from an extreme shortening of air mechanic.

Flying Bomb: see Doodlebug.

Focke-Wulf Fw190: this 1941 fighter evolved through forty variants but is typified by a maximum speed of 408 mph (355 knots), a time to 29,000 feet of twenty minutes, a ceiling of 37,000 feet, a range of 500 miles, and a combat endurance of one hour. Many carried four 7.92 mm (0.31 inch) calibre machine guns and two 20 mm (0.79 inch) calibre cannon; later versions employed 30 mm (1.18 inch) cannon and a wide range of underslung rockets. A comparison flight with a relatively early mark of Spitfire showed the FW190 to be superior in all respects except for turning capability.

Forty (40) mm Hg (mercury) **test**: a medical test, highly rated by aviation medics, introduced by researcher Martin William Flack in 1920. It required the candidate to sustain a 40 mm column of mercury in a U-shaped manometer for as long as possible with a single expiration. Pulse-reading variations showed the patient's response to the stress of the effort and to discomfort (breathlessness) generally.

General Duties: in an RAF context the term can translate (unfairly, and brazenly un-PC) as General Dogsbody. Not to be confused with the lofty General Duties (Flying) Branch.

Geodetic: the structure developed by aircraft designer (Sir) Barnes Wallis and most notably employed in the Wellington bomber. Essentially, it comprised triangular grids made up of aluminium strips to form a mutually-supportive shell of great strength. More properly, the component parts formed 'parts of a circle' – that is, geodetics, alternatively geodesics – on the structure, each element taking the shortest line across the curved surface.

Gharri (Gharry): Indian horse-drawn cart, hence lorry, or transport.

GI: an American soldier. Since the First World War taken as 'Government Issue', although at that time GI was also the frequently used stores listing for galvanized iron (in common use for buckets and so on).

Gong: medal.

Goniometer: an instrument that measures an angle, or rotates an apparatus to a certain angle.

Graf Zeppelin: celebrated German dirigible which flew scheduled services.

Gremlins: manikins whose *raison d'être* was to harass airmen by creating technical problems. They appeared in 1940, got into print in the *RAF Journal* in 1942, indoctrinated fighter pilot Roald Dahl a little later and subsequently Walt Disney: Known to be 'green, gamboge and gold; male, female and neuter; and both young and old', yet there were airmen who thought them fictitious.

Gunga Din: the water carrier in the 1892 poem by Rudyard Kipling.

Hairy: dangerous.

Heath Robinson: William Heath Robinson (1872–1944), a cartoonist who portrayed eccentric machines.

Hershey bar: Hershey's chocolate bar, 'The Great American Chocolate Bar', continues to be a segmented slab of milk chocolate containing almonds and peanuts.

Hutch: Leslie Arthur Julien Hutchinson (1900–1969) world-famous cabaret star in the 1920s and 1930s.

Ira Jones: Wing Commander James Ira Thomas 'Taffy' Jones, DSO, MC, DFC and bar, MM (1896–1960).

Jankers, or confined to camp (CC): a minor punishment in which otherwise free time is spent in reporting for kit inspections and carrying out fatigues.

John Snagge: John Derrick Mordaunt Snagge, OBE (1904–1996), a celebrated BBC radio newsreader and commentator.

Johnny Johnson: Air Vice-Marshal James Edgar 'Johnnie' Johnson, CB, CBE, DSO and two bars, DFC and bar (1915–2001), the highest scoring Allied pilot.

Kamikaze: (God Wind, or Divine Wind). A Japanese aircraft flown bodily into an Allied vessel, employed by the Japanese from October 1944.

Keep 'Em Flying: *'LET'S GO! U.S.A. KEEP 'EM FLYING!'* the rallying slogan coined by American Harry F. Dill in 1941.

Kesserine Pass: a gap in the Atlas Mountains where the largely untested Allied forces thrusting eastwards from Operation Torch were temporarily repulsed by the *Afrika Korps* in February 1943. The setback led to Allied command and control changes, and ultimate success.

(The) Kresy Wshodnie (borderland): in 1939, the Eastern Border of Poland. Effectively, land in Eastern Galicia seized during the 1919 war with Ukraine, then opened to Polish settlers.

Lady in White: throughout the Second World War, South African singer Perla Siedle Gibson (1888–1971), clad in a white dress and wearing a red hat, would position herself on Durban harbour and, using a megaphone, sing in and sing out troopships, not even missing the day when she learnt of her soldier son's death in action. A commemorative statue was unveiled by HM the Queen in 1995.

Leading Aircraftman/woman (LAC): the rank above aircraftman/woman class one (AC1). The next step up was Corporal, a supervisory grade. However, on 1 January 1951 the rank of senior aircraftwoman/man (SAC) was interposed to reflect the holder's advanced trade skills; designedly, it carried no supervisory status.

Link Trainer: a flight simulator originally designed in 1929 by Ed Link, an American organ maker.

LMF (Lack of moral fibre): the term the RAF used during the Second World War for combat fatigue or post-traumatic stress disorder. Since the 1700s also known as Nostalgia, Melancholia, Hysteria, Wavering, Shellshock, and Flying Sickness D (debility).

Messerschmitt Bf109: this 1935-designed, much modified fighter was typically powered by a 1,475 Daimler-Benz twelve-cylinder, liquid-cooled engine which gave it a maximum speed of 386 mph (335 knots) and an initial rate of climb of 3,346 feet a minute. It had a ceiling of 41,000 feet, an endurance of about an hour, and a range of 620 miles. It commonly carried two 7.9 mm (0.31 inch) machine guns and a 20 mm (0.79 inch) cannon; later, a 30 mm (1.18 inch) cannon. BF109 versus Spitfire trials showed them to be evenly matched between 12,000 and 17,000 feet with the Bf109 performing better above 20,000 feet.

Military Medal (MM): from 1916 until 1993 the award for 'Bravery in the Field' applicable to ranks below warrant officer. Since 1993, when the commissioned-non-commissioned divide was abolished in this respect, all recipients are awarded the Military Cross.

Montgomery: Field Marshal Bernard Law Montgomery, KG, GCB, DSO, PC, First Viscount Montgomery of Alamein (1891–1944). Architect of the desert victory won by the Eighth Army which drove German forces westwards from Egypt.

Morse: the morse code is named after one of its developers, Samuel Finley Breese Morse (1791–1872) an American painter-inventor. Although eponymous, the capital has long been dropped in aviation literature.

NAAFI: the Navy, Army, and Air Force Institutes, a British government organisation created in 1921 to provide refreshment and recreational facilities for the armed services.

Neville Chamberlain: see Chamberlain.

Norcross: the Service Personnel and Veterans' Agency located at Norcross, Blackpool.

Nous: 1670–80, Greek: mind, intellect, common sense.

Observer: see Air Observer, above.

Operation Aerial: an evacuation mounted by the Royal Navy from 15–25 June 1940, to take Allied troops from recently-occupied France (France formally capitulated on 22 June 1940). Some 192,000 troops were evacuated, including 24,400 Poles, 19,000 of the latter being evacuated from St-Jean-de-Luz (the last at 1430 hours on 25 June). Notably, 3,000 lives were lost when SS *Lancastria*, packed with some 6,000 troops, was bombed and sunk after leaving St Nazaire.

Phoney war: in September 1939 United States senator William Borah opined, 'There is something phoney about this war.' Churchill would refer to 'The Twilight War', the French to '*le drôle de guerre*'. This phase passed with the Battle of France in May 1940.

Pickard: Group Captain Percy Charles Pickard, DSO and two bars, DFC (1915–1944), starred in the 1941 film *Target for Tonight*. He was killed leading the 1944 precision raid on Amiens Prison (Operation Jericho) designed to enable French prisoners to escape.

Pitot tube: essentially, an open-ended tube, facing forwards to channel air into the airspeed indicator. The cover fitted to prevent the ingress of foreign bodies has to be removed before take-off.

Polish Resettlement Corps: formed in 1946 to accommodate Polish service personnel who were unwilling to return to by-then Communist Poland. The two-year engagement offered job training and the right to settle in Britain. Of the 115,000 who enlisted, 12,000 were airmen and 1,000 WAAFs.

Precautionary Landing: one where a pilot decides it is politic to put down, so permitting the selection of a suitable site: as opposed to a forced-landing.

Queen Mary: a 1938 low-loader trailer designed by Tasker's of Andover to transport aircraft. Over 4,000 were built.

RAFA ('Raffa'): the Royal Air Forces Association, a comradely and welfare organisation founded in 1929 and adopting its present title in 1943.

Raff: this pronunciation of the initialism RAF (Royal Air Force) was widely employed during the period and later among post-war National Servicemen, although it became anathema to post-war regulars.

RDF (radio direction finding): by the late 1930s the technique of fixing the direction of a target by use of radio waves had become commonplace. The term, RDF, therefore, served to hide the function of radio direction finding *and ranging*, or radar.

Reserved occupation: the 1938 Schedule of Reserved Occupations was aimed at avoiding a blanket conscription stripping key industries of workers (as happened in the First World War). The time came, however, when those volunteering for aircrew or for service in submarines could be released.

Rommel: Field Marshal (*Generalfeldmarschall*) Erwin Johannes Eugen Rommel (1891–1944). Rommel commanded the Axis forces in the North Africa campaign until ill health forced his withdrawal. Two months later, on 13 May 1943, his replacement surrendered the *Afrika Korps* to the Allies.

Routine Orders: RAF personnel were required to familiarise themselves with orders promulgated in such written forms as Daily Routine Orders, Station Routine Orders, and Station Standing Orders.

'Sailor' Malan: Group Captain Adolph Gysbert 'Sailor' Malan, DSO and bar, DFC and bar (1910–1963), South African commander of No. 74 Squadron during the Battle of Britain.

School Certificate: Britain's educational attainment qualification from 1918, taken at age 16. There was also a Higher School Certificate, taken at age 18, for those staying on at school. In 1951 both were replaced by the General Certificate of Education's Ordinary and Advanced Level examinations (GCE O-Level, and A-Level).

Self: the term employed to record one's own duty in RAF flying log books.

Sikorski: Władysław Eugeniusz Sikorski (1881–1943). Prime minister of the Polish government in exile, and Commander-in-Chief of the Polish armed forces. Killed on 4 July 1943 when his aircraft crashed shortly after leaving Gibraltar.

Snowdrop: RAF service policeman (SP). RAF police wore a white cap cover.

Spike Milligan: Terence Alan Patrick Seán Milligan, KBE (1918–2002). Writer and comedian who published a series of highly-entertaining books about his army service as a gunner from Operation Torch to Italy.

Spivs: 1930's racecourse slang, used for a flashily-dressed trader dealing with cut-price, often illegally-obtained, or (as coined in 1931) 'black-market' goods.

Splitarse: a hasty, very tight turn: both an emergency and a combat manoeuvre; usage from First World War.

Sprog: tyro; qualified, but still inexperienced.

Sten gun: a British 9 mm calibre sub-machine gun hurriedly produced when invasion threatened and the supply of Thompson machine guns dried up. Utilitarian and cheap (it was said to cost 7/6d to produce) it had a 32-round magazine. Sten is an acronym from designers **S**heperd and **T**urpin, and **En**field.

Stick (control column): despite some contemporary objection, 'stick' has always been the preferred term; 'pole' is equally acceptable but somewhat informal, 'joystick' antediluvially archaic, and 'control column' too pedantic even for Central Flying School. So stick it is, even where the aircraft in question has a wheel, or a yoke.

Stick and ball: the term for accustoming polo ponies to the mallet – not stick! – and ball

Suez Crisis: a political and military confrontation in which Egypt was opposed by Britain, France and Israel. It lasted from late 1956 until April 1957.

Tapes (stripes, chevrons): patchily from January 1939, and more generally from January 1940, non-commissioned trainees qualifying as aircrew automatically became sergeants.

The Jellicoe Express: Thurso to Inverness train named for Admiral Jellicoe; ran from 1917 and throughout the Second World War.

Tiffin: lunch.

Trenchard: Marshal of the Royal Air Force Hugh Trenchard, First Viscount Trenchard, GCB, OM, GCVO, DSO (1873–1956), 'Father of the RAF'.

U-boat: *Unterseeboot*, submarine.

V-1: see Flying Bomb.

V-2: *Vergeltungswaffe* 2 (Reprisal Weapon 2) A-4 ground-to-ground rocket carrying a 1,000 kg (2,000 pound) warhead. Being unguided, it had an eleven mile circle of error.

VE Day: 8 May 1945. Victory in Europe, end of hostilities in Europe.

Vichy: the collaborationist government of France, July 1940 to August 1944.

Victor McLaglen: Victor Andrew de Bier Everleigh McLaglen (1886–1959). An English (naturalized American) tough-guy actor, he appeared in 110 films.

VJ Day: Victory over Japan, end of Second World War. In UK, 15 August 1945. In the Pacific/Americas area, 14 August 1945 due to time-zone difference; also 2 September 1945, when the surrender was actually signed. Written too as V-J, and V-P [Pacific].

Walk-around inspection: pilot's visual pre-flight check. Essentially belt and braces after the technicians have cleared the aircraft for flight.

Warrant (officer): the sovereign's authority, issued by the Secretary of State for Defence, to those appointed to the highest non-commissioned rank.

Watson-Watt: Sir Robert Alexander Watson-Watt, KCB, FRS, FRAeS (1892–1973). British scientist who, from 1936, developed radar.

Whittle: Air Commodore Sir Frank Whittle, OM, KBE, CB, FRS, Hon FRAeS (1907–1996). RAF pilot and engineering officer, inventor of the turbojet engine.

Window: air-dropped strips of paper-backed aluminium foil cut to some correlation with the wavelength of the enemy's air-defence radars and designed to swamp their displays, so confusing their controllers.

Yarpie: white South-African, in Afrikaans, *japie*.

Zloty:(say 'zwottie'): Polish currency. In 1939 twenty-five zlotys were worth one pound sterling.

Selective References

Air Ministry (1937) *Royal Air Force Pocket Book, AP1081*. London: HMSO

Air Ministry (1943) *Elementary Flying Training, AP1979A*. London: HMSO

Air Ministry (1948) *The Rise and Fall of the German Air Force (1931 to 1945)*. London: HMSO

Air Ministry (1954) *Flying, Volumes 1 and 2, AP129*. (Sixth edition). London: HMSO

Bennett, D.C.T. (1936) *The Complete Air Navigator*. London: Pitman

Fellowes, P.F.M. (1942) *Britain's Wonderful Air Force*. London: Odhams

Hammerton, John. (1943) *ABC of the RAF*. Amalgamated Press: London

Handley Page Ltd (1949) *Forty Years On*. London: Handley Page

HMSO (1944) *Target: Germany*. London: Air Ministry

Monday, David (1982) *British Aircraft of World War II*. Chancellor Press: London

Stewart, Oliver. (1941) *The Royal Air Force in Pictures*. London: Country Life

Thetford, Owen (1958) *Aircraft of the Royal Air Force 1918-58*. London: Putnam

ND - #0194 - 270225 - C0 - 234/156/13 - PB - 9781780913759 - Gloss Lamination